FORTNEY ROAD

Life, Death, and Deception in a Christian Cult

Jeff C. Stevenson

Freethought House

Minneapolis–St. Paul

Library of Congress Control Number: 2015934173

Cover and interior design by Robaire Ream

ISBN: 9780988493827

Praise for *Fortney Road*

"A fine book . . . The difficult lessons learned by the followers of Reverend Hill at Fortney Road can inform, educate and serve as an important warning to people today."
—**Rick Ross**, executive director of the Cult Education Institute, author of *Cults Inside Out*

"A riveting portrait of the rise and fall of the Church of the Risen Christ, an Ohio-based cult . . . A sad, sordid story of sex, mind control, and rock 'n' roll."
—**Arthur Goldwag**, author of *Cults, Conspiracies & Secret Societies*

"A fascinating yet disturbing account of religious zeal gone haywire . . . I often thought the music of the All Saved Freak Band was weird, but the story behind them is so weird it almost seems like fiction!"
—**Dave Hollandsworth**, founder One-Way.org and davidhollandsworth.com

"*Fortney Road* is the well-told, harrowing story of a dangerous Christian cult."
—**William A. Gordon**, author of *Four Dead in Ohio*

"[Stevenson's] unwavering research over many years has brought to light those tragic times that controlled so many people's lives."
—**Ron Silverman**, co-founder of the James Gang

"An amazing story that needs to be told! Plenty of celebrities get their names dropped as the drama unfolds against the backdrop of a fascinating era. There was a band—a really good band that mixed blues guitar with classical cello—and there was prayer and fasting, and lots of Bible reading . . . also Tolkien . . . and there was a bullwhip and a garage full of guns . . . Wait! . . . Guns? Is it getting weird yet? Well, read on . . . you ain't seen nothin' yet!"
—**Mark Allan Powell**, Professor of New Testament, Trinity Lutheran Seminary

"Stevenson has deftly and painstakingly researched and documented the disturbing and violent culture that pervaded Fortney Road."
—**Darryl Berk**, musician

"Glenn Schwartz seemed to vanish at the peak of his powers. His downfall was a mystery to almost everyone. Stevenson's masterful tale of the cult on Fortney Road solves that mystery and many more . . . *Fortney Road* is an eye-opening, cautionary tale that informs and forewarns."
—**Jim Siegelman**, co-author with Flo Conway of *Snapping: America's Epidemic of Sudden Personality Change*

"I had the privilege of playing with Glenn Schwartz in Pacific Gas and Electric. I had never before nor since played with a better guitarist . . . Now that I know what he survived at Fortney Road, my admiration for him only increases."
—**Brent Block**, founding member of Pacific Gas and Electric

"*Fortney Road* is the incredible story of the Church of the Risen Christ . . . The community's survivors are finally able to tell their story."

—**David Di Sabatino**, documentary filmmaker of *Fallen Angel: The Outlaw Larry Norman*

"Stevenson has masterfully documented Glenn Schwartz's troubled journey and captured the zeitgeist of that era."

—**Mark N. Jones**, musician and artist

"*Fortney Road* traces the story of Pastor Larry Hill, world-class blues rock guitarist Glenn Schwartz, and the early Jesus Music group, the All Saved Freak Band, revealing how fundamentalist religion can become a tool to manipulate and abuse people."

—**Brian Quincy Newcomb**, veteran music critic, United Church of Christ minister

"This is a well-researched and deeply disturbing account of religious abuse and how the ideals of the 'Jesus Movement' of the sixties became horribly warped inside this isolated commune. A timely warning about charismatic leaders that take advantage of well-intended followers under the guise of religious devotion."

—**John Styll**, co-founder of CCM Magazine

"A fascinating story of one church's descent into depravity and the music it created."

—**Bob Gersztyn**, author of *Jesus Rocks The World*

"As a young believer and musician during the Jesus Movement, *Fortney Road* reminds me of how close I was to being caught up in one of the cults of the day."

—**Scott Wesley Brown**, artist and pastor

"*Fortney Road* is a cautionary tale in the mold of Jesus' parable of the talents. In other words, it doesn't have the happy ending of the other stories but it is well worth reading. For those that were there—and those that weren't—this is a great book!"

—**Bob Kilpatrick**, musician, author of *The Art of Being You*

"Nearly 50 people, most of them still in their twenties, went to live with 'Pastor' Larry Hill at his Fortney Road compound looking for salvation and a path to heaven. Instead, they found something closer to their own private Dachau. Stevenson has written a carefully researched account of Hill's short reign as a brutal cult leader."

—**Bob Frank**, musician and historian for the Cleveland Blues Society

"Stevenson has done his homework to bring this sad, compelling tale to light."

—**David Spero**, former disc jockey and artist manager

"Reads with all the intrigue and outlandishness of a modern novel . . . Stevenson's book not only raises disturbing questions about fringe Christian cults but also the hierarchies in many groups today that have grown out of a single vision of a dominant, seemingly well-intentioned visionary."

—**Jeff Johnson**, recording artist, ArkMusic

"A haunting masterpiece that walks us through the life of Larry Hill, the 'Manson' of Christianity, and his quenchless thirst for power, rock 'n' roll, and violence. *Fortney Road* is not just a book. It's a warning."

—**Bo Lane**, author of *Why Pastors Quit*

FORTNEY ROAD

For Mark Hill

Contents

I had no idea . . .

Why did we do these things? How do I answer that?

Each of us, I'm certain, had our own personal reasons. I was looking for a father and family. The music also played a powerful role, but good tunes and a father weren't that powerful a psychological factor. I'd lived without both before and "family" seemed sometimes overrated. Charlie Manson had a family.

I do not believe myself alone when I say we did it for the love of God—the same pure motivation that takes others to the priesthood, a convent, or the backside of a desert.

—*Statement by a former member of Larry Hill's Church of the Risen Christ*

I had no idea what was going on at Fortney Road. No idea at all. No one ever pulled me aside and told me the truth. If they had, I would have called the police immediately, I would have confronted Larry; I would have done anything necessary to help them.

I loved those people and the music we were making.

—*Statement by the All Saved Freak Band album producer*

Our group was no more a cult than the Baptist church is, and there was no physical abuse. The penalty for bad behavior was usually 10 push-ups. Any accusations of abuse are from a few disgruntled members made angry by the fact that developing spirituality meant losing money.

My relationship with the press has not been a happy one. What we do here has been twisted and distorted. We went through hell at that time. We were trying to minister to people . . . some got disgruntled.

Diane Sullivan never hurt anyone and children fought to be with her. It was not a cult. We were helping kids come off drugs.

—*Statement by Reverend Larry Hill, pastor of the Church of the Risen Christ*

Prologue

When America
was Losing Its Mind

I ran across Larry Hill and what's left of his "family"
very much by accident several weeks ago. I can
assure you he's still on the farm but seems only to
have a couple followers, mostly women from what I
could tell. I will say I came away from my encounter
there with a really bad vibe.

Only after an Internet search did I discover the
story and sordid details of this monster's life. I
hope all those who have gotten out from under his
control are moving on and gaining their lives back.

Very Scary Guy.

—*Internet posting at Exchristian.net forum, August 7, 2005*

I n the United States during the late 1960s and early
'70s every aspect of society was being dramatically
changed or challenged. "The decade was the furthest
thing from laid-back," Holland Cotter wrote in the May 25, 2007
edition of the *New York Times*. "It was wired, confused and con-
fusing, with constant clashes around race, class, gender and politics, idealism and ideology."[1]

Music, fashion, education, politics, along with sexual, social
and cultural mores, were all being re-evaluated. In 1965, 25,000
students marched on Washington to protest the Vietnam War. As
the decade progressed and tensions grew more heated in the wake
of political assassinations, civil rights issues, and the nuclear arms
race, the protests increased in size and frequency. It was a time,

as Cotter put it, "when America was losing its mind to save, some would say, its soul."[1]

The world seemed hell-bent on self-destruction, and the zeitgeist of the era was summed up on the cover of the April 8, 1966, issue of *Time* magazine, which asked in bold red letters: "Is God Dead?"

Meanwhile, on the West Coast, in direct rebuttal to the question posed by *Time*, a few individuals claimed they had been called by God to reach out to an obviously troubled, directionless, fearful, and angry generation. Those in the Jesus Movement, as it was soon to be called (or "Jesus Freaks" to those who opposed their message), looked like hippies but preferred the term "Jesus People." The Living Room coffeehouse opened in 1967 as an outreach to the growing population of youth and hippies in San Francisco's Haight-Ashbury district. These truth-starved young people were spiritually hungry, and it was clear that they had tried—and would try—anything to satisfy their appetites.

The climate of that time created the perfect breeding ground for any well-meaning or megalomaniacal charismatic leader to attract uncertain seekers as followers. Thousands of educated, middle-class youths abandoned traditional religions and embraced beliefs and practices that were culturally unprecedented. The term "cult" became a popular way of referring to these new Eastern religions or occult practices as well as to the more extreme forms of Christianity.

Among the most dangerous, demonic, and until now least recognized of the self-appointed messiahs of that time was Reverend Larry Hill. He was the self-proclaimed prophet, founder, and all-powerful leader of what came to be known as the Church of the Risen Christ, as well as the co-founder of one of the earliest Jesus Music groups, the All Saved Freak Band. Larry Hill preached a message of hellfire and brimstone but lived a life that would have been condemned under his own teaching. In public he demonstrated love and compassion to society's downtrodden, but in private he expressed rage and engaged in almost unbelievable abuse of the acolytes who lived in his commune on Fortney Road in Windsor, Ohio.

At about the same time Larry Hill was stepping into his power, the Jesus People were using their love of folk and rock to create

Jesus Music, a genre they could call their own. But their music didn't go over well with the traditional churches of the day, which were having a hard enough time dealing with "dirty hippies" who now claimed to be Christians and insisted on attending services in jeans and T-shirts.

Jeff Sharlet wrote in the December 2006 issue of *Harper's Magazine* that to those in the Jesus Movement, "'Church' was no longer a place you went to; it was an experience you consumed, and you wanted as much as you could get. You wore your jeans to worship and grew your hair long. You called yourself a Jesus Freak and you called Jesus a revolutionary. You listened to groups like The Way and Love Song and the All Saved Freak Band, and you read rags like *Right On!* and *The Fish* and *The Hollywood Free Paper*."[2]

I grew up in Southern California in the midst of the Jesus Movement, and it must have been in 1976 that I saw a very odd advertisement in a music magazine for an album by a Christian

Image 1: My Poor Generation ad.

rock group called the All Saved Freak Band featuring guitarist Glenn Schwartz. The album was a re-release called *My Poor Generation,* and while I had never heard of the band, I was well aware of Glenn Schwartz from when he had played with Pacific Gas & Electric, and before that, as a founding member of another band, the James Gang. I wondered how Glenn had ended up in this weird group whose album cover featured a bearded preacher wearing an Amish hat and pointing menacingly into the distance.

Curious, I ordered the record, and when it arrived, an enclosed note stated that the band had two more albums—*Brainwashed* and the oddly titled *For Christians, Elves, and Lovers.* I listened to *My Poor Generation,* and it was pretty good—especially Glenn's playing. The music and lyrics were so eccentric that I wanted to hear the other albums, so I bought those, too. And to this day, I've never heard any music like that recorded by the All Saved Freak Band.

Rachel Khong described it very well in the October 15, 2004 issue of the *Yale Herald*: "Truth be told, Jesus music was best served weird. The All Saved Freak Band had this down to a science. [They] lived on a five-acre lot of land in Windsor, Ohio [and] wrote songs and recorded in Cleveland, eventually releasing *My Poor Generation* in 1973. It was surprisingly good—part folk, part garage, part psychedelic, part blues, and part who-knows-what. There was Glenn Schwartz on the electric guitar, classically trained Kim and Pam Massmann singing backup and playing harpsichord, cello, violin, and assorted woodwind instruments, and Larry Hill's lead singing."[3]

"There is an extraordinary urgency to the All Saved Freak Band," Erik Davis wrote in *Slate,* "whose combination of righteousness and rock anticipates the stance of straight-edge hardcore but who also manage, at least sometimes, to be good-humored, down-home, and lovely. Living collectively, the band made a handful of intense and very strange records, including the Tolkien-inspired folk-rock rarity *For Christians, Elves, and Lovers.*"[4]

I met Glenn Kaiser of Resurrection Band while at a potluck dinner at Keith and Melody Green's house in the mid-1970s. I asked him if he knew anything at all about the All Saved Freak Band. He had encountered them a few times while on tour, but in his only recollection, he said "The women can't look at the men in the eye, they always have to look at the ground." He didn't know why they did this and it would take me more than thirty years to find out the reason.

In 1980, I added the All Saved Freak Band's final studio album, *Sower*, to my collection. The extensive apocalyptic commentary on the back cover and inside sleeve, written by the Reverend Larry Hill himself, was both fascinating and repelling. Erik Davis agreed, writing, "[Y]ou can hear Hill's increasingly creepy mania best on *Sower*, which, though it was recorded in the late '70s—a time when the growing industry of [Jesus Music] was making its saccharine pact with the pop devil—crackles with apocalyptic power and the desire to use the rock song as a vehicle of total transformation."[4]

When I moved to New York in 1983, dozens of boxes containing my albums, including the four LPs by the All Saved Freak Band, moved with me. I looked over the album covers and glanced at the liner notes again as I unpacked. There was something about them that I still found captivating, and what little I could find out about Larry Hill and the band intrigued me. However, at the time I was focusing my attention on my new job as a copywriter at an ad agency, getting acquainted with a new city and making new friends. Also new at the time was the advent of the CD. Over time I, like everyone else, began to replace my favorite albums with CDs.

In 1998, I saw an ad for the CD of *My Poor Generation*. In 2000, a combo CD was released containing the All Saved Freak Band's third and fourth albums, *Brainwashed* and *Sower*, followed in 2004 by the CD release of their second album, *For Christians, Elves, and Lovers*. Since I'd been without a turntable for years, I hadn't heard the band in some time, but once I received the CDs and heard them again, my curiosity was rekindled.

Over the years, I had read rumors on the Internet about the All Saved Freak Band's very dark history, a behind-the-music story like no other. There were horrific allegations about what went on in the Christian commune where they lived during late 1960s and early 1970s. Had peace, love, and rock and roll for Jesus really turned into something sinister?

Erik Davis thought so. "The All Saved Freak Band is a different kettle of fish—at once more powerful and more disturbing, and a reminder of how apocalyptic convictions, Christian or otherwise, can go sour."[4]

One day I came across the All Saved Freak Band website and contacted Joe Markko, who co-founded the band with Larry Hill. We struck up a friendship via the Internet and email. He told me he was putting together a "best of" CD called *Harps on Willows*, and I volunteered to market and promote it. At that time, I conducted an extensive interview with Joe about the band and the recording of their four albums. I titled it "Everything You Always Wanted To Know About the All Saved Freak Band (But Never Had The Chance To Ask)," and Joe posted it on the site.

This was in May 2006 and by the end of the year, *Cross Rhythms* online music magazine had named *Harps on Willows* "One of the 20 Best Albums of the Year" out of the more than 1,500 CDs submitted. The music of Switchfoot and Bob Dylan was also honored. All the CD reissues of the All Saved Freak Band albums had immediately sold out and the original albums were fetching hundreds of dollars online. Clearly, there was still an audience for this music.

By this time, I probably knew more about the All Saved Freak Band and their music than anyone else—except for the band members themselves. But I still didn't know what really had happened at the commune on Fortney Road where they had all lived.

So I asked Joe if he would tell me his story. After thinking about it for several days, he agreed to talk to me about his time with the All Saved Freak Band and the Church of the Risen Christ. He wrote to me, "This is a story, among other things, of the dark side of the Jesus Movement and the wealth of lessons that might be learned and applied. America is currently overstocked with Larry Hills, particularly in the Pentecostal ranks. Your work has the potential to be more than just another cult story because it will read like current history for many other souls bound in the name of Christ, religion or oppressive patriarchies."

He promised to call some of the other band members and others who had lived at Fortney Road to see if they would speak to me as well.

Word soon got out about my project, and that's when reporters started to phone and send me emails. For example, Dick Feagler of the *Cleveland Plain Dealer* said to me, "I've written a *lot* of stories over the years but Larry Hill left me with a real impression of something; he was creepy, spooky . . . It's going to make a *great* story—I'm glad you're telling it!"

Another reporter who works for a paper in the town where Larry lives told me, "On the day you hear Reverend Larry Hill has died, remember to wear thick-soled shoes because hell will be stoked up extra hot."

A former member of Larry's church emailed me, "The full, monstrous tale of Larry Hill's betrayals against men, women and children in the name of Christ needs to be told . . . child molestation, rape and brutality—he was nothing more than a Shadow Prophet—a dark, empty reflection of the real thing. A destroyer of families, his own included, none of his children want anything to do with him, his two sons running away as soon as they were able."

In August 2007, I was invited to Ohio to attend the second reunion of former members of the Church of the Risen Christ and the All Saved Freak Band. Of course, I was eager to meet them, and while I was there I also hoped to visit Fortney Road and maybe even speak to Reverend Larry Hill himself.

"Larry Hill is a chicken. He's a coward," that local reporter had warned me. "He's a psychopath. Really. Be careful. Larry Hill is the devil incarnate."

With a warning like that and the others I'd received, how could I not pursue the story?

Chapter 1

Where a Breaking Occurred

I t was the evening of Wednesday, February 16, 1977, and eleven-year-old Bethy Goodenough was cowering in the corner of an upstairs bedroom of the house on Fortney Road.[5]

Thirty-year-old Diane "Dee Dee" Sullivan, Reverend Larry Hill's second-in-command, chief prophetess, and one of four constant female companions, stood on the other side of the room ferociously beating Bethy with a six-foot-long buggy whip known to Hill's followers as the "White Judge." Diane had to stand that far away because the whip was so long. Bethy's hands were up around her head as she tried in vain to ward off the blows. Again and again the lashes rained down the length of her body, ripping the clothes off her back and drawing blood.[5]

In August 2007, I met Diane's parents, a sweet and gentle couple in their late 80s. They knew of this book and told me several times, "Whatever you write, we know it's true but that woman is not the daughter we raised. We are good Christian people, she was raised a Christian, and that is not our daughter in the book."

Finally Bethy managed to escape and career down the stairs, running toward the dining room and screaming for help as Diane chased her relentlessly. At that point Larry Hill, 42, furious at being disturbed by the commotion, came into the dining room demanding to know what was going on. Instead of putting an end

1

to the beating, however, he grabbed the whip out of Diane's hands and shouted, "You're not hitting her right! You're not breaking her spirit!"[5]

With that, he shoved the child to the floor and continued to horsewhip her for another ten to fifteen minutes while Bethy frantically tried to protect her legs, head, face, and chest with her hands.[5]

Finally, her strength depleted, Bethy's agonized shrieks and pleas gradually diminished, but Larry kept on whipping her until she was completely still and silent. Then he stopped, his discipline a success, her heart and spirit completely broken.

There were more than a dozen people living in the house on Fortney Road at the time. How is it possible that no one witnessed the horrific beating, no one tried to stop it? The truth is, there were at least two witnesses.

Twenty-eight-year-old Carole King (now Carole King Hough), a blonde Georgia Peach with a husky voice, had joined the church in 1972 and taught Sunday school at Fortney Road. Her friend Millie Romanchik, also 28, had never been out of Ohio and had married her high school sweetheart. Their only child, Lisa, was four years old, and they had lived at the farm for several years.

Why neither of them rushed in to rescue Bethy speaks to the level of fear and intimidation instilled by Larry Hill in his acolytes. It had literally been beaten into them that Diane held final authority over all the women in the Church of the Risen Christ and could command and execute punishment on any of them. As a result, when Carole and Millie saw what she was doing to Bethy they didn't dare speak out. They just stood very, very still and prayed she didn't notice them.

A year earlier, Millie's own daughter, Lisa, had been whipped. Millie and her husband had been away from Fortney Road for an evening, and when they returned, they checked on their four-year-old daughter. Lisa was pretending to be asleep, and when her parents quietly approached her bed, she sprang up and cried out happily, "Oh, Mama, you're home!"[5]

Larry Hill strictly enforced the discipline that when children were put to bed they were to remain in bed, silent, until the morning. So when he heard about Lisa only pretending to be asleep, he immediately ordered another woman to whip the little girl. She

was taken into the farmhouse den and when she had been suffi-
ciently beaten, "Lisa came back and started sniffling," Millie said.
Since the child was still whimpering and not silent, Larry yanked
her into another room and furiously whipped her some more,
until she stopped crying.[5]

Fearful that if she spoke up now Lisa might be beaten again,
Millie simply stood there as Bethy was whipped into silence. "I
could only stand there," she said, "because I didn't know what to
do."[5]

As Larry wheezed and caught his breath, Carole and Millie
held theirs, and tried not to faint from terror and guilt. They had
done nothing to intervene and had not even covered their ears to
muffle the sounds that they would hear forever.

Once Bethy's punishment was over, Carole and Millie's greatest fear was that Larry or Diane would turn on them. The women
held hands and pressed themselves against the wall, wishing they
could disappear into the paneling. Carole remembered that her
silent prayer at that moment was, "Oh God, please don't let me be
next! Please, Jesus!"

Less than a year later, as various members of the group began
to defect, Larry grew to fear that word of his abuse would leak to
local authorities, and so he too left Fortney Road and went into
hiding in Pennsylvania. With their shepherd gone, many of the
flock found the courage to scatter. Several members of the church
went to the authorities, and eventually the FBI was brought into
the investigation.

Although there were dozens of charges that could have been
brought against Larry Hill, the only ones that were accepted in
court were those involving eyewitnesses. Consequently, Carole
and Millie were called to testify against Diane Sullivan and Larry
Hill for the beating of Bethy Goodenough. According to Carole's
testimony, during the five years she spent with the Church of the
Risen Christ, "all the church members' children were whipped at
one time or another, all done in order to 'break their spirit.' I don't
ever recall anyone getting it with just a hand. They usually got it
with an instrument of some sort—and very, very, *very* brutally."[5]

With the exception of Carole and Millie, the community
members who testified were still under Larry's mind-altering control. All perjured themselves and denied the beatings and abuse.

Even Bethy Goodenough said that the whipping hadn't hurt her very much, and that she needed and deserved the discipline.

When I met Bethy in 2007 she was in her early forties and didn't shy away from answering my questions. I sensed that she had managed to separate the childhood she had experienced from the life she was now leading. "I want everyone to know," she said, "that I do not blame them for what happened to me at Fortney Road. As an adult I understand how things like this can happen. I realize that no one knew the severity of my abuse. How could they? It was hidden from everyone. And there are still a lot of parts that are hidden deep within me as well, and that may be the best place for them."

When she looks back at her time at Fortney Road, Bethy calls it "a hell that I passed through." We talked about that word 'hell' and the fact that religious traditions describe it in various ways: where the dead dwell, or a fiery landscape, or a place of intense shame, contempt and rejection. Hell is said to be where a breaking occurs and where remoteness or separation from God is experienced.

"It was a place of breaking," she agreed after thinking for a moment. "It didn't so much break me, but it did break off and destroy parts of my childhood—I lost innocence, so much joy, and the safety and security that all children should have . . . I know that what happened there continues to affect my life every day. Life has not always been as good as it is now and I have been through times of trying to figure myself out on my own."

I asked her if she ever told anyone about her time at Fortney Road and, if so, what their responses had been.

"I have told my story to people with different reactions," she said. "Mostly they suggest that I go back there and end the lives of the people who abused me, Larry and Diane. Others want to know what the hell was wrong with my parents. Why would they allow anyone to take their child away from them?"

She hesitated for a moment, then smiled slightly and said, "My favorite is when people say, 'It's done, it's over, just get over it!'"

Bethy admits there are gaps in her memory that she attributes to the traumas she experienced as a child, but some memories are still very vivid. "I remember coming home one day when I was very young and there were strangers at our house. It must have been Larry and Diane and others from the church. They stayed for a long time and returned often, always taking up a lot of Mom and Dad's time."

Her first trip to Fortney Road was at night. After several meetings with church members, Larry apparently trusted her parents enough for them to attend a church service at his home. Bethy had fallen asleep in the car during the drive over and her parents decided to let her sleep.

"I remember waking up in the back seat of the car. I could hear people talking and singing in the house. I started crying but no one heard me. I was scared and I called for Mom and Dad but no one came, so eventually I got out of the car. I had no idea where I was. It seemed like a long dark walk to the house, a place I had not seen before. I really don't recall what happened when I did go in the house."

In 1972, Bethy was seven years old and her parents, after much prayer, decided to join Larry Hill's ministry. They moved their family into a rented house a few blocks from Larry's home on Fortney Road. In the beginning, she said, "Things were pretty good. I was happiest playing with the other children." She remembers playing outside by the clothesline where a billy goat once kicked her in the stomach; a mustang horse that bucked everyone off; and swinging on the swing set all alone.

But three years later, everything changed for Bethy and her parents. According to Carole King, "The Lord supposedly spoke to Larry in 1975 and told him that Bethy was to be taken from her parents and put into Diane Sullivan's hands."[5]

"At some point," Bethy told me, "I was taken from the rented house where I lived with my parents and siblings and moved several blocks away into the main house on Fortney Road with Larry and Diane. I was not allowed to talk to my parents or see them. The fear I felt, as well as the disappointment in my family for allowing that to happen, made me feel like I was on my own.

"At first I didn't know that it was going to be permanent, but as time passed I realized that I might never see my parents again. I was so confused as to why my parents didn't come to get me.

Image 2: The house on Fortney Road in 2005.

I was their daughter! How could they just let someone take me away from them? It was like a black cloud was over my head. The feeling of being abandoned grew stronger. I felt so alone."

Bethy recalled that once she was separated from her parents there wasn't much playtime. "It was always work, work, work. There were chores to do every day and the house always had to be spotless. To earn money—we always needed money—we would go and clean houses outside the farm. When we went to one house to clean, the family had a little girl I played with. One day I took her out in the backyard and she would not stop crying, so I did what I was taught, I slapped her and kept hitting her until she was quiet. Little did I know that when she woke up from her nap she would have a horrible bruise on her face. After that we did not go back to clean that house anymore."

When the child's furious parents called Diane, she did the best she could to make amends, promising a complimentary house cleaning if the neighbor didn't mention the incident to other clients. And she also promised to discipline Bethy. "When Diane asked me what had happened to the little girl, I lied and told her she had fallen down," Bethy said. "But she didn't believe me."

Diane yanked Bethy by the arm and dragged her upstairs to a bedroom. "She grabbed the back of my head and slammed it through the wall, telling me that I had caused them to possibly lose a client and income because of how stupid I was. She screamed at me that I had disappointed her and Larry and, as with any beating, afterwards I had to go to the tiny, cramped, dark storage area under the stairs called 'the spot' and pray and pray and pray until God forgave me."

From then on, Bethy said, she was constantly being punished, every day, several times a day. "Larry and Diane were always telling me that I was lying or stealing or thinking things I shouldn't think. I remember thinking about running out the front door, but Larry would seem to read my mind and he would always say, 'If you run the niggers will find you and kill you!' He also told me all the time that no one wanted me and no one would ever want me."

Bethy soon began to believe that if her parents didn't love her enough to take her away from Fortney Road, or even to see her, Larry must be right: No one cared about her; no one wanted her.

But the punishments, beatings and the verbal abuse and threats were not the worst that Bethy experienced as a child.

"One day, Diane took me into the master bedroom upstairs. When I walked in, Larry was under the covers. Diane closed and locked the door behind us and started taking her clothes off. I was so scared. I didn't know what they were doing."

They told her that it was time for her to see how adults loved each other.

"They had sex while Larry made me touch him," Bethy said. "From then on, I do not remember what happened. But I know that a part of me died that day and I gave up on love and what it really was supposed to be. I was very confused. I wanted to please Larry and Diane because I was afraid of the consequences, but I was disgusted with what was being done to me."

Everything changed after that encounter. It was as if Larry and Diane never wanted her out of their sight. Bethy was no longer allowed to sleep or dress alone, bathe or even use the facilities alone. She was not allowed to look at anyone or talk to anyone unless Larry or Diane was present.

"Larry was always there, trying to touch me or to make me touch him and telling me that he loved me and that I was special to him. He told me that whenever he touched himself while we were with other people it meant that I was going to have to be with him when we were alone later. He would bring me into the study or his room and make me perform oral sex on him while he fondled me. And he showed me how to French kiss, always saying that I needed to know these things because someday I was going to have to do them with the man I loved and I should be the best at it. There was never a moment's peace.

"I recall thinking that if this is what it was like to be with a man, I did not want that. But at the same time I wanted Larry's approval, and I thought that if I made him happy, possibly he would not beat me or make me do these awful things. I always tried to hide from him, but he would always find me, or one of the girls would find me and tell him where I was."

Bethy also told me that Larry would wake her up in the middle of the night and make her listen to him talk about God. And she remembers his taking her into the study, swinging a pocket watch in front of her face and say things to her. It wasn't until years later that she realized it was a type of hypnotism. Now she says, "I can only imagine what he told me or suggested to me during those times."

Once a vibrant, happy, inquisitive child—a normal child—Bethy gradually became overly compliant, shy, and somewhat uncommunicative. Other members of the community noticed these changes but never suspected the cause, and besides, her parents lived only a few blocks away, surely they had noticed.

"I cried so much, wishing my parents would just come and take me away from this awful man and woman. Diane became even more hateful the more Larry spent time with me. I remember having to get up very early in the morning and running for miles, while Diane would come behind me with a horsewhip. Sometimes she would slap me so hard that my ears hurt and my head pounded. I remember wishing that someone would help me and wanting these people to die, wanting my parents to come rescue me. I really thought they knew what was going on, but then I realized that they were blinded by what Larry told them. I thought I was going to die there, all alone and forgotten.

"I am now a forty-something-year-old woman who has done an almost 180-degree turnaround in her life. I have moved on and take only the positive from my life. I leave the negative experiences of Fortney Road in hell, where they belong."

Chapter 2

Corrupt Seed

C ults are as old as recorded history and they tend to flourish during periods of social and political turbulence. There is evidence of their existence after the fall of Rome, during the French Revolution, during England's Industrial Revolution, in Japan after World War II, and in Eastern Europe after the breakup of the Communist regime.

Unlike most established religions that usually incorporate some type of elected board to ensure checks and balances, cults usually have a pyramid structure with one strong authority figure at the top who demands complete obedience from subordinates. Control is always the goal of the leader and he or she must constantly monitor the group to ensure all members remain loyal to the community and its teachings and purposes.

When I began researching this book, I was surprised to discover that many of today's modern day cult leaders, self-proclaimed prophets and heretical bible teachers were born within years of one another. And they all claimed to have supernatural visions, hear voices from God or angels and were all told they had a great work to do while here on Earth.

This is exactly what the Reverend Larry Hill experienced early in 1965. He had the first of his five visions from God, and how he used those revelations to draw a congregation of young people to himself is the story of what happened at Fortney Road.

A quick overview of these men—they are almost always men—shows an alarming pattern that has been followed dozens of times, and almost always includes physical, sexual and mental abuse, and often death.

William Branham, the first of nine children, was born in a log cabin in Kentucky on April 6, 1909. Branham claimed that in his early childhood he heard the voice of the Angel of the Lord who told him "never to drink, smoke or defile his body for there would be a work for him when he got older." In 1946, he testified to having received an angelic visitation, commissioning his worldwide ministry of evangelism and faith healing. Although he was embraced by many in the burgeoning Pentecostal movement, in hindsight his "prophecies" and visions were shown to be false or never substantiated, and his doctrines about the Trinity and the role of women in the Fall of Man have now been denounced by mainstream Christianity. He was killed in a car accident in 1965, but Branham still has followers to this day.

In 1911, Lafayette Ronald Hubbard, an American author and the founder of the Church of Scientology, was born.

In 1916, Victor Paul Wierwille was born and would be remembered for founding The Way International in 1957. He claimed to have heard from God in 1942: "He spoke to me audibly, just like I am talking to you now. He said he would teach me the Word as it had not been known since the first century, if I would teach it to others." Wierwille died in 1985.

Oral Roberts was born in 1918 and his claims of having healing power, seeing visions and hearing from God directly are well documented. Most famously, he claimed God told him to build the City of Faith Medical and Research Center and later said he saw a 900-foot-tall Jesus who told him that the vision would soon be realized and that the hospital would be a success; it closed in 1989. Roberts passed away in 2009.

Also in 1918, Mark L. Prophet was born and claims he was first contacted by the Ascended Masters at the age of 18. He would become a religious figure, self-proclaimed prophet, orator, and husband of Elizabeth Prophet. They founded The Summit Lighthouse organization in 1958 and after his death, his wife renamed the organization the Church Universal and Triumphant in 1975. She died in 2009.

In February of 1919, David Berg was born in Oakland, CA. He married in 1944 and between 1948 and 1954, Berg was a minister in the Christian and Missionary Alliance but was expelled from the organization for differences in teachings and alleged sexual misconduct with a 17-year-old female church employee. Berg moved his family to Fred Jordan's American Soul Clinic in Mingus, Texas, and he enrolled in a three-month religion course. Larry Hill's first wife said that Larry also took religious studies at the clinic but I have no evidence that Hill and Berg ever met. Berg worked with the organization until 1967, and in 1968 he formed the Children of God organization (now The Family). Berg died in 1994.

In 1920 Sun Myung Moon was born, and as a self-proclaimed messiah, he founded the Unification Church in 1954.

In 1921, Harold Camping was born and would later become infamous for predicting that Judgment Day would occur on or about September 6, 1994 and then, after a robust promotional campaign, he predicted May 21, 2011 was the day of judgment, followed by a physical Rapture that would occur on October 21, 2011. Camping died in 2013.

Modern-day apostle and prophet Sam Fife was born in 1926. In the mid-1960s, he felt he was experiencing a "move of God" and created the organization The Move, which focused on believing the Tribulation and Second Coming of Christ were near. He died in 1979.

The 1930s saw the birth of future televangelists Pat Robertson, Paul Crouch, David Wilkerson, Jerry Falwell, and Jimmy Swaggart, cult leaders Jim Jones (People's Temple), Marshall Applewhite Jr. (Heaven's Gate), Rajneesh (Indian mystic, guru and spiritual teacher with an international following), Charles Manson, Werner Erhard (EST training), and Stewart Tanner Traill (Forever Family and Church of Bible Understanding).

And on May 21, 1935, Charles Lawrence Hill was born into the family of Charlie and Thelma Hill of Ashtabula, Ohio, a brother to 14-year-old Claudine.

What was the world like when Larry Hill was born and is it possible it influenced the man he would become?

The 1930s started parched and dry, especially in the East.

Soon after President Roosevelt was inaugurated in 1933, drought and erosion combined to cause the Dust Bowl. In addition to the ominous atmosperic conditions, much of the 1930s was spent trying to survive and recover from the 1929 Wall Street Crash that resulted in the Great Depression.

In the coalfields of Pennsylvania, several families crowded together in one-room shacks, living on wild weeds. In Arkansas, some families lived in caves, while in Oakland, California, they lived in sewer pipes. In Ohio, the unemployment rate for all residents reached 37% by 1932.

Drought and depression—a double whammy—was soon joined by a rising and increasingly violent crime rate.

In the 1930s, Ohio was known as a safe haven for criminals, while Cleveland was considered the nation's most dangerous city due to its high incidence of traffic accidents, organized crime and its woefully understaffed police force.

Less than 60 miles northeast of Cleveland was the community of Ashtabula, Ohio, located on Lake Erie's coastline. Founded in 1803 and incorporated in 1891, the name "Ashtabula" means "river of many fish" and in the 1930s, approximately 20,000 people called Ashtabula home.

It's amid the dust, death, crime and the Great Depression of the 1930s that Larry Hill was born in the small township of Ashtabula.

With national unemployment still running at 20%, even men like Larry's father, Charlie Hill, a veteran of World War I with a small pension, had to work long and hard to support his family. He made a steady but meager living as a door-to-door salesman, peddling Watkins liniments, spices, herbs, and dietary supplements. Charlie was now part of the first international direct sales company in the world, a "Watkins man." He was given a large black leather products case with the Watkins label in gold letters on the outside. The case opened up like a large tackle box with multiple shelves. Some people commented that looking into that case each month was like gazing under a present-laden tree on Christmas morning.

Charlie hunted and fished, not for sport but to put food on the table. He processed honey from bees kept in his backyard to add to the family income, and also to put beer money into his pocket. He had a thirst for cold ones and was a regular at the recently opened Jewel's Dance Hall in nearby Austinburg. Formerly a dairy creamery, Jewel's—"The most fun you can have with your boots on!"—had evolved into a gathering place where people went to drink and polka dance.

Larry Hill's mother, Thelma Hill, didn't drink or dance. A plump and temperate woman, she regularly attended the neighborhood Assemblies of God (AOG) church, where Pentecostal experiences and miracles were sought after in earnest.

The AOG denomination traces its roots back to a religious revival that started during the late 1800's. The revival was characterized by speaking in tongues and claims of supernatural healing, both of which gave birth to the Pentecostal movement. Thelma was taught that speaking in tongues was a sign of a special anointing from God, and the "Baptism in the Holy Spirit" was a unique experience that gave believers extra power to witness and call for signs and wonders in the name of Jesus.

By the time Larry Hill was born in 1935, his father Charlie was already in his late 40s or early 50s and had little time to spend with his newborn son.

Larry was rambunctious and, with a frequently absent father and preoccupied mother, was left alone to run wild at home, in school, and throughout the neighborhood. A thin—some would say scrawny—country boy, Larry was a big talker with fast legs that allowed him to flee whenever his mouth got him in trouble.

"I have a humorous story about Larry Hill as a child and the lengths he would go to in order to get attention," a family acquaintance told me. "He lived down the road from my stepfather. There was poison ivy out and Larry claimed he wasn't allergic to it when the other kids warned him to stay away from it. He rolled in the poison ivy and guess what? He got a horrible rash!"

Joe Markko was fourteen when he first met Larry in 1962. He said, "I once worked with two fellows who went to school with him when he was little. They told me of a small, rather puny kid who said offensive things to classmates as he ran off the school bus to hide behind his mom, waiting on the porch. I pictured him sticking out his tongue from behind her skirt. Unaware I possessed such potentially embarrassing information, Larry once told me about a time when his schoolmates finally caught him. He said they held him down and urinated on him. In his mind he was persecuted, even as a child, because 'God's hand' was on him and the Devil didn't want him to make it. Whatever. He shouldn't have habitually pissed off his classmates. He's one of the few people I've ever known who has consistently refused to live with the consequences of his choices."

As a young man, Larry did not hesitate to strike his mother if he felt she wasn't responding quickly enough to his demands. Joe recalled, "Larry's mother, Thelma, told me herself that Larry beat her up when he was younger."

Joe also told me about the Clays who lived just up the road from Larry's family when he was a child. Priscilla Clay's older sister was a classmate of Larry's throughout their school years. Like many rural Ashtabula County schools, Cork Elementary School often doubled up classes, placing second and third graders or fourth and fifth graders in the same room. By the time they were out of the sixth grade, Larry's reputation for troublemaking was such that Priscilla's parents repeatedly told all their children to stay away from Larry Hill. (Ironically, Priscilla's sister died in 1964 and Larry officiated her funeral.)

While in high school, Larry had a reputation for acting up and causing disruptions in the classroom. Larry's son, Tim Hill, related the story of an exasperated teacher named Mr. Sherman, who demanded that Larry stop disturbing the class. Larry was warned that if he didn't settle down immediately, he would be sent to the principal's office. The oft-told anecdote ends with Larry throwing the teacher out of the window.

In the late 1940s, when Larry was a teenager, he was involved in a horrible car accident. According to Larry's son, Tim, "It was in February and my dad and five or six people were driving over a narrow bridge with cement guardrails. He was asleep in the back seat behind the driver, his right leg stretched out into the front seat. The driver hit another car head-on and two people were killed. Dad was thrown out of the car with such force that his right leg was left in the car. His body fell into the creek below and he was the last to be rescued—the police thought he was already dead."

After the accident, having lost his right leg, Larry moved about with the assistance of an ever-rattling pair of forearm, or Canadian, crutches. According to Joe, "Because those white

Canadian crutches rattled and creaked when he walked, he thought it suggested that his presence was a precursor to a judgment that was to come."

By the early 1950s, Larry's growing interest in music led him to vanish for days on end to visit the crowded, smoky jazz clubs of New York. He spent time at Birdland, Arthur's Tavern, Village Vanguard, Minton's Playhouse, Lenox Lounge, and Monroe's, all the places where the new sound—hard bop—was making its mark.

Larry watched Sonny Rollins and Art Blakey take the influences of rhythm and blues and gospel music and incorporate them into their piano and saxophone performances. Joe told me this is where Larry developed his own rolling, left-handed style of piano playing.

New York in the 1950s was its own universe of creativity and nothing could match it. Beat literature, abstract expressionism and method acting were all reshaping the arts, and nothing was off limits. Everything was subject to change. Artists, writers and musicians met and listened to the newest of the new and then recreated it overnight so everything was always fresh and dynamic.

Larry thrived in this environment, enjoyed the bars and the popular drugs of the day, and even spent a night in a New York City jail. When he recalled this time of his life, Larry said with his gravelly voice, "I used dope, cursed my parents and dared my father to strike me. I played rock and roll, made big money hustling, mixed with the underworld, and hated cops to my guts!"[6]

In 1955, not yet twenty, Larry was earning a living as a traveling magazine salesman. It was a skill that served him well professionally and later when he gathered his congregation.

"To be successful at what he later did, he had to be the most charming, intelligent and caring man you would ever meet," his son Tim says. "And the whole missing leg thing would work in his favor because people would say, 'This poor man is so upbeat and positive!'"

That same year, Larry Hill fell in love with, and married nineteen-year-old Carol. With little income, they had no choice but to move in with Larry's parents, at the time residing in Harpersfield, Ohio.[6] Later that year, they had a son, Brett.

Then, in the spring of 1955, Larry shocked his wife and friends. He abruptly gave up his rough ways and had a radical conversion experience, surrendering his life to Christ.

"It was after he was arrested in New York for carrying a switchblade knife and told to leave the state," his wife Carol Hill says. "That's when he began his religious career."[7]

Larry wrote passionately about his conversion experience:

> I got on my knees and mustered all the faith I could. I began to cry out to God in Jesus's name. I knew I had no merit in myself and asked God to hear me because of Christ's sacrifice, and praise God, I felt His presence. I felt my sins washed away, what joy and release! A new power entered my soul that made me a new man. Through surrendering to Christ, He broke my drug habit and gave me peace and love within toward myself and for others.[6]

Later, Larry wrote of his spiritual experiences in the *Freedom Bell* broadsheet. Larry used the newspaper, first published by his community in 1968, to proclaim his teachings and prophecies.

Both the AOG church and the form of Pentecostalism that Larry embraced were in the midst of resurgence in the mid-1950s. This was the time of Billy Graham's tent revivals, William Branham's and Oral Roberts's faith-healing crusades, Eisenhower's television commercial urging Americans to go to church, and his approval of a Joint Resolution of the 84th Congress declaring IN GOD WE TRUST as the national motto of the United States.

The AOG churches practiced an expressive form of worship that includes shouting and crying, dancing and shaking and "going under the power," which involved falling to the floor in a trancelike state. During this period, all AOG churches allotted time during the Sunday services for the congregants to give testimonies of salvation and miracles, and to pray for divine healing. They passionately believed that separation from the world was essential to preparing themselves to be a faithful remnant, a bride for whom Christ would soon return. The pastors and leaders of these congregations determined the extent to which charismatic manifestations were part of the regular services, and prophecy was always the priority.

After only a few months of attending church and studying his Bible, Larry grew convinced that God had called him to be an

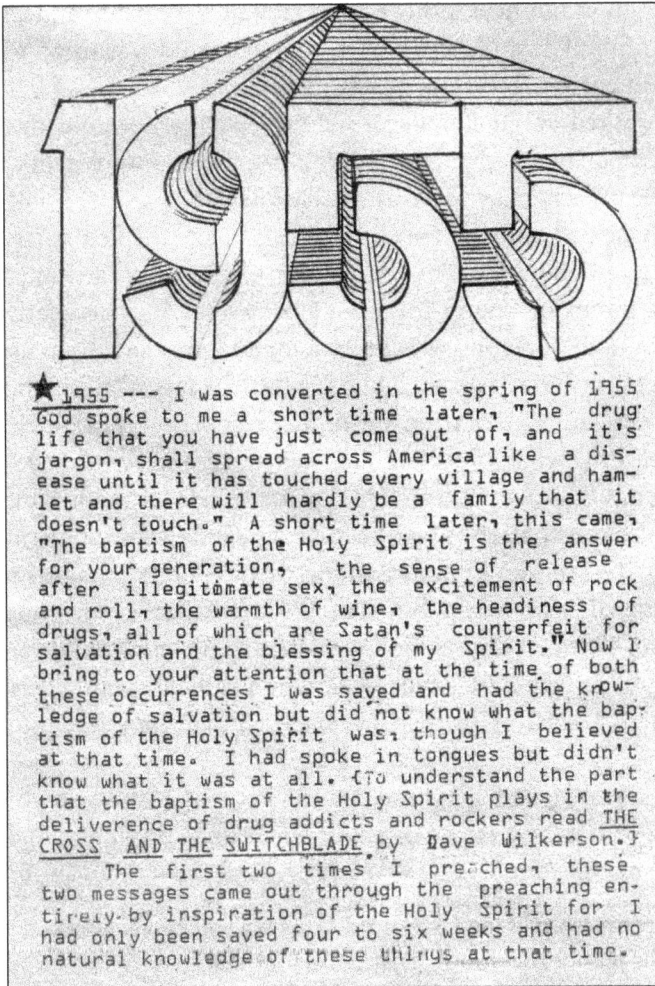

★ 1955 --- I was converted in the spring of 1955 God spoke to me a short time later, "The drug life that you have just come out of, and it's jargon, shall spread across America like a disease until it has touched every village and hamlet and there will hardly be a family that it doesn't touch." A short time later, this came, "The baptism of the Holy Spirit is the answer for your generation, the sense of release after illegitimate sex, the excitement of rock and roll, the warmth of wine, the headiness of drugs, all of which are Satan's counterfeit for salvation and the blessing of my Spirit." Now I bring to your attention that at the time of both these occurrences I was saved and had the knowledge of salvation but did not know what the baptism of the Holy Spirit was, though I believed at that time. I had spoke in tongues but didn't know what it was at all. {To understand the part that the baptism of the Holy Spirit plays in the deliverence of drug addicts and rockers read THE CROSS AND THE SWITCHBLADE by Dave Wilkerson.}

The first two times I preached, these two messages came out through the preaching entirely by inspiration of the Holy Spirit for I had only been saved four to six weeks and had no natural knowledge of these things at that time.

Image 3: Freedom Bell.

evangelist, wanted him to pastor a church one day, and had given him the gift of prophecy:

In the summer of 1955 I saw myself organizing a non-denominational church in Geneva, Ohio and training many young people for the ministry. I didn't see how this could be. At the time I was only nineteen years old and hadn't finished high school. I pondered over this a good deal and was troubled much. In eighteen years this has happened not by planning or forethought but by following God day by day. The work started in Geneva and has now moved to Kent[6]

Although brand new in his faith, Larry quickly made a local name for himself as a fiery preacher, someone God was using to speak about current and future events.

When asked about Larry's preaching abilities, Joe told me, "Early on, when he filled pulpits, he was one of the most dynamic, evangelistic preachers I've ever heard. He knew the Bible by book, chapter, verse . . . book, chapter, verse . . . book, chapter, verse. The man knew the Bible like you wouldn't believe. What would impress a group of young idealists during the late '60s, early '70s? It would be someone who knew a lot and presented it in an unapologetic fashion. Larry's biblically-based rants against 'the machine' were unheard of from any other preachers of the day. He was to preaching what Johnny Winter was to guitar playing: he let it all hang out, mistakes and all. He didn't care. He just kept right on going as if it was all coming directly from God in the moment. Eventually, the rants and political indoctrination—the conspiracy theories, the visions—began to replace his methodical expositions of scripture. The man is gifted in the Word and he knows when to use it for greatest effect. If you had heard him early on, you'd likely have a different sense of the man. He just eventually morphed into a monster."

Larry claimed that he made one of his first prophecies in 1956, concerning the election of a Roman Catholic president. In a 1973 issue of *Freedom Bell*, he wrote:

> In 1956, the word of the Lord came, "America will have a Roman Catholic president, a young senator from the east coast. When he comes to office, the judgment of America is just off its shores."[6]

To bolster Larry's after-the-fact prophecy credentials, *Freedom Bell* also stated that his wife, Carol Hill, had a notary public witness her statement that Larry had indeed made prophecies that John Kennedy—"a young senator from the east coast"—would be elected president, and later, Martin Luther King, Jr. would be assassinated:

> I, Carol Hill, do hereby affirm with my word and honor, that I heard my husband prophesy in 1956 the election of a Roman Catholic president, a young senator from Massachusetts.
>   That he prophesied "the coming of the Pope to the U.N. with a policy of peace" well over a year before it was publicized.

That in 1965 he had a dream-vision of "a hearse pulled through the streets by white horses. And, a Negro woman standing by (my) side." He told me he believed it meant the assassination of Martin Luther King.

In the beginning of 1968, he prophesied a deep wound to the colored people in America. Just a few months after this, Dr. King was shot.[6]

Although Larry felt that this process validated his claims, technically a notary is simply an impartial witness who verifies that the person who is making the statement has been properly identified. The notary is not required to confirm the truth of the testimony.

According to Joe, "Carol Hill became the unfortunate template for Larry's idea of holiness in women. Though more intelligent and possessed of a quicker wit than her husband, she followed the biblical admonition for submission to her man. I'm not certain he would have gotten anywhere without her as his partner. She made him credible. As far as he was concerned, that was just part of her job description."

In addition to the spiritual gifts he believed God had given him at his conversion, Larry also embraced any and all anti-Catholic rhetoric that he came across.

Whether Catholic or Protestant, in the 1950s, Americans had a solid and unwavering belief in God. In fact, a 1954 Gallup poll found that an astonishing 96 percent of Americans believed in God, with 79 percent identifying themselves as regular churchgoers. Church attendance was seen as a form of social conformity, and non-conformity was seen as un-American and pro-communist. And atheism was akin with Communism.

And to Larry Hill, the only movements worse than Communism were the false doctrines he perceived to be in the Catholic Church. Believing that the Communists had already infiltrated the Catholic Church, he stated that God had informed him that the Roman Catholic Church was the "great whore" as mentioned in the Book of Revelation:

The Roman Catholic church is the great whore as described in the 17th Chapter of the Revelation and the protestant churches who are like her; lost in education, pomp, money, and the worldly power are her daughters, harlots, and they shall make

Mystery Babylon and shall become a world power to be used by the Antichrist. [6]

The Whore of Babylon is one of several figures of supreme evil mentioned in the Book of Revelation, one who is closely associated with the Antichrist and the Beast. Popular television evangelists and figures including Jack Chick, the author of numerous religious pamphlets and tracts condemning Catholics, Muslims, and Freemasons, kept the idea of a link between the Roman Catholic Church and the Whore of Babylon, and the concept of the Pope as the Antichrist, alive. The Protestant reformers Martin Luther, John Calvin, and John Knox all identified the Roman Catholic Church with the Whore of Babylon, and this opinion influenced several generations in England and Scotland.

So although Larry claimed to have insights and revelations from God as to the true nature of the Whore of Babylon, he was merely repeating anti-Catholic statements that originated centuries ago. And like many Protestant church leaders before and after, he would later declare that "the Pope is a false prophet and the Antichrist."[6]

Larry Hill was twenty-four in 1959 and had received another direct message from the Lord:

> In 1959, the Lord reaffirmed the raising up of the Roman World Church order and the Pope as a false prophet. The Lord spoke to me in the last part of 1959 that America had crossed the line of no return, and John F. Kennedy would be elected president. The Lord said, "The time will come when the Pentecostals will run to the sign of the Antichrist and turn around and point and say, 'Come on you poor uneducated fools before it's too late.'"[6]

Nervously, Larry searched the newspapers each morning, watched the evening news, and listened carefully to the radio. Then, what he feared most came true: On January 2, 1960, John F. Kennedy initiated his campaign for President in the Democratic primary election.

In September of 1960, Larry listened through gritted teeth as Kennedy said, "I am not the Catholic candidate for President. I am the Democratic Party candidate for President who also happens to be a Catholic. I do not speak for my Church on public matters– and the Church does not speak for me."

Larry was not impressed. He knew the man was lying. *America has crossed the line!* Larry thought, pleased yet apprehensive to see that his prophecies were coming true. *We are at the point of no return! The United States will become the Whore of Babylon!*

Two months later, Kennedy defeated Nixon in one of the closest presidential elections of the 20th century. Larry had fasted and prayed that it would not occur but the Antichrist spirit that now ruled this godless nation was too powerful.

Ominously, an unexpected snowstorm on the eve of Kennedy's inauguration caused massive traffic jams. Temperatures plunged to 10 degrees below freezing. Larry was certain it was a sign, God's last ditch effort to prevent the Roman Catholic from taking his place of authority.

But on January 20, 1961, John F. Kennedy succeeded Dwight Eisenhower as President of the United States of America.

It had all fallen into place, exactly as Larry prophesied back in 1956. Humbled and in awe at the power and anointing given him by the most high, Larry Hill pondered what the future would hold and what role he would play as God's spokesman to a wicked and rebellious generation.

By 1961, Larry and Carol Hill had two sons, firstborn Brett, and Tim, who was born in May 1960. Carol Hill was pleased with the change in her husband after his conversion, accepted that he had a prophetic gift from God, and loved that they had two boys to raise. "Larry has put behind him his wild years of taking drugs and drinking alcohol," Carol Hill said. "He studies religion at the American Soul Clinic in Mingus, Texas. It was there he found his calling."[7]

The American Soul Clinic was founded by Fred Jordan, one of the first television evangelists. In 1952, Jordan met David Berg when Berg enrolled in a three-month course at the clinic. "I never heard that Larry had anything to do with David Berg," Joe told me. "In fact, Larry often used the Children of God to demonstrate to us how far off a group could get. He had no fondness for any of that."

Carol Hill said that there was one man at the school "who is the director and he, of course, taught different aspects of the Bible than what the Bible taught about family life."[7] It's at this school that Larry learned a method to train children to obey God. The premise was that if a child is taught to fear his or her parent, he or she will then fear God.

"In order to do this, you take the child at a very early age, before they are a year old and if they have an occasion where they disobey or don't do what you want them to do, you spank them," Carol Hill said. "Only the school director doesn't say 'spank them,' he says 'beat them.' He says, 'Beat them and don't stop until they stop crying.' Other students attending the school heard the same teaching, but they didn't beat their children. Larry takes this teaching straight to heart and proceeds as he's taught."[7]

Larry began practicing on Carol Hill, beating her regularly, and even breaking her nose on two occasions. He also applied what he had learned to his sons. When Brett was crying at night, instead of comforting the infant and seeing what he needed, Larry picked him up and spanked him until he was silent.[7]

Tim Hill told me, "One of my earliest memories is that I am wearing blue pajamas and just learning to walk. I have a hard time of it and I remember my Dad screaming at me, 'Get up and walk or I will beat you!'"

Undoubtedly this method of discipline came naturally to Larry since, as a young man, he never hesitated to strike his mother if he felt she wasn't responding quickly enough to his demands.

In 1962, Larry and Carol Hill settled in Chicago and sons Brett and Tim had a new baby brother, Mark. Larry soon became a street evangelist with the Teen Challenge Center on South Ashland Avenue, working closely under the supervision of Grady Fannin.

AOG pastor and evangelist Grady L. Fannin was invited to Chicago in 1961 to become the director of the second Teen Challenge Center in the United States. Founded by David Wilkerson among the Latino and African American gangs of New York in 1958, the Teen Challenge youth outreach projects were opening in several major metropolitan areas across the country. Wilkerson's ministry was showcased in the 1970 film *The Cross and the Switchblade* which starred Pat Boone and Erik Estrada. Fannin eventually served as Wilkerson's associate evangelist across the U.S. and Canada, so it was a great opportunity for Larry to work with such a well respected and high-profile ministry.

One evening in October 1962, while making his rounds on the streets as part of the Teen Challenge outreach team, Larry spotted a group of tough-looking kids on the corner of Southport and Waveland on Chicago's North Side.

Joe and some friends, including his girlfriend and future wife, Sandy, were hanging out on a corner when they noticed someone coming up the sidewalk toward them.

"He was hard to miss," Joe recalled. "His right leg was gone and so he was forced to walk with these rattling crutches." Joe was fourteen in 1962 and had just dropped out of school.

The man shambled purposefully toward the teenagers as if he was expected. Religious pamphlet in hand, crutches rattling and squeaking, Larry smiled broadly and introduced himself. "Hi, I'm Larry Hill."

Before they could respond, the one-legged minister began to preach hard at the young people.

"I was a little taken aback by his curt approach to me and my friends," Joe said, "and he came on strong and very decisive when talking about God. I politely listened to what he said. Even though I lived my life by my own rules, I did have a cultural respect for religion and I had been taught manners."

Image 4: Larry Hill handing out pamphlets on the streets with David Wilkerson's Teen Challenge ministry. Photo by Chuck Mace.

Joe listened reverently and followed along as Larry pointed at the illustrations in his religious pamphlet and explained how they represent God's plan for salvation. Joe ignored his friends as they fell up against the wall, laughing and hooting and mocking the one-legged man with the gravelly voice.

But despite Joe's tough exterior street smarts, he admitted that Larry's words got through. "He talked to me about my soul, about a Father and a family at Teen Challenge that would care about me, a place where I would fit right in."

Touched by how emotional and emphatic Larry was about religion and God, Joe found himself nodding in agreement as Larry explained God's love for Joe and how it's possible to escape judgment and eternal damnation. Larry's eyes teared up as he spoke and several times his gruff voice caught as he made his impassioned plea for Joe's soul.

Larry locked all of his attention on Joe, knowing that a spiritual battle was at hand, one he was determined to win. Both of them ignored the boisterous teenagers who continued to laugh and cruelly mimic the preacher.

Suddenly, the preacher grabbed both of Joe's hands to pray and Joe was startled by the firm, hard grip the scrawny, one-legged man had. But there was something more than just simple physical strength or charisma emanating from Larry Hill. There was a powerful sense of purpose and conviction, a confidence and certainty about what he was saying and the God he was talking about.

Together, Joe and Larry bowed their heads as Larry prayed. And Joe felt something: maybe it was a transfer of power from the preacher and his prayers, or evidence of God's presence that's like that fluttery, nervous feeling before a performance or ball game. Regardless of the source, something good was stirring inside of Joe and he assumed it was God.

Joe knowingly made an eternal commitment to God, but at the same time, he was unknowingly binding himself to Larry Hill for the next sixteen years.

In hindsight, Joe admits to often pondering what his life would be like today if he had laughed with his friends instead of praying with Larry Hill.

Chapter 3

Something Waiting

"Before turning seven, I was arrested twice by the Chicago police for breaking and entering," Joe said. He also had a younger brother by 18 months, Randy, who became his partner in crime. Together, they were raised in a tough Chicago neighborhood and the harsh environment became ingrained in them.

In 1956, when Joe was eight years old and in the third grade, his classroom assignment was to stand beside his desk and answer two questions: What age would he be if he could be any age he wanted, and why?

"Standing slowly beside my desk, I said, 'I want to be old,' and sat down. I have no idea why I said that. Realizing the teacher wasn't going to let me get away without finishing, I stood up again and said, 'I think there's something waiting for me out there.'"

Within four years, sisters Laura and Esther and youngest brother Matt joined Joe and Randy. "My memory goes back to when I was about four years old," Randy said. "One of my first recollections is of my [dad] punching around my [mom]."[6]

Their mother was never much of a homebody and would often steal money from Joe's stepfather, Gilbert, and disappear for days, enjoying the company of other men. Joe said, "Ultimately, eight children from four fathers called her Mom."

Joe had a love and aptitude for music and by the time he was twelve, he played four instruments, had performed publicly, and had written his first songs. He and Randy regularly attended the local Congregational Church where Joe became a Boy Scout.

"I spent an entire year working toward the 'God and Country' award," Joe said. "Of the many tasks essential to secure the award, I needed to teach an adult Sunday school class. Along with a growing respect for sacred things, a desire to be a good man was awakening in my little boy heart."

With their mother unable to care for them and rarely around, the siblings eventually ended up living with their stepfather, Gilbert, and his new wife, in a cramped, run-down, three-bedroom apartment.

Randy said, "We lived in our alleyway apartment with the big city rats that my stepdad was forever setting traps for."[6]

Even with Gilbert and his wife working, there was little to show for it. The children were forced to steal the clothes they wore or do without. Randy said, "I shoplifted my clothes all the time. The kids used to laugh at the socks hanging out of my shoes, or the way my brother's clothes fit me. Gilbert and his wife were forever fighting. I used to steal a purse once in a while, or take the pop bottles off of someone's porch for the money."[6]

Life became a source of drudgery and humiliation because most of Joe and Randy's friends came from homes that were better, larger, or simply nicer. Dangerous though they were, the streets became the place to be.

Randy said, "In the summertime, we would sleep at the lake in the day and run around all night. Joe was learning to drive, so we broke into a car dealership and took three cars right out of the showroom garage. I used to break into a lot of places just to see if I could get into them. Ten other boys and I destroyed a lot of property at the school. That was the first of many times in Chicago courts because of my behavior."[6]

Joe recalled, "If we wanted alcohol we broke into the local liquor store and took it. If we wanted amphetamines or barbiturates we broke into the drugstore and took them. If we wanted money, the first person walking by found it wise to accommodate our demands. When we later needed microphones for the band we started, we broke into a local church and took the sound system marked for use by the hearing impaired."

Randy said, "This one guy didn't have any dad—at least not around—and his mom worked, so it was by his house that we started drinking. Needless to say, I was already smoking. We used to have some real sex parties up there, and pills once in a while."[6]

Such was the life Joe and Randy were leading when Joe encountered Larry Hill on that street corner in October 1962. While his friends made derisive and then incredulous comments, Joe bowed his head when Larry invited him to repeat a sinner's prayer: *Heavenly Father, I know that I have sinned against You and that my sins separate me from You. I am truly sorry. I now want to turn away from my sinful past and turn to You for forgiveness.*

At the age of fourteen, Joe acknowledged Christ as his savior. "It really was just that simple," Joe said. "Larry came along and touched my spirit at the precise moment in time that I was discovering I even had a spirit."

Although Randy visited the Teen Challenge Center off and on, he also managed to continue to get into trouble and was committed to the Illinois Youth Commission for eight months in the spring of 1964.

Randy would eventually return two more times before he was finally released on parole in April of 1969.

Image 5: Randy Markko's 1964 mug shot. Photo courtesy of Joe Markko.

While Randy continued to cross paths with the law, Joe quickly adapted to life as a Christian. Larry took pains to be sure his new ward received all the support and attention he needed. The Teen Challenge organization sent a van to take Joe to weekly Bible studies as well as services at Central Assembly of God Church in Chicago.

Joe began traveling with Larry and the Teen Challenge leaders, giving his testimony. Together they visited churches in New York and Chicago where Joe told the crowds how he had left behind a life of drugs and crime. Then Larry would follow up with a dynamic evangelistic message.

Larry became well known in the organization, and when the Detroit Teen Challenge Center had its grand opening, Larry was invited to sit on the stage with the Teen Challenge founder, David Wilkerson, while Joe, "the token convert for Teen Challenge," sat near Larry.

Joe grew to like Larry, even though he knew the man seemed to slightly exaggerate his own history. "He tried awfully hard to be 'hip' for the youth he was trying to reach, which were all kids behaving like I had. His persona always seemed a bit forced to me. I could never see this little, one-legged man being as bad as he professed he once was. But there was genuineness about his motives and that did impress me. He had a very forceful temperament and was able to take command of your attention, a skill the best politicians have perfected."

Also, Larry had a cause. "I'd never known anyone with a cause. Neither had I ever met anyone who said, 'The Lord spoke to me,' as if it were a commonly accepted thing."

Larry's ability to reach the youth of the day is evident in the testimonies that were published in the *Freedom Bell* over the years:

> I won't forget the time Randy Markko and Larry Hill came up to see me after I got busted. My heart was hard, and I didn't care to see anyone, but my mother called around and got a group of kids together for a meeting. Randy and Larry spoke. I went along. During the meeting I really felt a need for Jesus and the filling of the Holy Ghost. Then I dedicated my life to Him.[6]

Those who encountered Larry usually spoke about how unlike he was from other ministers and preachers they knew. One young woman said, "The first time I met Larry Hill, there was something different about him . . . he was talking to us with real concern for us. To me, a minister just wasn't where it was at."[6]

Never knowing the significance of her statement, she finished by saying, "Larry was different though. He wasn't like other ministers."[6]

Chapter 4

Disturbing Visions

L arry Hill's faith was a rigid one, and his idea of an obedient walk with God mandated abstinence from things like alcohol, tobacco, movies, card playing, makeup and anything else associated with "the world." Proponents of this creed were labeled "clothesline preachers" because they seemed so hung up on what people wore but Larry practiced what he preached.

"I'd never known anyone who could say no so easily," Joe recalled.

Larry had a kind and loving exterior, and he was known to spend hours with a soul in need of salvation. But even a saint has a limit and Larry's always-simmering rage would often explode when he was challenged as a man of God or when his authority or God-given insight was put to the test.

So it was no great surprise that Larry didn't do well in structured organizations if he wasn't the one in charge. His time with Chicago's Teen Challenge lasted less than six months.

"The best I've been able to understand is that Larry's departure occurred under less than desirable circumstances," Joe said. Supposedly, Larry didn't seem to feel that Grady Fannin was the one who should have been in charge and he didn't agree with how the director of the Chicago organization said things should be done.

When I contacted David Wilkerson in May of 2007 to gather any recollections he had about Larry Hill, Wilkerson's spokesperson, Barbara Mackery, said the name was not familiar to him now or in relation to the Chicago Teen Challenge. "David didn't recall the name at all," Barbara said. Wilkerson was killed in a car accident in 2011.

This was one of the first instances I came across where Larry may have exaggerated his involvement or influence with another individual or ministry. Over the years, as David Wilkerson became more well-known and respected amongst both the religious and mainstream audience, Larry would continue to mention to the press that he was "formerly associated with David Wilkerson and Teen Challenge."

With no money or local job prospects after leaving Teen Challenge, Larry and Carol Hill and their children moved back to Ohio to live with Larry's parents. Joe remained in the Windy City and soon became lost again without his spiritual advisor.

When Larry returned home, he wasn't able to pay his parents any rent.

"Dad barely worked a job in his life," Tim Hill told me. "I understand from my Aunt Claudine that my grandpa and grandma graciously opened their home to us many times over the years and they were generous to a fault. They didn't have much of their own and yet they made room for their son, daughter-in-law, and three grandkids—really a houseful."

The family would eventually grow to include two more children, Rebecca and Lucas. Tim's own childhood memories and those of his siblings are dark and painful ones. Larry was known for telling racist jokes and he believed that Carol Hill was cheating on him with the black men in the neighborhood. When Lucas—the baby of the family—was born two-and-a-half months premature, Tim remembered Larry saying, "Your mother was always a cheater, always busy having sex with the niggers on the church altar! And this one [meaning Lucas] isn't even mine!"

Larry would spitefully tell his children, "We know where your Mom got all that rhythm, don't we? She got it from all those niggers!"

Tim said, "Although we all were beaten on a regular basis, Larry attacked Lucas the most."

Larry also believed his son Mark was a "mama's boy" and beat him regularly, calling him a "devil child."

I wasn't able to comprehend all I was hearing from Tim when I interviewed him by phone. Surely his father showed some sort of affection toward his children? Was he always a monster, never exhibiting any compassion or kindness?

When pressed to recall any affection from his father, the closest Tim could come up with was when he had the chicken pox. Due to serious complications, Tim was in a coma for four or five days. "Once I had recovered, all I could eat was soup. I recall that one day I sat on Larry's lap and he fed me soup, but I couldn't hold it down. I threw up and that ended it. He set me aside."

In 1965, Larry and his family moved into an old Victorian home on Creek Road just outside of Jefferson, Ohio, ten miles from Austinburg, where his mother—now a widow—had relocated. "Charlie Hill had smoked himself to death at the V.A. Hospital outside Brecksville," Joe said.

What happened next was the turning point that would ultimately have a devastating impact on anyone who ever came into contact with Larry Hill.

It was during this time—1965—that he had the first four of his five visions, with the final one occurring in 1971. Each one graphically revealed a looming Armageddon, a Great War that involved the United States of America being invaded and overtaken by various world powers. Larry eventually wrote commentaries and interpretations about his visions and even had them diagramed as a chart and illustrated.

According to what Larry published in the *Freedom Bell* (and wrote in the third person, referring to himself as "Elder C. Larry Hill"), there were:

[A] series of visions that God gave to Elder C. Larry Hill in 1965, of the beginning of the Viet Nam War and its climax on the North American continent. We are setting forth here a prophetic message revealed to Elder Hill which has been confirmed several times by supernatural signs as he has told it before hundreds of people. The signs were visions revealing various things concerning people in the congregations to which he was preaching. This has happened many times in churches and among people that he has never been acquainted with before. The visions have been something besides (although sometimes including) sickness, and have gone deeper into the personality and family backgrounds in vivid details. They have lasted as long as forty-five minutes at a time as problems in individuals were worked out. Many healings in mind and body have taken place. Up to this time this ministry has had no great amount of publicity but it is the only ministry that we know of that has showed forth the turning of world events in accurate detail months and years ahead in such a consistent and abundant manner.[6]

One red flag that is common to all cults and sects is a statement like, "It is the only ministry that we know of . . ." By setting this ministry—which is Larry Hill—apart from others and claiming to have exclusive and hidden revelations from God, Larry has begun to make himself the only conduit to God. If Larry Hill is getting insights and people are experiencing "healings in mind and body" then it's best not to doubt what the man says.

A clipping from the *Freedom Bell* states that the staff spent "over a year of study" to uncover the Satanic conspiracy to "rule the world." Unfortunately, space did not permit them to publish all of their findings. This tease—the promise of further revelation—is common in cults and sects because if you don't continue to follow and listen to the leader, you won't be prepared for what God has planned. And since God is only revealing His plan to this leader, everyone else is deceived if they are not part of this congregation.

Of course, Larry wrote all of this—he is the 'we' of "We are setting forth here"—and he gave himself the title of "Elder Hill," making it up as he went along. He never was accurate at prophecy. If it was raining today, he would be quick to say, "Remember I told you last week it would rain today?" And if no one recalled, he'd simply say, "Well, I did."

Joe said, "We felt Larry was a special man, someone with prophetic powers. He seemed to know things about people and circumstances beyond natural knowledge."

How'd he do it? Ruth [not her real name] told me, "Larry and others would snoop in member's belongings to prophesy against them."

Image 6: Larry had his visions illustrated. This detail is from Part 1, the Chinese preparing to invade the United States.

Since no one can argue with a man who has had a vision from God, Larry eventually concocted five of them to leave no room for doubt. He said that it was in the beginning of 1965 that he was sitting at a sewing machine when:

> [S]omething said to me, "Get your Bible and read the sixth chapter of Revelation." I did so, and as I read it, was as though a veil was lifting off of the chapter. As I read, understanding was given to me concerning many things, and I continued to read until at the tenth chapter, seventh verse I felt the Spirit going up.[6]

At that point, Larry says that he had a dream, which was his first vision:

> I had a dream that I was fleeing through the countryside with American people. Some were pulling cart wagons, and some who were with me were carrying sacks. I looked back along the dark lined horizon and saw thousands of heads appearing.
>
> Immediately I was brought into a close-up scene of these numerous soldiers. I could see their color and features distinctly. They were young slender men, watching the fleeing people intently. The sufficiency of the soldiers radiated their whole being. They were yellow, dressed in blue uniforms. The interpretation of the vision was plain. America was going to war with a yellow skinned people, and was losing.
>
> It should be specially noted that for two and a half years after this vision, whenever I would tell the visions in church services or to the public, I would say that I didn't understand the blue

uniforms. In 1967 I learned that Red Chinese and Vietnam's soldiers were wearing blue uniforms.[6]

Larry interpreted that first vision-dream to be "America at war with an oriental people,"[6] and that it would conclude in this country with citizens fleeing.

Six months later, in the summer of 1965, Larry had his second vision.

It was a pleasant day, partly cloudy in the mid-70s with mild westerly winds, and Larry went to visit his mother. When he arrived she was in the living room with another woman, snapping beans for canning. Larry later wrote that while the two women chatted and snapped green beans, the room abruptly darkened around him. It was as if storm clouds had suddenly eclipsed the sun. He glanced up to see what was happening. Neither woman seemed to notice the change in the light.[6]

Larry sat in a chair, his right arm over his stomach, using it as a surface on which to rest his left arm. Bending his left elbow, using his left hand, he stroked his chin. He grew very quiet and began rocking back and forth:

> I immediately fell into a vision. My eyes were looking at a map my mother had hung on the wall. I saw a soldier in a military-billed cap step out of the center of the Soviet Union. An old-fashioned cannon stood to his left. The soldier began to walk through the Soviet Union down into Red China, down through Vietnam, the Philippines, then Australia and stopped. I then looked back at Red China and saw a black arrow go from Red China to Hawaii . . .[6]

Image 7: Larry's second vision reveals how the Great War would progress.

Image 8: Larry's third vision.

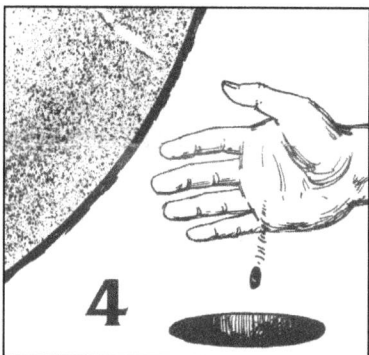

Image 9: Larry's fourth vision.

Larry interpreted this second vision as "how the war would progress, reaching Australia then a black arrow streaks from Red China pointing to Hawaii and from Northern Russia to the Alaska area."[6]

A few weeks after his second vision, Larry's third vision [image 8] revealed that Latin American paratroopers would invade the United States.[6]

The third vision revealed how the enemy had finally reached this continent. Now in this vision, Red China was in my mind constantly, but the only face I saw was that of a Latin American. Therefore, South America will be involved.[6]

He believed his fourth vision [image 9] was a prophetic dream that emphasized the need for the Church to repent and return to its original, New Testament state of purity. He felt that God was going to send America into vast and destructive judgment for its sins. Larry saw a large hand drop a seed into the ground and an "audible voice" told him that the church must return to its original state of purity, like a seed being planted.[6]

The 1960s were a popular time for visions, signs, wonders and God speaking to preachers. In fact, two years before Larry Hill received his 1965 visions of the Great War, another minister and prophet received his own revelations from God.

In February of 1963, Pentecostal pastor William Branham—who founded the post–World War II faith-healing movement—climbed Sunset Mountain in northwestern Arizona. It was there he met with seven angels who revealed to him the meaning of the seven seals from the Book of Revelation. These revelations eventually led him to predict that Jesus would return to earth in 1977.

Even though Branham was very well respected among the leading evangelicals of the day—such as Demos Shakarian who founded the Full Gospel Business Men's Fellowship International, Oral Roberts, T.L. Osborn, Gordon Lindsay, the founder of Christ for the Nations, and many others—and had a successful ministry with thousands of followers, God told Larry Hill that something was wrong with Branham's doctrine:

> In July or August, 1964, the Lord spoke that He was going to take home Brother William Branham, and that he was going to die. About three or four months later I was at a friend's house who said he had Branham's tape and wanted me to hear it. I was more than glad to listen for I had heard such Branham tapes before and greatly enjoyed them. But from the beginning of this one something seemed wrong.[6]

Larry doesn't like what the popular preacher says about the Holy Trinity, speaking in tongues, and the Baptism of the Holy Spirit:

> I questioned the Lord and said, "God, this is going to confuse hundreds of people . . ." And this came, "Remember I told you in the summer that I will take Branham home and that I called him My servant? He has been under much strain and loneliness in his life. Where there is much revelation there is danger and the chance of misunderstanding. I will correct this in My servant. I will take him home." Many witnesses heard me speak of Branham's death several months before it occurred.[6]

On December 18, 1965, William Branham was traveling to Tucson when a drunk driver hit his car. Branham was taken to a hospital where he went into shock, and never regained consciousness. Branham died on December 24, 1965. For many days after his death, several well-known ministers supposedly prayed over his body in an attempt to raise Branham from the dead, while some of his followers predicted he would return to life during Easter.

Today, almost one hundred loosely affiliated churches worldwide with two million followers—known as Message Churches—adhere to and teach what Larry Hill (and God Himself) said are the heretical doctrines of William Branham.

When Larry first went public with his first four visions in 1968, he exhorted people to "begin stockpiling nonperishable foods and the fundamentals for camping and survival."[6] According to Larry's visions, God was going to gather together small groups of believers to form pockets of resistance all over America. These chosen ones would live off the land, run and hide from the coming invaders, and stand and fight when necessary. With God's miraculous interventions, they would eventually drive out the enemy.

"He believed that this remnant of warrior-poet, philosopher-kings would then rebuild America's government, each of the groups being responsible to administer Godly government in specific geographic areas," Joe said. "The Church, now restored to a thoroughly God-dependent state, would thus become 'the head and not the tail,' awaiting the momentary return of Christ in a unified bliss."

With his dark visions and revelations in place, Larry Hill—like every cult leader before and after—was ready to search for converts and build a congregation.

Chapter 5

Nothing Left To Do
but Run

W hen Larry and his family had moved back to Ohio, Joe was left behind in Chicago without his spiritual mentor. He soon fell back into his old ways and before long, petty crimes and a string of jail time followed. Ironically, at the age of sixteen, Joe found himself at the Teen Challenge detention farm in Rehrersburg, Pennsylvania. Through it all, his childhood sweetheart, Sandy, continued to write, phone and keep in touch.

When he was seventeen, Joe was housed at the Illinois State Training School for Boys just outside St. Charles. Nine months into his incarceration, he was surprised to hear he had a visitor.

"Turns out it was one-legged Larry from Ohio," Joe said. "Hoping he might help me, my family had informed him of my situation. He offered to let me live with his family and newly formed church but I didn't imagine the State of Illinois would allow a parolee to be released to an out-of-state non-family member. But it happened, and next thing I knew I was on a Greyhound bus headed for Cleveland."

Larry had his visions in the summer of 1965. "He formed his church," his wife, Carol Hill said, "because he believed he had something special to tell the world."[7]

His mother and a few families from area churches in Ohio joined Larry's household in making up the majority of the flock, but that wasn't enough for the now Reverend Larry Hill. He was intent on growing his own church and sought to make a name for himself preaching as an evangelist among the other churches in his community.

He sought out African American congregations—the varied offshoots of the Church of God in Christ as well as the Apostolic Faith churches—because he felt accepted and validated there. They tended to see him as unique for a white man and this was where he developed much of his fire-and-brimstone preaching style.

And, since he was one of God's end-time prophets, Larry was intent on speaking "words of knowledge" into people's lives and directing them as God told him to. Larry knew that when they listened and obeyed him, they were listening to and obeying God.

"I sat there many times when he told the group in meetings that whatever words came out of his mouth, if they were not obeyed, it's just like not obeying God," Carol Hill said. "Those words were put there by God."[7]

It was during this time that Larry began to grow a beard since he realized that in the Bible, Jesus and the kings and—most importantly—the prophets all had beards.

When Joe arrived in Ohio, he immediately found that life with Reverend Hill wasn't much better than incarceration. Larry and his family lived in an old, two-story country house. There was very little money coming in. Larry did odd jobs in town, selling Amway and Christmas trees during the holidays.

But it wasn't a happy time for anyone who cares to remember.

"It was all work and all church. Work hard, then go to church. Often. Then work some more. That was life with Larry and his family," Joe recalled. "Eating potato sandwiches for lunch, I worked twelve hours a day, six days a week. 'You don't work, you don't eat,' was Larry's approach."

Larry was desperate to fulfill God's call on his life and was trying to get an independent church established. But he had little success with the congregation since it consisted of only a handful of people, his mother and a few families from the area. He had a loose affiliation with the local AOG but he wrote a letter to them, severing his relationship. "I never knew the details," Joe said. "But it was inevitable. Larry saw everyone as against him from the beginning of his life."

Reverend Hill now only had to answer to God.

Joe participated in all the church activities at Larry's insistence, but his heart was never really in it. "I was with Larry because there was no place else to go. And I had to behave and do as he said because I was still on parole and subject to Larry's care and supervision."

Larry thought of himself as Joe's spiritual father and he desired to impart all of God's wisdom and revelation into his "spiritual son." Since Larry frequently saw God reveal His will via nature and the interaction of animals, birds, the weather and the changes in season, he would often walk in the fields with Joe and wait for insights and visions.

One of his earliest documented visions involved what he called the "Parable of the Hawks" which he published in the *Freedom Bell.* According to Larry, the strange aerodynamics and presence of hawks were used by God to confirm to Larry the soon-coming invasion of the United States:

> It was in the summer of 1966 that I and Joe Markko were walking across the pasture of the old Jim Craig farm in Harpersfield. Suddenly from high over my left shoulder a hawk came screeching. He was coming out of the West and the sun had gone over the horizon, but the sky was still bright and rose-colored. The hawk immediately got my attention for a curious thing had been happening to me.
>
> About two months later I prayed, "God when are you going to help me understand this parable of the hawks?" Immediately a question flashed into my mind: "What happens in nature at this time of the day?" Before my mind could even begin to ponder the question, the answer came with great power: "The birds go to roost." And with that the whole thing opened up.
>
> The hawk flew into the south and disappeared a moment and came back quickly! That is the attack on the United States! [See my 1965 visions.] The hawk then flew back into the fading light where he originally came from. We are past the time, but God in His mercy waits on the few that have not come to Christ. The Son is passing the Gentiles now, and is leaving the evangelism now to the few that will be saved.[6]

Since Larry was both the leader and only prophet of his church, whatever interpretation he wanted to assign an event became a "word from the Lord," regardless of whether or not it made sense or was at all practical when explained.

After Joe had toiled in Larry's church for several months, he was overjoyed when his longtime girlfriend, Sandy, finally joined him in Ohio. Even better, they decided it was time to get married. "We settled on August 13, 1966, as the day. We'd been sweethearts, through thick and thin, since I was thirteen. Unfortunately, I had only $100 with which to buy the ring and a suit for the wedding. I wasn't real confident I was going to accomplish either one with that amount of money."

In a rare moment of compassion and kindness, Reverend Hill stepped in and met Joe's need.

Larry took Joe to a jeweler and a men's clothing store in Ashtabula. "He was like a father or best friend," Joe recalled, "gently doing what he could to help, trying to encourage my efforts at doing something for others. In order for me to afford the ring, Larry co-signed and vouched for me and, at the end of the day, I had everything I needed and $20 left over."

Randy was Joe's best man and soon after the wedding, Joe and Sandy found a small apartment in Jefferson. They loved their independence when away from the church services. It was such a contrast to the strict Christian lifestyle that Larry required. In the end, it was far too demanding and stringent for two newly married people who simply wanted to enjoy life together. "Our hearts weren't in step with the sacrifices Larry demanded," Joe said, "so as soon as I was released from parole, Sandy and I moved back to Chicago, both of us quietly glad to be done with Larry."

Once again separated from Larry, Joe immediately returned to his old ways. This time, psychedelics were in full bloom and Joe took his first LSD trip on Christmas Eve, 1966, just as his younger brother Randy started to experiment with heroin.

In 1967, Kurt Cobain was born and Lyndon Baines Johnson was president. And that summer, the corner of Haight and Ashbury in San Francisco was the destination for thousands of young people from around the world. As many as 100,000 converged on the neighborhood for the "Summer of Love," a defining moment of the era that brought the hippie counterculture into middle-American living rooms via the evening news. The Summer of Love was a time of unbridled freedom: free food, free drugs, and free love were available, along with a free clinic and a free store that gave away basic necessities to anyone who asked.

In Chicago, Joe was enjoying the freedom of his own summer of love. At nineteen he was married to his childhood sweetheart, expecting a baby, and had money for essentials plus enough left over to purchase good, cheap drugs. "My life was really about drugs and music at that time. Jefferson Airplane, Steppenwolf, Iron Butterfly, and the Paul Butterfield Blues Band were touring and we saw them all. Sandy was pregnant with our daughter, Shannon, and I was playing guitar with local musicians, having fun, doing whatever I wanted, no real responsibility."

Life was good.

The following summer—July of 1968—Joe learned that his stepfather Gilbert had contacted Larry and spent a week working with Larry's church in Ohio. "Gilbert came back to Chicago all fired up about relocating to become a permanent part of their group," Joe said. "I told him I had no intention of moving my family to Ohio; I'd had all the religious experiences a normal body could tolerate and, as far as I could see, it hadn't done me enough good to warrant the inconvenience."

A month later, there was a knock at Joe's apartment door. When he opened it, Reverend Larry Hill was standing there. Since Joe, Sandy, and their newborn daughter wouldn't go to Ohio, Ohio came to them.

"God laid you on my heart," Larry said.

Larry and church member Harold Sullivan had arrived in Chicago about ten days before the start of the 1968 Democratic National Convention. Harold and his family had left their AOG church to help Larry begin his new ministry, now called the Harpersfield Community Bible Church.

Harold's twenty-one-year-old daughter, Diane—or Dee Dee—headed the youth ministry at Larry's new church. She had heard Larry speak years earlier when he was a guest evangelist at her family's AOG church and she had never forgotten him. From the moment she met Larry, she idolized him, committed herself to

Image 10: Diane Sullivan, age 10, and her sister in 1957. Image provided by anonymous individual.

him, and would do anything for him. He was the commander and she was his general, ready at a moment's notice to do his bidding.

Many whom I interviewed believe that in the final days of Larry Hill's community, Diane Sullivan may have surpassed Larry in the number and extent of atrocities that occurred at Fortney Road.

"Diane Sullivan was what I considered a 'weak-chinned' person," former member Leon [not his real name] told me. He now heads a cult information center. "She was one of those people who were never going to do or be anything on her own. She became the ideal hatchet person for Larry. He called her a 'prophetess of God' so she was now in charge, had respect, but it was based on fear, of course. She never would have had any of that without Larry. It was very much a case of, 'Without you, I'm nothing.'"

One of Diane's relatives recalled her first impressions on meeting Larry. At the 2007 reunion I attended, she told me, "Larry used to be a very godly man when he started out. I think—if I remember correctly—that we started going to his church, but then as he started to change we left, but Dee Dee didn't. She came home and told us she was moving in with the Hills. Dee Dee was twenty-one when she left and we never saw her again until our grandfather died, and that had to be about twelve years later at least. Christmastime was always kind of different after that because one person was missing. It was like a part of us died."

The family would see Diane infrequently over the years. "Dad saw her once. He saw her with a bruise on her face that was somewhat hidden by her hair."

I soon discovered that the Sullivan family didn't want to speak much about Diane. Their contact with her became sporadic over the years and their recollections are vague. Talking with the few family members I met, I was only able to piece together the following statements:

"Diane always wanted to be in control and important."

"She could not tell how far a car could go on a tank of gas and was always running out and getting stranded. And she could not judge distance at all either. I remember one night she tried to drive my dad's new car between two poles in the park and ended up ripping the chrome off of the side of the car."

Speaking with those who lived at Fortney Road, it became clear that Diane provoked almost as much fear and disgust as when they spoke of Larry. I spoke with her once on the phone but never had the chance to meet her. Again, I was left piecing together a woman based on descriptions by people who were terrified of her:

At six feet, Diane Sullivan towered over many of the people in Larry's church. Light brown hair framed a narrow face with penetrating, wide-set eyes that always seemed to be reading your diary. Hidden away in her skull was a brain that was always thinking but produced little intellect. Flat chested, with an extremely thin, almost skeletal figure, her odd appearance caused people to shy away from her or feel uncomfortable if caught in her presence. Her temperament was that of a ravenous bird of prey, always scanning the horizon for a victim, eager to pounce, attack, and devour.

No wonder she was Larry's right-hand woman. Based on that cobbled together description, they obviously shared the same values. Because she was in charge of the church youth, I'm certain

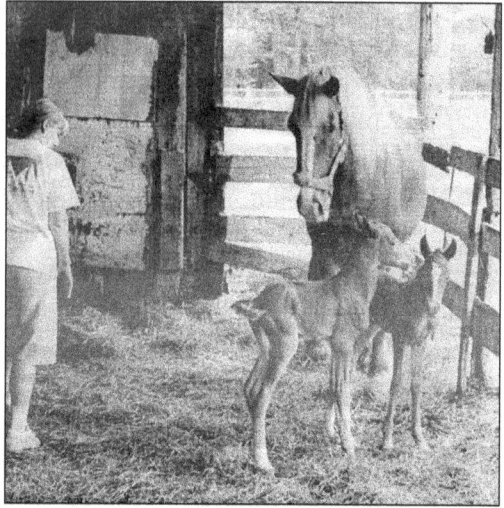

Image 11: Diane Sullivan in 1999. Photo is courtesy of Douglas E. Fair, The Valley News.

it was an extremely well behaved, unusually quiet, and spiritless group of children.

"Think Nurse Ratched in the *Cuckoo's Nest*," Joe said, agreeing with me. "Several believe her to have been a sadist since she could be so cruel to people. She became a pure, brutal monster with a smile and a head full of Scripture, and that's why I use the reference of Nurse Ratched to describe her.

"When Diane talked at public meetings, everyone cringed because you never knew who she was going to name in her criticisms. Think Chairman Mao's wife. She was an unflinching taskmaster, directly in charge of the household and all the women at the farm. At some point she went from victim to perpetrator, and is as despised as much as Larry is by everyone who left Fortney Road. She's become a very scary person who's been doing Larry's dirty work for decades."

When Larry showed up at Joe's Chicago apartment in August 1968, Joe appreciated his spiritual mentor's concern but said, "My life was going in a completely different direction than his. I was now a family man and for the first time in my life was actually beginning to put down some roots. The only area of concern I had at that time was the growing tension in the streets of Chicago due to the upcoming Democratic convention."

It had already been a tumultuous year for the United States, with the assassinations of Martin Luther King, Jr. and Senator Robert F. Kennedy, plus the ongoing and widespread protests of the Vietnam War. Chicago Mayor Richard J. Daley expected sizable and unruly protests and he repeatedly declared, "Law and order will be maintained!" and implemented an 11:00 p.m. curfew.

It seemed that every radical group in the country was already represented in Chicago and word was starting to circulate that bad things could happen—riots, an assassination attempt on presidential candidate George McGovern, fire bombs—and horrible things probably would when the convention began at the end of August.

"There was only one appropriate way to deal with all the tension," Joe said. "It was time to get high."

Joe's brother Randy was already "taking LSD, smoking a lot of pot, and going into other drugs . . . shooting up."[6]

To deal with the stress of everything going down, Sandy Markko joined her husband and brother-in-law and decided to take her first LSD trip—and it was a bad one. The drug-induced hallucinations terrified her and she came home that night absolutely paranoid, thoroughly convinced the city was going up in flames. Hysterical, she told Joe she was getting out of Chicago and taking their daughter to Ohio.

Joe said, "And she wasn't leaving next month or next week, she was leaving *that* night! I should've held her down until help arrived but all I could think of was the sudden possibility of losing my child and the only woman I ever loved. I should've stayed. But I'd never seen her like that and I wasn't positive she would come back. The stakes were far too high for me and I wasn't willing to gamble the loss of that which meant most to me."

Many of Joe's siblings felt the same way Sandy did—they needed a change, a break from all the stressful events around them. So when they heard about Reverend Hill's offer to get them all out of the city and relocated to the country, they immediately made up their minds to go.

Joe said, "So, believe it or not, within twenty-four hours of the 'Prophet Larry Hill' appearing on my doorstep, my wife, daughter, brother Randy, and many of my other brothers and sisters had packed all our belongings into our cars and rented a U-Haul trailer. We were heading someplace I didn't want to go. And a few months later, Randy's girlfriend, 'Cookie,' who later became his wife, and my sister Laura followed.

"I still remember my brother Randy muttering as he looked off into space, stroking his beard, 'Living with a prophet. Hmm. Yeah!' By now, years of nonstop drug abuse had wrecked us. We were true children of our era, dysfunctional beyond understanding and thoroughly out of touch with the real world."

When everything and everyone was packed in tight, the car doors were slammed and locked, and the engines rumbled to life. Joe pushed the 8-track tape in and he can still clearly remember the ominous song and chords that crept out of the car's speakers. It was The Doors' "Not to Touch the Earth:"

> Not to touch the earth, not to see the sun
> Nothing left to do, but run, run, run,
> Let's run, let's run . . .[8]

The caravan traveled east on Interstate 90 toward a time and a place that, as Joe said, "was a destructive delusion that would cost us more than our combined imaginations could bear. Of the seven souls in that car, two would not live beyond their twenties, a third would lie on a death bed for nine months, and it would be thirty years before I felt my life belonged to me again."

Chapter 6

The Guitarist from a Different Planet

"G"rowing up in Cleveland, you'd hear about a wild guy in town who could really play guitar," former Clevelander and guitarist Darryl Berk told me. "Back then, there were a lot of local bands playing what became known as psychedelic music. I was just a teenager and I'd hear about this guy who could play while he was slung over someone's shoulders, and could even change strings while playing."

Mark Jones said, "My cousin told me that he saw the James Gang play at a bat mitzvah in Beachwood, Ohio. He said their lead guitar player would hang upside down from the other guitar player's shoulders and play his ass off. A total wild man! And there was the rumor about him having played with Jeff Beck while in the army in Europe."

Glenn Schwartz was born March 20, 1940, and raised in Euclid, Ohio. He had one passion: playing rapid, fluid, blues guitar. His love affair with the instrument started "when I saw Gene Autry strum his guitar on TV. I asked my dad to buy me a guitar."

Glenn's brother, Gene, said, "His first guitar, I believe, was a Gene Autry acoustic. It was during that time Glenn started listening to a lot of the old blues records. We'd go to the Giant Tiger Department Store and go through all these records in the used record department and find albums by B.B. King and Jimmy Reed, all for about a nickel a piece."[9]

At the age of eleven, Glenn started taking lessons and it was clear to his teacher that his student had a gift. Glenn's father William knew his son had talent and because he was footing the bills for the lessons, he pushed the teacher to make Glenn learn a week's worth of lessons in a day. Glenn was more than up for the challenge and the boy wonder was soon playing along with his favorite blues songs of the 1950s.

By the time he was twelve, he was playing in polka bands and performing at the old Slovenian Home on Cleveland's East Side.

When I interviewed Glenn by phone in June of 2007, he remembered that as a youth he sensed a spiritual calling and a craving for more. "Even as a young boy, I had a hunger and thirst for the Bible and I would carry a hymn book around with me as a child."

That thirst would eventually lead him to Fortney Road.

Glenn Schwartz was known to never give interviews and rarely allows his photo to be taken. That's changed a bit in the past few years, but back in 2007, he was known to be a bit of a recluse in Cleveland, was said to live in an old van covered with Bible scriptures but still played electric guitar in such a way that it was as if the guitar was electrifying him.

I knew Glenn lived with his brother Gene in the home they grew up in so I plugged the address into Google and the phone number came up.

I called, got the answering machine and left my information.

My phone rang at 8 p.m.

"Is this Jeff? This is Glenn Schwartz."

For a second, I thought it was a joke but I recognized his gruff voice from his recordings with the All Saved Freak Band.

I was absolutely stunned that he had returned my call but I quickly started asking questions. It was certainly the oddest conversation and interview I had ever been a part of.

It was like we were driving down a road at night, calmly conversing and he'd startle me by suddenly yelling that we missed a turn or to watch out for that pothole or we were about to go over a cliff. Or think of a radio dial and someone was rapidly switching from elevator music to death metal to smooth jazz to industrial to the hit parade of the 1940s and '50s to classical to house music. He was like a pinball, bouncing off every question I asked and then hitting another one, spinning to a new topic, yelling his answers, whispering some Bible warnings at me, and sometimes having a very calm and dry sense of humor.

Glenn just let it rip and it went on for two-and-a-half hours. Most of the time, he recited Scripture to me and he was very focused on the end-times we were living in. He repeatedly said that Satan's power was growing on Earth and he claimed that most Christians didn't fear God and we needed to walk under a continual fear of "missing it" with God.

He didn't hold to the basic Christian doctrine that if you "accepted Jesus into your heart, you were going to heaven." No, Glenn believed that we could never really know for certain if we will get into heaven or not. One false move and you were damned to hell.

No "Jesus loves me, this I know" and none of that "God loves you and has a wonderful plan for your life."

I realized that if I just let him rant, the conversation would go nowhere. And the entire time I spoke with him, I couldn't shake the thought that I was listening to Larry Hill channeled through Glenn Schwartz. It made me wonder again what the hell Larry Hill had taught those people at Fortney Road.

By the time he was fourteen, Glenn had won an international guitar-playing prize. After high school, he helped to support his family for a year.

Glenn spent most of his time kicking around with local bands. He briefly played in what has been regarded as one of Cleveland's first rock 'n' roll bands, Frank Samson and the Wailers. Like most bands of the era, it was primarily a guitar and sax-dominated instrumental dance combo or "East Side twist band" whose repertoire was R&B-dominated. With his fiery lead guitar playing, Glenn quickly became a focal point of Samson's group and his signature song was "Rock The House."

He married young, to a woman named Marlene, in 1961, and had two sons, Glenn in 1961 and Bob in 1963, but he wasn't a domestic type. He spent most of his time picking up gigs from the endless supply of newly formed bands and he toured locally to earn money to send home to his wife and sons.

In July of 2014 I spoke to his son Bob who told me, "Growing up, he was a great dad. He was real friendly and kind of goofy and childlike. He liked pranks, and he'd walk along with people and would pretend to trip and fall. He'd do pratfalls to make everyone laugh. He acted like a big kid himself, and that's how I am with my own two kids."

One of Glenn's earliest bands was the Pilgrims, formed in 1964, and they were soon popular enough to play at CKLW, Detroit's legendary regional radio station. Program Director Dave Shaffer had the band backing live performances by artists such as the Isley Brothers, the Supremes, the Temptations, the Four Tops, Marvin Gaye, and Smokey Robinson, among many others.

A local label, The Note, had the band record a single, "Plymouth Rock," at Ken Hamann's Cleveland Recording Studio, which was where Glenn would later record with the All Saved Freak Band. The A-side of the single, "Plymouth Rock," charted locally, and the flip side of the record was the song "Maudy" which was written by John Lee Hooker and arranged by Glenn Schwartz. This is Glenn's first known recording.

During his stint with the Pilgrims, Glenn missed an arranged swear-in date with an Army National Guard officer. With an un-timely draft notice served, a promised contract for the Pilgrims to be Motown's first white group went unsigned. (That honor went to the Messengers in 1967.)

"It was a vibrant scene for musicians back then," blues legend Bill "Mr. Stress" Miller said of the Sixties. "In those days, a lot of musicians would perform with ones from other bands. Whoever was around would play together."[9] Glenn teamed up with Bill and some other players and soon Cleveland's first white blues band, Mr. Stress Blues Band, was born.

It was during this time that Glenn and Marlene divorced. His life on the road had simply put too much distance between Glenn and his family. (Marlene and Glenn were married and divorced twice, with the second divorce occurring in 1972.)

In 1966, Jim Fox was looking for a lead guitarist for his band the James Gang.

Formed earlier that year with guitarist Ron Silverman—who also came up with the band's name—Silverman soon departed for military service. Guitarists Greg Grandillo and then Dennis

Image 12: Glenn Schwartz in 1966. Photo courtesy of Ramona Shay.

Chandler were briefly in the band, while Tom Kriss played bass and Phil Giallombardo was on keyboards.

"During this time we heard Glenn Schwartz was out of the army and looking for something to do," Jim Fox said. "I'd never heard Glenn play but I'd heard rumors about him and how talented he was. He was quite a bit older than us—Phil and Tom were just in tenth grade at this point. Glenn came to listen to us play at the English Grille, two doors down from La Cave. At one point during the set, Glenn came up on stage and started playing 'Jeff's Boogie' with us, and of course, he was phenomenal."[9]

Image 13: The James Gang in 1967: Ron Silverman, Glenn Schwartz, Phil Giallombardo, Jim Fox and Tom Kriss. Photo courtesy of Ron Silverman.

The James Gang quickly became the city's most promising band.

Cleveland-born and raised guitarist Butch Armstrong recalled his first impressions of Glenn in the James Gang. "I was thirteen-years-old and the first time me and my friends saw Glenn, we all thought he looked like Jesus. We didn't know his name so we just called him Jesus. He had hair down to his shoulders and wore sandals. And I remember he had the biggest hands in the world! There was a sound going around back then, something Clapton and the Stones were introducing to music and we just couldn't figure out how they did it. We could not get the licks right. Then we saw Glenn Schwartz and he knew how to do it and he created that sound right in front of us! He used his fingers with the whammy bar and that was it! He became God to us in that moment."

Glenn immediately had a following and became known as 'the Guitar Godfather of Cleveland' or 'the Pied Piper'. "Everywhere he played, we'd go," Butch said. "Wherever Jesus went, we followed. Some of the best guitar players around today got to be so good because of Glenn Schwartz."

The Black Keys singer-guitarist Dan Auerbach, an Akron native, is a huge fan of Glenn's sound and agrees with Butch. "He does insane stuff—his personality comes through in his guitar-playing. No fences. Totally unrestrained. I love the fact that he's ours—Ohio's—and nobody else's."[10]

The music scene in Cleveland in the 1960s was a hotbed of aspiring musicians who, while competitive, also appreciated one another's talents and, for the most part, remained loyal to one another over the years. Back then, few were famous and everyone seemed to know someone in a band.

Born and raised in Cleveland, Darryl Berk told me he began studying guitar at age 12. "I knew Jim Fox since my great-aunt would play mahjong with his mom, and I think the first time I met Glenn Schwartz was when he was playing at La Cave with the James Gang. Everyone played at La Cave back then. He was amazing to watch, really knew his blues. After the concert, I spoke to him and he was very approachable, very personable."

Ohio guitarist Rick Kalister recalled the first time he saw Glenn play with the James Gang. "To this day, I have not recovered from that experience. When I heard Glenn Schwartz, my life changed."

The first thing Rick noticed as the band was setting up was that some of them had long hair, which was very unusual for Cleveland at the time. Their clothes resembled the style the hippies wore in San Francisco and Glenn had a little goatee. Just by the look of the band, Rick knew it would be a different sound.

Glenn played a natural finish Epiphone Riviera hollow-body guitar that he had decorated himself. Among other things, it had a peace sign and flowers painted on it, and the words "Help Me." He plugged into a tiny Fender Champ amp and from there went into a Twin Reverb. He told Rick that running one channel into another gave him his distinctive sound.

"When they began to play, it was like a fucking hurricane had hit the building!" Kallister said. "I was hearing feedback and crazy distortion—all like something from a different planet. The audience gasped in amazement and their jaws collectively dropped. The stage show was outrageous . . . I had seen Hendrix, Jeff Beck, Jimmy Page, the Doors and everyone else popular at the time but that night with the James Gang was the most incredible case of rock-and-roll anarchy that I have ever seen!"

After the show, Rick, though he felt a little intimidated, had to meet what he considered to be a "guitarist from a different planet." Rick remembered Glenn as very friendly, approachable, with no ego whatsoever. "I said something like, 'Uh, how did you get so good?' and Glenn said, 'I was stationed in Europe when I was in the National Guard and while traveling through England, I took a few lessons from Jeff Beck.'"

When the James Gang played locally, Ramona Shay, a friend of Glenn's, was often there. She'd first heard Glenn in Cleveland in 1966. "After spending a few hours watching and listening to him, transfixed, I was transformed into a complete and utter blues freak!" Ramona said.

"On stage, Glenn would step out in front of the band and sometimes even move into the audience and play," she remembered. "He played like he had been playing for centuries, never missed a lick, a beat, or a note. The James Gang was musically tight, but they had wide-open fun, too."

It didn't matter if Glenn was among friends or with a crowd of fans, he was always comfortable, fun, and easy to be with. "He was spontaneous, with an honest simplicity, and a tender straightforwardness," she said. "You'd looked into his laughing, gray-green eyes and never doubted that you could trust him with your life, your money, or your wife! He was polite and respectful to all people."

Glenn openly and sometimes gleefully enjoyed the camaraderie of the band, taking part in their familial joking and pranks. He was all about the blues and living the high life of an up-and-coming rock star.

When the James Gang's original rhythm guitarist left, their drummer, Jim Fox, brought Bill Jeric in, an ideal choice since Jeric had studied Glenn's guitar work from a distance. "I said, 'Boy, could I learn a lot from this guy!'" Jeric recalled, thrilled to be part of the band. "Glenn had a big smile and this ebullient personality. His whole attitude was, 'I'm the underdog. I've got to fight.' He had this drive in him."[10]

Like Hendrix and the Who—the most talked about performers at the time—Glenn wanted to give audiences an unforgettable show that would leave them stunned, so he was always thinking of something new and memorable to do.

The James Gang would often end their performances with the Yardbirds' "Jeff's Boogie" and it was known to be a spectacle and a favorite among fans: Glenn would throw his legs over Jeric's shoulders, then play guitar hanging upside down as Jeric turned his torso, spinning them both around in a circle. It was a true moment of rock-and-roll mayhem, with plenty of feedback and chaos on stage and in the audience. Glenn would play entire lines one-handed and upside down while Fox knocked over his drum set à la Keith Moon.

"I'd bang Glenn's head against the stage while I spun around," Jeric said. "He loved it when I drew blood, and he never missed a note!"[10]

Glenn was at the top of his game, acclaimed for his talent, playing most nights in sold-out halls to screaming, adoring fans, and actively participating in a life of sex and high times. Having succeeded in the natural realm, Glenn—like many youth of that era—began to explore popular spiritual beliefs of the day, such as Hare Krishna and Transcendental Meditation. It was during this time that he stopped eating meat for a time, and as Larry Hill would later say, "freaked out in voodoo."[6] Glenn's spiritual searching continued at the same time he enjoyed the success of the James Gang, but eventually one of the two passions would win out.

When I spoke to Glenn on the phone in 2007, he would not mention Larry Hill by name.

He referred to Larry as "the one-legged preacher" or the "Preacher Man" or "the Dark Man." When he talked about his time on Fortney Road—and it was clear, he didn't want to talk about it—he often made it sound like it was a positive experience for him. He told me that much of the teaching was good, but he and the others who lived there simply were not strong enough to take it or reach the level of perfection that God demanded.

And yet Glenn would also acknowledge to me that something was terribly wrong about Fortney Road and that he had seen things and experienced things that he knew were depraved. I noticed his tenses would change, sounding at times as if he was still living there and not recalling events from decades ago.

"That one-legged preacher . . . he put a terrific burden on the women and the men. I was going twenty days without food because I couldn't please God. I had too much ego! The one-legged preacher would always warn us that we were going to lose out if we didn't obey. So I'd fast Monday but it wasn't enough so I'd fast another day. I was always under fear so I fasted all week and then eat on Saturday. Man, I was so tired, I could barely push the pedals on the truck. The Word condemned me all the time.

"Some people would eat only dog food to humble themselves, to keep themselves low. I would slap and punch myself in the face to punish myself so I wouldn't lose out in the end.

"Some of the women got fat, and they have to get under the yoke, deny themselves. I was always under fear. Fear of the Lord is the beginning of wisdom!

"I wanted to endure to the end. Most of the people couldn't take it and left the farm or God struck them down, just like the Preacher Man said He would. You have to stay humble or God will beat you down! Those old hymn writers, they get a little proud and they are never heard from again, are they? Some of the writers in the All Saved Freak Band got proud and they aren't around anymore, are they? And that was never God's name for the band. He doesn't make freaks!"

Glenn told me that he thought most former members of the community are no longer following the Lord or have too much pride.

"They are too high-minded, think too much of themselves! You have to stay low. I'm hanging on by thread all these years, but it's a mighty strong thread."

In 1967, Glenn was only twenty-seven years old, had been nick-named "the White Hendrix," and was considered by some to be one of the top five blues guitarists of the day, yet he couldn't shake the growing emptiness and spiritual void in his life. Ultimately, the constant touring, drugs, and exhausting stage shows over-whelmed Glenn.

As Jim Fox put it, "Glenn Schwartz's life caught up with him. It turns out he was AWOL, behind in his alimony, and his dues were unpaid in the musicians' union. He wanted to go to California. He sat us down after a gig one night and said, 'I'm leaving town. I don't have a choice.' We felt terrible; we felt that the band would end because Glenn had become so important that we would be unable to replace him. Our attitude was that we'd talk about it in a week, after the holidays. We were shattered."[11]

Almost all of the James Gang biographies contain the same er-ror repeated over and over again. They state that Glenn Schwartz left in April of 1969 and Joe Walsh joined the band at that time. However, it was actually toward the end of November 1967 that Glenn left Ohio—and the James Gang—for California in hopes that a change of scenery would help him clear his head and calm his spiritually confused heart.

Eventually Joe Walsh, the guitarist in one of Kent, Ohio's top bands, the Measles, replaced Glenn. Walsh told BBC Publications in 1981, "They had heard I was hot stuff, so they asked me to join. I had some big shoes to fill."

"Many local music fans in Cleveland were stunned when we heard Glenn had quit the James Gang and moved to California," Rick Kalister told me. "We didn't even bother to go see the James Gang for a while. After all, how could this new guitarist, Joe Walsh, be anywhere close to Glenn Schwartz?!"

Guitarist Butch Armstrong felt the same way. "I was a big James Gang fan because of Glenn Schwartz. I was bummed out when he left the group—where had Jesus gone? I didn't think anyone could take his place."

When Joe Walsh appeared with the James Gang at the Chesterland Hullabaloo, Butch and his friends didn't bother to attend. "Who was this skinny white guy? Where was Jesus? Of course, the next day at school, I heard all about how great Joe was! And he became our next guitar hero, but we never forgot Glenn."

Glenn's brother Gene recalls that a friend drove Glenn out West. "He got dropped off on a corner with just a suitcase and his guitar. At one of his first pick-up gigs out there, Duane Allman saw him and asked him to join the Allman Brothers, but he turned him down."[9]

Charlie Allen, vocalist and drummer for the highly eclectic California blues, gospel, soul, jazz, and rock band called Pacific Gas & Electric (PG&E), found Glenn playing at a local club in California. He asked Glenn to the join the group and word soon got back to fans in Cleveland that Glenn had joined a new band.

PG&E bass player and founding member Brent Block told me, "We were all blown away by Glenn's talent. I had a very hard time keeping up with him. He was nearly a decade older than the rest of us, and had way more experience than we did. Glenn was also an acrobat of sorts. Glenn thought nothing of jumping off stacks of amplifiers and rolling around on stage. One night at the Cheetah

Club, I saw him roll off the stage, fall maybe twenty feet, and he never missed a note!"

Former Canned Heat drummer Frank Cook was interested in managing PG&E and he began to call his contacts in the music industry. Frank decided that Charlie was a natural front man, so Frank joined PG&E, took over on drums, and continued to manage the band.

Frank said, "We were playing at the Shrine Auditorium in Los Angeles and Freddy DeMann came up and introduced himself. Freddy was a producer for Kent/Modern Records and got us a small amount of up-front money to record an album."

Glenn's friend Ramona said, "With PG&E, Glenn displayed a wise music business-sense, doing his job and enjoying it, willing to be the team player, but always the consummate bluesman. PG&E shared gigs up and down California with all the big artists of the time and Glenn thoroughly enjoyed meeting and often jamming with these great bands."

However, by late spring of that year, Ramona told me she detected that a change was taking place. "Glenn's developing spiritual interests in yoga and East Indian religious practices had been

Image 14: Tom Marshall, Glenn Schwartz, Freddy DeMann, Frank Cook, Charlie Allen, and Brent Block. DeMann went on to manage the careers of Madonna and Michael Jackson.

replaced with one that focused on the Bible. He told me later that he was feeling troubled much of the time, and I sensed he had become ungrounded mentally and physically. The music business in Hollywood was a pretty harsh, heartless, and competitive scene, and I think the lifestyle was beginning to eat away at the sense of peace and love and balance Glenn had once had."

What happened next has been debated for decades. Was it the result of Glenn tripping on acid as some claim, the consequences of simply spinning too fast on the carousel of success, or a modern day road to Damascus conversion experience?

Chapter 7

The Revolution Inside

P G&E was a hot ticket in California and Glenn had pretty much everything and anything a man could want before the age of thirty, but a man named Arthur Blessitt was about to offer Glenn something more.

Blessitt was a well-known sidewalk evangelist who proselytized to the youth drawn to the drug culture of the 1960s. Eventually he began traveling through America and around the world carrying a twelve-foot cross. When he met people along the way he greeted them with his famous opening line: "Have you tried the world's greatest drug? It's Jesus Christ! He'll give you a high that will keep you until eternity!"

Early in the summer of 1968, Glenn strolled onto the infamous Sunset Strip in Los Angeles and stopped next to a small group of people listening to Blessitt. Glenn found himself drawn to what was being said. Even though the message was wrapped up in drug culture references and bad puns such as, "You don't have to drop downers, man. All you got to do is start dropping Matthew and Mark, Luke, or John!" and presented by a hyper-charismatic hippie and a small team of followers, the truth of forgiveness, love, and the chance for a clean slate made perfect sense. Stoned or not, to the best of his ability at the time, Glenn chose Christ.

Glenn said, "I was finally blessed by mercy, for I heard the Gospel of Christ on Sunset Strip as a man of God preached Christ with tears in his eyes. Soon my tears joined his as he gave the invitation to pray, to come forward from the crowd, to accept Jesus, and I did so."[6]

In March of 2007, Arthur Blessitt and I exchanged emails about his encounter with Glenn Schwartz. "It was in the summer of 1968 that Glenn came to Jesus at His Place, my coffee shop. I do know that I prayed with him after one of our team had also talked with him about giving his heart to Jesus. I knew he meant business with Jesus and Jesus changed him from that moment forward. I do remember talking with him about following Jesus and answering questions and his great passion for Jesus and desire to witness to other people in rock bands and bringing them to Jesus."

It was as if a powerful switch had been flicked on and all at once, Glenn Schwartz became an unstoppable zealot for Jesus Christ. He shared Arthur Blessitt's enthusiasm and passion, and he began to tell everyone about his new faith.

Darryl Berk told me, "I remember hearing that Glenn was in California and he was really tripping and he had gone into a revival meeting and become a Jesus Freak."

Glenn immediately began preaching to reporters and anyone within earshot. He also expressed his concern about the music he played and the power he felt it had. "A lot of rock music becomes idolatrous. Psychedelic stuff can be like witchcraft. You know what I'm talking about? That psychedelic stuff can be like sorcery. A lot of times I find myself on an ego trip and I'm proud. You know, everyone in the audience bowing down to you. The music really gets far out, spaced out. But I pray before I go on and the Lord keeps it pretty well under control."[12]

Glenn's newly acquired faith did not sit well with his band, his family, or his friends. Few were swayed by his sermons or his testimony, most just wanted him to shut up and play his guitar. So he tried to temper his enthusiasm when he realized that most musicians really were not interested in hearing about Jesus, but Glenn often couldn't contain himself. "I ask the Lord to use me to get the Word out to everybody."[12]

Doing their best to ignore Glenn's sudden and very vocal and continuous preaching—and having signed with Kent/Modern records—PG&E needed to produce an album. In 1968, the band quickly recorded the well-reviewed *Get It On*, which entered the *Billboard 200* album chart at number 159 in November of that year.

Each band member wrote a brief note directed to the fans that bought *Get It On*, and Glenn's message stated that, "Together we can make everything all rite [sic], if you just clear your mind and let your heart be your guide. Pray for peace and may the good Lord Jesus be with you all."

In September 1968, Glenn returned to Cleveland as part of PG&E and former James Gang fans turned out to hear their hometown hero. Rick Kalister remembered counting the days until PG&E appeared at La Cave. "Glenn absolutely played his ass off that first night back home. Much of his wild stage show from the James Gang days was gone, but Glenn transferred all that energy into his playing. I actually saw people weep when he played a slow blues; it was so sweet and beautiful. A friend of mine told me that he saw Glenn's eyeballs roll back into his head and drool come out of his mouth once while playing. The point of it is that this was no crappy 'entertainer.' This was not an 'act' or a 'show.' This was a guy ripping his heart out while playing for the people. Sometimes he would even appear to collapse from the intensity of it all, and he would play on his knees until he had the strength to stand up again."

In the midst of PG&E's rapidly growing success and expanding fan base, Glenn always insisted on sharing his newfound faith, regardless of where he was at the time.

"Once, when they played at a club called Euphoria on Euclid Avenue, Glenn walked up to the front of the stage, which jutted out into the audience, and threw tiny red Bibles out to people," Mark Jones told me. "We just rolled our eyes."

Darryl said, "Off stage when you'd see him he would sometimes hand you a little red booklet and inside there would be a Bible verse, like, 'What shall it profit a man if he gains the world but loses his soul?' Simple little things like that. I kept mine for years since Glenn had given it to me. And every now and then he'd make a passing comment about God, but it was always in that gentle way of his so it wasn't offensive at all. He was into the Jesus thing but he was not proselytizing or pushing his beliefs on anyone."

In 2007, Glenn told me over the phone that, "The Preacher Man came to Hoopples' bar a few weeks ago to see me play and I remember him back from when I lived on the farm. He had books on witchcraft that I saw and I felt the doom coming over me—but

I was okay because I fear God. I wasn't allowed to say anything at the farm—I kept out of trouble by keeping my mouth shut. But I didn't last at Fortney Road, I just couldn't make the grade, so I had to leave."

"Frank Cook had got us that first big tour," bassist Brent Block remembered. "It was supposed to be three cities. Cleveland, Detroit, and New York City. The New York job landed us a spot at the Miami Pop Festival, just after *Get It On* was released, and that got us about seven more weeks on the road. We were now a touring band. All that playing made us really tight musically."

The 1968 Miami Pop Festival was a turning point for PG&E's popularity. From December 28–30, 1968, the Gulfstream Park Racetrack in Hallandale Florida hosted the festival. The Saturday, Sunday, and Monday event was post-Monterey and pre-Woodstock and drew a total of almost 100,000 fans over three beautiful winter days. Many seminal acts of the time were featured, including Iron Butterfly, Steppenwolf, Canned Heat, the Grateful Dead, and Creedence Clearwater Revival. PG&E played the first day, sharing the stage with Fleetwood Mac, Country Joe and the Fish, and Three Dog Night, among others.

Glenn told me, "Whenever I did my first solo—pretty much everywhere we played—I would get an immediate standing ovation. When we played 'Stormy Times' from our first album, the whole place would go absolutely crazy, screaming and cheering."

All the acclaim had a troubling effect on Glenn. Now that he was in a successful and in-demand rock band, he saw the other rock icons of the day up close. He was friendly with Janis Joplin and Jim Morrison of the Doors and he knew the vices they struggled with.

"He felt the devil was after them," Butch Armstrong told me, "and he felt that the more famous he became, the bigger target he would have on his back. So for Glenn, fame was often something he attributed to the devil. I tried to explain to him that when people applauded and cheered, they were showing their appreciation for his talent, but he didn't think so."

The enthusiastic crowds, ideal weather and environment ensured every band at the Miami Pop Festival played at their peak. PG&E was no exception and, after wowing the audience with a blistering set of blues-rock, Glenn finished a blazing solo and stepped up to the microphone. His Riviera Semi Hollow guitar reflected and flashed off the sun like a bolt of lightning from the stage. The adoring fans clapped and roared their approval, still reeling from what they had just heard. Glenn eyed the more than 80,000 people. It was as if the whole world, a true sea of humanity, was before him.

From his vantage point, Glenn could see what many of them were doing, could smell what many of them were smoking, and knew what he, his fellow bandmates and the other artists at the festival had available to them. The world and all of its pleasures had truly been laid at his feet.

He grasped the microphone and the audience hushed a bit to hear their blues messiah speak. His bandmates looked on with apprehension.

"You know, my life seemed all right to me for a while until I was no longer in control. Then I was afraid . . . there was a revolution . . . and it took place inside me," Glenn said, looking intently at the restless mob before him. Someone whistled, the sound piercing but then it was immediately swallowed up.

What he said next shocked everyone.

With his guitar strapped in front of him, Glenn Schwartz pointed one hand to the sky and the other at the mass of people before him. "The revolution that took place in me . . . it happened when I was saved through Jesus Christ. I accepted Jesus through a real need. I want you to know I've kicked drugs!" he shouted into the microphone. "No more drugs, man! And I'll tell you something else. Christ is my savior now. Yeah, Jesus has saved me. He can save you too! Turn to Jesus, man—He's the only way to heaven. Ask Him into your heart!"

Disc jockey Dale Yancy was there and he remembered it well. "The place came apart and it blew the rock world's mind!"

In Ohio, Larry Hill thoughtfully read the newspaper stories about local guitar player Glenn Schwartz who was now traveling the country and "playing for Jesus."

Chapter 8

Sharing the Vision

W hile Glenn Schwartz was adjusting to the heady acclaim of being in a successful rock band, Joe, his wife Sandy, and an assortment of Joe's siblings were adjusting to the demands of a life lived with Reverend Larry Hill.

"When he began I think he had a truly humble heart before God," Joe said. "In all honesty we felt ourselves unique by association with Larry. It was like God had provided a prophet and teacher just for us, and the closer we got to the prophet, the closer we were to God. Once Sandy and me and my daughter and much of my family had relocated to Ohio from Chicago, all at once I was suddenly surrounded by Christians and church services."

By this time, Larry led a congregation of about thirty people and they met in the Harpersfield Town Hall Sunday mornings and

Image 15: Outside of Harpersfield Town Hall after a Sunday service in February1969: [Front] Joe's stepfather, Gilbert; Laura Markko; Randy Markko and his girlfriend, Cookie. [Back] Joe's daughter Shannon, Joe, his brother Matt, and two friends visiting from Chicago. Photo courtesy of Joe Markko.

evenings, and held midweek Bible studies in members' homes. They had also purchased five acres of land in the hopes of one day building their own church building.

Harpersfield Community Bible Church (HCBC) was made up of families from Michigan, Illinois, and Ohio. Drawing on the at times extreme Pentecostal evangelism of Oral Roberts as well as T.L. Osborne and Kathryn Kuhlman, Joe said, "The focus for this small group of willing, passionate hearts was that each and every person they met had to hear the gospel." (Although this was Larry Hill's first ministry, the majority of the congregation did not remain with him when he moved to Fortney Road, so I was unable to identify them and have focused on those who eventually became part of his Church of the Risen Christ ministry.)

The HCBC produced their own literature and had soon published the first edition of their *Freedom Bell* newspaper, which they filled with testimonies, Bible studies, poems, and topics relevant to the local community and culture.

Church members were on the streets witnessing all weekend and almost every night. The successful results of the HCBC outreaches were published in the *Freedom Bell* for all to see. Written like a revival testimony, the ministry boasted: "One confirmed pill popper and grass smoker delivered by the power of Christ" and "A young man that has been burning pot and tripping on LSD is completely delivered through Christ! HAVE FAITH IN GOD!"[6]

Larry continued to use nature, animals, birds and the weather to lead his flock and reveal to them the secret and mysterious insights God was showing him by revelation knowledge. However, his spiritual logic rarely made sense, yet no one was in the position to question the man of God. For example, Larry uses a divinely appointed peach tree to remind his parishioners about his vision of an eminent invasion of the United States by the Chinese. He wrote in the *Freedom Bell*:

> The Lord told us to cut the branch of an almond tree. We found the closest thing we have here to an almond tree is a peach tree. A young man went and cut the branch of a peach tree and I noticed it had four green peaches on it. The four green peaches were [my] visions about to mature into fruition. We also found the peach

tree comes from China. The Chinese name for the peach tree is tao mao. Also in [my] third vision Red China was constantly on my mind.[6]

In those days Cleveland was known as "the mistake by the lake" because it was a magnet for prostitutes, addicts of everything and anything, and the notorious Hell's Angels. During the 1960s, the motorcycle gang roared its way through the American Dream, its leather-jacketed and swastika-wearing members terrorizing entire towns with lead pipes and bike chains. The members of Larry's congregation never blinked in the face of any of these "mistakes," they just looked at everyone as a mission field and every weekend, they invaded the area.

"We went where the mission field was," Joe said. "No excuses. The mission and the moment might never come again. Jesus was coming back! This was the unction, the holy grease that drove the entire Jesus Movement."

But it was one thing to speak to the bikers on the streets, another to invite them to your house. Tim Hill recalled that his father would often bring home the bikers, terrifying his mother because of their rough appearance and behavior. Larry would occasionally encourage the men to stay a few days, which only intensified Carol Hill's discomfort.

Publicly, Larry Hill was a passionate, charismatic and loving minister, writing in the *Freedom Bell*:

> After years of Bible study I have finally discovered the true love of a father. A father manifests his love for his children by the rules he gives them to guide them to, and in, life. This is the Bible. It is the father's love letter, the map of life to His children.[6]

Larry stoked a true evangelical fever into his congregation and they literally went to the four corners of their world to tell people about Jesus and that He was coming soon. According to Joe, "Between 1968 and 1971 every household in the towns of Geneva, Rock Creek, Jefferson, New Lyme, Andover and Austinburg, Ohio had the gospel hand-delivered to their door" by one of Larry's congregants.

Each August, the Ashtabula Country Fair was held and HCBC leased a small, circus-type tent where they held services

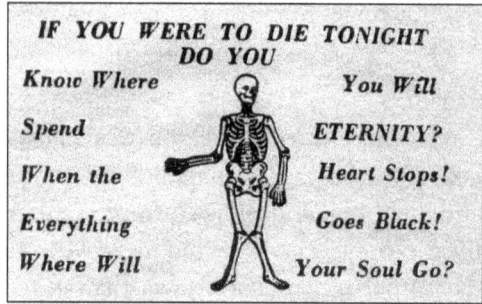

IF YOU WERE TO DIE TONIGHT DO YOU

Know Where You Will

Spend ETERNITY?

When the Heart Stops!

Everything Goes Black!

Where Will Your Soul Go?

Image 16: Members of Larry's church handed out thousands of copies of this salvation pamphlet or "tract" which they referred to as "The Skeleton Tract."

and invited the fair-goers in for refreshments. During the day, the women from the church staffed the tent and in the evening, the men took over when they returned from work. Both shifts handed out religious tracts and reminded everyone that Jesus was coming soon.

"But that wasn't enough," Joe said. "Sandy and I went to the farm camps of migrant workers from Mexico who came to Northeast Ohio to pick grapes. We had an interpreter and held church services one Sunday afternoon each month."

Larry's growing congregation was also kept busy with visits to the Ashtabula County Jail and local nursing homes, as well as creating a community action group called The Way Out. Joe said, "It was an attempt to mobilize people of influence in Ashtabula County for an anti-drug campaign."

Harold Fuller was one man of influence and he and his wife served on the anti-drug committee. Voted 1968's Man of the Year by the Orwell Chamber of Commerce, Fuller's photo was featured on the cover of the *Freedom Bell* and he speaks highly of Larry Hill's efforts:

> I serve on "The Way Out" committee because I am concerned about the problems our teenagers must face and are involved with today. Many young people are looking for help and I feel "The Way Out" has more to offer than possibly any other agency. I feel this way because it has definite proof of teenagers that have had this problem that are genuinely cured. I serve on the committee with these young people and have heard their stories of how deeply they have been involved in drugs. I have seen the change [in their lives] and what a fine group they are and [I have] told many others about them. I attribute this to the fine efforts of "The Way Out" committee and its leadership.[6]

All of these very high profile community activities served to give Larry Hill and his congregation a very positive identity in the community. But unbeknownst to his loyal and growing congregation and the community who was sending drug addicts to him for help, the Reverend continued to regularly and violently beat his wife and children.

Larry's son Tim remembered that when he was about seven years old he was having a difficult time learning his letters at school. "Dad made me hold my hands out in front of me and he started beating them." When Larry finished, Tim's hands were so swollen and bloody and he was in such pain that he wasn't able to go to school for a week.

In 1968 Larry decided God had given him the go ahead to share his 1965 visions and revelations with his congregation. He claimed that his prophesied invasion of the United States was about to take place.[6]

"I don't know if we all believed everything that Larry said when he shared his visions of a coming Great War," Joe explained, "but we did believe revolution in America was a possibility."

During this time, the United States was dealing with increasingly complex cultural and political trends, an escalating civil rights movement, and a real-life social revolution that was actively changing society. The Black Panthers, Students for a Democratic Society, the Weathermen and dozens of lesser-known radical groups were all convinced that war on American soil was imminent.

"We believed chaos in the streets would open the door to invasion and our personal survival was superseded by the survival of the Church in America," Joe explained. "Larry's 'Great War' would purge the dross from the Church and survivors would help rebuild the nation. We felt fortunate to have a prophet at our helm."

Once Larry told his congregation of his visions, he said that the invasion would soon occur and his group of former drug addicts, students of religion and young people would make up his "lasting generation."[6]

Joe said, "In the Bible, God always has 'a remnant,' a group of people who survived from which He would rebuild. And God also would always have a prophet through whom He would speak, guiding His people." Larry considered himself that prophet and those in his congregation would be that remnant.

To be part of what Larry called God's lasting generation—the remnant who would survive the Great War—it was imperative that adults and children learn self-control and obedience. And they would need a place to hide when God's wrath rained down on the United States.

The city of Geneva, Ohio, is located about nine minutes north of where Larry's congregation met and in the winter of 1968–69, almost 6000 people lived there. And none of them ever suspected— or could even have imagined—what was occurring while they slept.

That winter, Larry ordered his followers to "slip secretly into the woods at night near Geneva to dig out a cave to harbor his lasting generation."[13] When his prophesied attack came, this would be where they would hide. At that time, one member of his congregation said, "I would be afraid of him now, because he doesn't advocate being a pacifist, and he is preparing for war."[13]

Joe said, "In preparation for the Great War Larry had foreseen, we dug underground tunnels near high vantage points along the Grand River. Complete with battery powered lighting systems, they were designed to hide people and materials. Bethy's father set up the bracing and lighting for the tunnels. A small group of us would get dropped off in different remote locations each night around midnight. The driver would turn off the headlights to hide his activities from local residents. We would then follow paths and game trails through the woods until we arrived at the site of that night's work. Lookouts were set up and a password system was established to challenge anyone approaching."

Tim told me, "The challenge word was 'Zero' and the correct password was 'Freezing.'"

After a few hours of digging, the community members camouflaged the tunnels so they wouldn't be seen by anyone during the day and then silently marched through the woods to a designated pickup area. This continued night after night after night.

"We'd get home with just enough time to get a couple hours of sleep before the 4:00 a.m. alarm and then we'd be off to our day jobs," Joe said.

Tim said, "My brother Brett would often say that he was so exhausted, he could fall asleep anytime, in any position, standing up or outside, even at high noon."

And where was Larry Hill during those late, late nights? One former member said that Mark Hill told them, "On the nights when you guys were out freezing your asses off we'd be in downtown Cleveland eating at the best restaurants and staying at the best hotel."

By severely reducing their amount of sleep and convincing them that they were doing God's work—and that the Armageddon clock was ticking—everyone in the community was motivated to work impossibly long hours. "I can remember telling a friend how well I thought I could function if we could only average three hours of sleep per night, but we didn't even get that," another member told me. "I thought about sleeping all the time."

"Not sleeping much took its toll on me," Bob Tidd told me. "When I first moved to the farm in May of 1972, I worked 40 miles away. I normally hitchhiked to work. The first year or so I had already totaled two cars by falling asleep at the wheel. I ran a VW Beetle into a culvert, and I put my head through the windshield of another car when I ran into the back of a car that was stopped for car trouble. That was before seat belts.

"On one trip home from work one day I ran an older lady in a Cadillac off the road by swerving over into her lane while dosing off. But I was ready. I stopped and came to her aid. I made sure that she was alright and gave her our skeleton gospel tract that says 'If you were to die tonight do you know where you will spend eternity?' I wasn't ten miles down the road when I dozed off again and the police stopped me, I believe for weaving. The police officer made me walk a straight line to see if I was sober. I could walk straighter than I could drive!"

The damaging effects of sleep deprivation—commonly used in all cults—result in individuals who are highly suggestible, and who exhibit severe intellectual and motor impairment. Common symptoms of severe sleep deprivation include problems with concentration and long-term memory, verbal learning, and a difficulty in communicating with others due to the inability to find the right words. All of this makes the sleep-deprived person someone who is easy to intimidate.

And it always works. As a former member described it to me, "Unfortunately, we gave our love and loyalty to a pastor who morphed from purveyor to perverter of the truth over a period of twelve years. We were led to believe that God both required and rejoiced in our sacrifices. Second, we believed we were doing it for a heavenly Father who loved us. Third, we believed Jesus was really coming back. If those last three pieces weren't present, we would neither have tolerated nor endured the things we did."

One woman told me, "The sleep deprivation really took its toll on me. I felt so out of it, physically feeling like I was on something all day long, but I learned how to push through, just like we all did. Then home to more all-nighters and exercises, things I now know were meant to break us down. It worked. But I thoroughly believed I was doing what God wanted me to do. My purpose was to win the lost at any cost, even my own lifestyle."

A former member of the cult who suffered years of sexual and physical abuse and no longer considers herself a person of faith, wrote me, "I want to know from God, 'What glory did my pain bring to You?' I will know in the world to come, only then, I won't care."

In the mid-60s, Pentecostal Christianity was filled with "prophets." The entire generation was more open to such profession of spiritual insights and Larry's visions seemed reasonable and laudable within that context. One woman explained, "I had heard of the Great Tribulation occurring before the Rapture all of my life. I think I associated Larry's visions of the Great War with that."

Now that his small but growing congregation knew of his visions and were on board for preparing for the coming Great War, Larry felt it was imperative that they get the Word out faster and to a broader demographic. Larry began broadcasting a radio program on Sunday mornings. He called it "Time for the Risen Christ" and it was on WREO in Ashtabula County. The radio program did help to draw more people to the church services, but it was really a singer and his guitar and a simple song that caused the surrounding community to take notice and be drawn to Larry Hill and his ministry.

Chapter 9

Preacher and
the Witness

J oe hadn't touched his guitar since he arrived in Ohio, wanting to focus on the things of God and not be distracted with music. Late one night, feeling that enough time had passed, he went outside and played. "I remember it was late and very quiet," Joe said. "As I sat strumming my guitar beneath the glow of the deep night, I came up with what I felt was a reasonably good tune but couldn't think of any lyrics."

Glancing around in the darkness, he saw the words "There Is Still Hope In Jesus" written on the tailgate of a red pickup truck. Repeating those words a few times, he found they fit with the tune he was strumming. Then more words came, but only a few:

"There is still hope in Jesus
Let Him pick up the pieces of your life
And start anew
There's so much good you can do."[14]

"That was all I had," Joe said. "But that was enough. It pretty much said it all." Later he sat in Larry's living room and played the section with words, using it as a chorus, and then simply hummed where the unwritten verses would have been. As it turned out the humming was perfect for Larry to overlay the closing words of his radio broadcast. Unbeknownst to them, the first two pieces of an interesting, musical synergy had just come together.

It was September of 1968. "Although there was really no intention to form a musical group," Joe said, "I suppose you could say that Larry and I started one that night."

Image 17: An early incarnation of Preacher and the Witness: Joe Markko on guitar, Mike [last name unknown] on drums, Larry Hill on piano, and Randy Markko, seated, on bass.

A few of the church members had some musical skills or experience, so when the band—christened Preacher and the Witness—began, it was very primitive with a basic line-up that usually included Joe on guitar, Larry Hill on piano and Randy Markko on bass.

"No one had any experience in writing songs. In fact, I had to teach my brother Randy how to play bass," Joe said. "Larry was a wordsmith and gifted poet, and I'd performed publicly as a musician since I was nine so, between us all, we managed to hammer out enough songs to constitute a set."

Larry often wore a broad-brimmed, Amish hat and a long black priest's cassock during concerts. Preacher and the Witness began playing on street corners, in coffee houses and churches, and the folk band began to get attention in northeast Ohio.

While Preacher and the Witness grew in popularity, the church's outreach continued in earnest. There were hundreds of encounters with a wide assortment of street people, some willing to hear the message being presented to them and join the congregation while others shrugged with indifference or shouted away the persistent church members.

Even the "want ads" placed in the *Freedom Bell* were evangelistic, proclaiming:

WANTED:
A dope fiend, whore, gang member,
hippie or teeny bopper in desperate need of HELP!
If you're willing to let JESUS CHRIST work in your life,
CALL: GENEVA, OHIO 466-2210.[6]

Larry was very specific when he spoke to his congregation about how to evangelize their community:

Be courteous and kind but firm. If you have a Gospel tract with you, hold it out boldly to the person and say, "Here's something you will like to read!" NOT, "Would you like to read this?" With an elevator operator, if you're going up, you can look at the operator and say something like, "I don't want to go down." They'll look at you like you're out of your mind, and if you say it enough times they'll probably inform you that you're going up. Then you can say that you know the elevator is going up, but you meant that you didn't want to go to hell, how about them? If the elevator is going down, work out something of your own for that. At a service station one day an attendant said, "Man, it's hotter than hell, ain't it?" I immediately smiled, stuck out my hand and said, "I'm really glad to meet you because I've accepted Jesus as my Savior and I'll never have to go to hell. Now you, evidently, have been there. Is it really as hot as they say it is?" Even if this irritates some, they're usually under conviction from the start. Press your point.[15]

Joe's sister Laura had visited the congregation several times but it wasn't until November of 1968 that she made a commitment to the group, as she wrote in the *Freedom Bell*:

I had coffee with Brother Hill on Saturday November 2. We talked about things I was in, and how Jesus could help me. I noticed how my brother Randy had started to change. How happy my father seemed to be! I'd sit and listen to everyone talking about how Jesus loved everyone. I watched the people get together for prayer meetings, and even then I could feel like a peaceful unity among them. After that we went to Larry's house and started praying. The next thing I knew, my arms were up in

Image 18: A photo of Laura Markko from the Freedom Bell.

the air and I was praising the Lord! I was feeling the love, peace and happiness I always wanted all at once. I felt the love of Jesus Christ inside and opening my mind, heart and soul. That night was the most glorious night of my life.[6]

When Laura joined the church, she bragged to Carol Hill and members of the congregation that she and a former boyfriend were closely associated with several men who were very much involved with the disruption of the 1968 Democratic Convention in Chicago, including the rioting that took place between the demonstrators and the Chicago Police Department:

> Toward the summer [of 1968] I started to get into demonstrations. Then I got into the thing that was happening on Sundays in Lincoln Park. I met more people there. I met people who you might say were instigators of the Yippie, or who came up with the idea.[6]

Founded in 1967, the Yippies stood for the Youth International Party, and they were part of the counterculture, anti-war movement. The term was created by Abbie Hoffman and Jerry Rubin who were social and political activists and symbols of youth rebellion.

In typical fashion, Larry greatly embellished Laura's story as part of his introduction to his *Scripture Lessons for Modern Man*, a bound collection of his teachings on basic Christianity he published years later. In the introduction, he wrote:

It may bless you to know that after they were converted, such individuals as Tom Miller, the young revolutionary that started the fires at Kent Campus when the students were shot; Laura Markko, a former dope pusher that aided Jerry Rubin with the Chicago Yippie; Glenn Schwartz, world famous guitarist; some family members of President Ford's cabinet, ministers and laymen from all classes have studied SCRIPTURE LESSONS FOR MODERN MAN.[15]

When asked about these claims, Laura's brother Joe told me, "To say my sister Laura 'aided Jerry Rubin with the Chicago Yippie' is a clear distortion of the truth. Laura had nothing to do with planning anything relative to the demonstrations in 1968. We've all learned that Larry had a way of stretching the truth to make his ministry seem more powerful than it ever really was."

Laura's false claims about being involved with the Yippies revealed a young woman who was hungry for recognition. When she joined Larry's congregation, she sensed immediately how the chain of command was organized and sought out the one woman who could hopefully grant her the esteem and attention she desired.

Diane Sullivan—the woman Laura's brother Joe referred to as the sadistic Nurse Ratched from the *Cuckoo's Nest*—was to become Laura's closest friend.

Chapter 10

Moving to
Fortney Road

B y the late 1960s, hippie communes were springing up all over the country, as alternatives to the traditional family, and it was an idea that appealed to Larry. Although most of the church members already spent as much time together as possible, the thought of combining their resources was tempting.

"We felt the whole would be significantly greater than the sum of its parts," Joe said. However, this radical idea didn't sit well with everyone. Those who had formerly given great chunks of money to the work of Larry's ministry began to hold back, uncertain where things were headed. Living in a commune and putting everyone's money into one pot wasn't what they had signed on for.

Meetings were held, voices and opinions were heard, argued and prayed over but it was clear that the church was splitting. Attendance at the services began to decline as whole families stopped coming. Soon it was clear there wasn't going to be much of a congregation left to form a commune or a church. Larry—speaking on God's behalf—overruled all objections. When the dust settled, many members including Joe's stepfather, Gilbert, along with Larry's mother, Thelma, and Diane's father, Harold Sullivan, and most of his family, left the church. Diane Sullivan stayed, choosing Larry over her family. In appreciation for her loyalty, Larry invited Diane to move in with him and Carol Hill and their children to more closely assist him in the ministry.

When Larry's mother Thelma left the church, he severed his relationship with her as he did the others, labeling them all enemies and saying they were examples of how anyone could be used by the devil and become a Judas. Larry proclaimed the entire experience a test, that as the Great War grew closer, the loyalty of *everyone* would be examined. God was simply separating the wheat from the chaff. It was time to close ranks.

After the church split, the remaining members of HCBC consisted of about forty-five men, women and children. Reverend Larry Hill was now in his early thirties and the oldest member of the congregation, both chronologically and spiritually. "Because we were so young in so many ways, there was no one to correct him or challenge his thinking," Joe said. "He was the pastor, he was the authority figure, and because he was never challenged, this provided the root for his eventual corruption."

Since Larry was never able to raise the money to construct a building for the HCBC, he decided that the members would now live as a commune and share everything in common. He sold the acreage and with the funds purchased a small farm straddling both sides of Fortney Road, outside Windsor, Ohio. The owner, Mrs. Seymour, sold the property to the church below market value. As a Christian woman, she rejoiced that it would be used "for the Lord's work."

With only a large red barn on the east side of the road and a two-story farmhouse on the other, it would take time to make it livable for the growing group's purposes. But the congregation provided an almost unending supply of willing and enthusiastic labor. As Joe said, "Sanctified sweat was a small price to pay when you believe you're building a legacy for God." And with Larry's Great War coming soon, there was no time to waste.

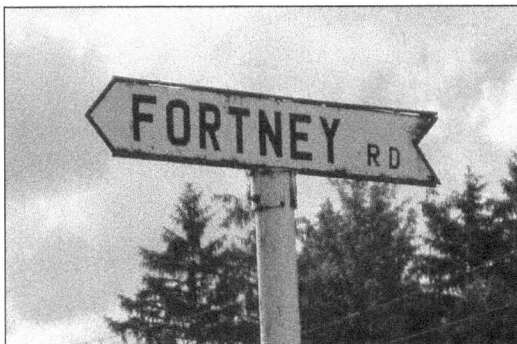

Image 19: The Fortney Road street sign in 2005.

Image 20: The barn on Fortney Road in 2005.

The community busied themselves setting acres of fence posts, corncribs, and additions to the house. Treadle sewing machines were collected and all the women learned to sew, making clothes from scratch. The women canned jars of food and learned to dry food and preserve meats. Carole King Hough told me, "We canned everything, and I mean everything. We cleaned people's fields after they'd finished their harvest, and canned the leavings. The basement was full."

When asked about their farming skills, Leon, who joined the community in 1971, said, "We were rarely successful at raising any crops and the vegetable gardens were often allowed to become overgrown with weeds. Few farmers can profitably raise livestock by purchasing all of their feed, grain, and hay, and yet this was the way we operated. I knew little if any of our farming activity was paying off, but because Larry claimed so many times to be directed by God, it was impossible to argue with God's cost accounting. In addition to the aforementioned problems, we kept many horses, ponies, and other unproductive livestock. At times we had as many as fifty ponies, three milk cows, a couple bulls, twenty-five or more cattle, ten or fifteen horses, forty pigs, and twenty goats."

One former member recalls that his chore was butchering the farm animals for food. Several times he was asked to butcher

Image 21: The farmhouse on Fortney Road in 2005.

Image 22: The second residence on Fortney Road in 2005.

ponies when they died in the mud on the farm. "I literally broke a knife trying to cut it," he said, recalling a meal of pony meat.[16]

The single men slept in the barn until a dormitory-like addition could be built, and they were not permitted in the farmhouse unless Larry was present.[13] Single women and married couples found beds and floor space throughout the farmhouse, some occupying one of the four bedrooms while others laid claim to the study, front porch, living room or whatever space they could find. Eventually, a second house (Image 22) was secured a half-mile south on Fortney Road to accommodate the needs of families.

"That other house was another good idea turned slowly sour because it eventually became viewed as second-class housing." Joe said. "Larry never wanted to put any money into it, so those who lived there endured broken windows and drafty, dingy rooms."

Morgan King was single and recalled that he "slept in the barn one winter and in the winter before that, I slept in the second house that had no heat, no electricity, just four walls."[13]

According to Larry's son, Tim, Larry's bedroom was nicely finished with silk knotty pine while Joe said the living room in Larry's house had handcrafted tongue and groove cherry paneling.

To bury the name and memory of those of the HCBC who had betrayed him and put behind him the failed attempts to raise money to build a church, Larry decided to rename the ministry the Church of the Risen Christ or CRC. The words "CRC Farm" were painted in large black letters over the red barn door for everyone to see.

The community's final sign of ownership was to carve onto a cross-section of a tree trunk a portion of a poem by J.R.R. Tolkien, "All That Is Gold Does Not Glitter":

> All that is gold does not glitter,
> Not all those who wander are lost;
> The old that is strong does not wither,
> Deep roots are not reached by the frost.[17]

Larry had read *The Lord of the Rings* and discovered J.R.R. Tolkien was a Christian. He became obsessed with the story and the author's writings. After the words had been carved into the tree trunk, it was suspended by a hook and chain from a tree by the driveway. That tree and some of the children who lived at Fortney Road are shown in image 23: Bethy Goodenough is the third child from the left, wearing the bandana. Joe Markko's daughter Shannon is the tall girl in the

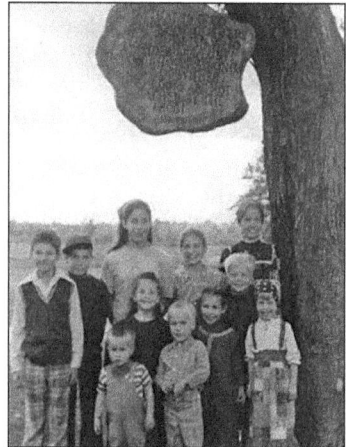

Image 23: Some of the children who lived at Fortney Road. Photo courtesy of Joe Markko.

back. The Tolkien poem "All That Is Gold Does Not Glitter" is carved into the suspended tree trunk.

Joe recalled that Larry presented the new congregation with his constitution and bylaws, which admonished in part:

> No member shall use tobacco in any form, be a habitual user of drugs or alcoholic beverages, attend theaters or moving pictures or indulge in any gambling activities or card games as such.

Pretty standard stuff for any devout Christian but some of the rules had darker implications:

> Christians shall dress as those professing godliness and shall sweetly obey those that have the rule over them.

The growing congregation at Fortney Road could never have fathomed what kind of rules they would be expected to "sweetly obey."

Chapter 11

From Offstage to Onstage

W hile Larry's flock was growing, so was Glenn Schwartz's faith and his boldness in sharing it.

For example, when PG&E opened for Fleetwood Mac, which at the time featured three guitarists—Peter Green, Danny Kirwan and Jeremy Spencer—Jeremy remembers a significant encounter with Glenn.

"Before a concert in San Francisco's Fillmore West, Glenn Schwartz asked me if I believed in Jesus. I said I did—and I guess I actually did, in a mental sort of way. 'Then say something about Jesus on stage tonight,' Glenn said to me. 'It would make Him happy.'"[18]

That night during the concert, Jeremy waited for the right time to say something. Finally, before one song, he spoke up. "I want to say something about Jesus!" He hesitated, not sure what he wanted to say, and some members of the crowd shouted in disdain. The crowd waited. Finally, he finished his statement. "Yes . . . just . . . just read what He has to say!"[18]

In 2012, in response to my email about his encounter with Glenn, Jeremy wrote,

Image 24: Glenn Schwartz in 1969. Photo courtesy of Stephanie Landry

"After the gig, Glenn told me about asking Jesus into my heart, a concept I had never heard about in my homeland of England. That night alone in my hotel room, I did. I felt no sensations or anything right then, but I sensed my life, conceptions and perceptions changing over the coming year or so, and I began praying for a change in my life and direction. The Lord answered that prayer when He led me to leave Fleetwood Mac in early 1971 and pursue a different calling."

Following PG&E's well-received performance at the Miami Pop Festival, twenty-six-year-old talent scout David Geffen told Frank Cook that Clive Davis wanted the band on the Columbia label. After Columbia Records signed the red-hot group, a self-titled album was released in August 1969 and fared better than their debut, reaching number 91 on the *Billboard* charts.

"While soloing, Glenn would often raise his right hand to his forehead," Darryl said. "It was sort of his version of a Pete Townsend windmill, so to speak. I asked Glenn to raise his hand with that gesture when this picture [image 25] was taken."

Image 25: Euclid, Ohio, May 1969: Glenn Schwartz, Mark Jones, Darryl Berk. Photo courtesy of Darryl Berk.

Even in the midst of the success of PG&E, Glenn never lost his desire to tell the guitar heroes of the day about his newfound faith in Christ. Bible in hand, he sought out Johnny Winter, Jimmy Page and Gregg and Duane Allman of the Allman Brothers Band.

Glenn told me in 2007, "Although I was never a close friend of Jimi Hendrix, Eric Clapton, Jeff Beck or Jimmy Page, we all knew of one another, but they were all *much* better players than I was. You couldn't get real close to Jimi Hendrix because he was so popular, but I kept praying for him. I remember walking the streets of New York City one cold, cold winter night. I was just praying about Jimi and next thing I knew, a Cadillac pulled up next to me. Inside were some of Jimi's people—they had recognized me—and they invited me back to where Jimi was having a party." Glenn recalled that it was Jim Fox, the James Gang drummer, who was in the Cadillac with Jimi's people and had spotted Glenn on the street.

For decades there has been a story circulating that Jimi Hendrix requested that Glenn Schwartz—"one of his favorite guitar players"—perform at what turned out to be Hendrix's last birthday, November 27, 1969. The story isn't true. Glenn himself told me when I spoke to him in 2007. Larry Hill, who tended to exaggerate whenever it served his purposes, most likely started the rumor. First, in the *Freedom Bell*, Larry wrote:

> Schwartz . . . impressed the late Jimi Hendrix when he played at Hendrix's last birthday party.[6]

Then in the liner notes for 1976's *Brainwashed* album, Larry wrote:

> But the rock world knew they had more than a propaganda-produced superstar when Honor of Honors came running down. Jimi Hendrix himself requested Glenn to play at what turned out to be his last birthday party.[19]

And finally, in the liner notes of the 1980 *Sower* album, Larry wrote:

> Jimi Hendrix wanted the best. That's why he asked Glenn Schwartz to play for him at what turned out to be his last birthday party.[20]

The truth is that Jimi spent his last birthday at the Rolling Stones concert at Madison Square Garden. The Stones' dressing room was so crowded with people coming and going throughout the day that the band decided to stay out and they retreated to a back room.[21] When Glenn arrived in the packed, backstage dressing room, he told me he jammed with the drummer and bassist for Jimi's newly formed but ever-changing Band of Gypsies.

"I was playing this blues riff with the guys," Glenn said, demonstrating to me over the phone his still extraordinary talents, "and Jimi stopped by and listened for a bit and nodded his head. But nobody cared who I was."

According to Glenn, by this time relationships were strained with his PG&E bandmates. "Tom Marshall hated me when he saw me with a Bible. The whole band hated me and I hated playing with them."

When asked to comment, PG&E bassist and band co-founder Brent Block told me, "While there was hostility and tension, I don't think anyone in the band 'hated' Glenn. Well, speaking for myself, I know I didn't hate him. But, simply put, I think Glenn is right that the band didn't want to be around him, but I don't think Glenn wanted to be around the rest of us in the band as well. To the best of my memory, it was more Glenn distancing himself from the band and what he would often call the 'evils of rock and roll' than it was us. I remember thinking at first that this was hopefully just some phase he was going through. Business-wise, Glenn was too valuable to the band to simply kick him out for his radical religious behavior."

But the band's frustration only increased when Glenn took his proselytizing from offstage to onstage. It was during a show at the Fillmore West, to a mostly stoned audience, that Glenn decided to begin preaching from the stage.

Brent told me, "We're playing a slow blues number and the lyrics of the song were about dying from a sexually transmitted disease! Glenn's in the middle of one of his solos and all of the sudden, he starts exhorting the audience! I'm sure he felt that he had to reach people where they were. Still, a band on stage is a collective personality and not an individual using it as a platform to expose personal beliefs."

It was after that incident that the band sat down and had a talk with Glenn.

"I remember a band meeting where we attempted to reason with Glenn concerning voicing his beliefs from the stage," Brent said. "People didn't pay to come hear a sermon. They paid to come hear a great blues band, something that we worked hard to become, and that included developing a fan base. For me, his personal life is just that, personal, and it has no business on the stage."

Glenn took the confrontation with his bandmates as evidence that the guys in PG&E loved his talent but detested his Christian beliefs. But he was undeterred by the intervention and remained intent on preaching the gospel to everyone he encountered, and he soon crossed paths with a superstar singer known as "the Queen of Psychedelic Soul."

Janis Joplin and Glenn Schwartz had come to musical prominence in the mid-to-late 60s, so they frequently crossed paths while touring, and several times, PG&E shared a bill with Janis.

Janis asked that her friends call her Pearl and when Glenn heard this, he immediately told her the parable of the Pearl of Great Price. "It's all about the great value of God's kingdom," he had told her excitedly. "It's like the value of a pearl—" Janis rolled her eyes and walked away, shaking her head. "Oh Glenn, Glenn, Glenn."

Glenn told me about another time he tried to convince Janis to turn to Christ. "I had some Christian friends who had some round stickers that read 'Real Peace Is In Jesus' and we stuck those all over our clothes. We put some on Janis but she didn't like it and took them off. I remember she got pretty upset."

He had read that Janis had once jokingly said, "People, whether they know it or not, like their blues singers miserable! They like their blues singers to die afterwards." He had cringed when he'd heard that, and promised the Lord that he'd pray more fervently for Janis.

While Glenn was testifying before PG&E's thousands of fans and trying to convert Janis Joplin and others, Reverend Larry Hill was busy on a much smaller scale with his popular little folk-rock band, Preacher and the Witness.

Both Glenn and Larry were ferverently praying for God to lead them and reveal His will to them, and within a year they would meet and begin recording together. They were both certain it was God's will, and certainly an answered prayer.

But as Saint Teresa of Avila once said, *more tears are shed over answered prayers than unanswered ones.*

Chapter 12

The All Saved Freak Band

B y 1970, Larry had gradually incorporated more people and musical talents and instruments into Preacher and the Witness and with each addition, the sound began to change from simple folk music to incorporate a more contemporary sound, so Larry decided to give the band a new name.

"We were practicing on the front porch at the farm," Joe told me, "and Larry mentioned he felt a need for a name change for the band. It turned into a comedy break with everyone contributing serious and funny names, making little Bible jokes and puns and plays on words and so on."

Joe threw out a name that suggested they were all just a bunch of freaks, a group of ex-druggies and hippies, runaways and rebels. A bunch of saved freaks was how he put it.

After a few chuckles and comments Larry zeroed in on that name and it stuck: The All Saved Freak Band.

The Church of the Risen Christ community and the All Saved Freak Band may have remained secluded and faded into obscurity, their dark secrets their own, if it wasn't for what happened in the spring of 1970. It was a violent local event that quickly impacted the nation.

Richard M. Nixon was sworn in as the 37th President of the United States on January 20, 1969, promising to bring an end to the Vietnam War. More than 40,000 American soldiers had been killed in that conflict by the end of 1969.

In April of 1970, Nixon stunned the country by announcing a US and South Vietnamese invasion into Cambodia to end the war in Vietnam and win a "just peace." The announcement generated an immediate, nationwide outcry against him and his war policy. Attendance and frequency of anti-war demonstrations increased, American college campuses erupted in protest, and Nixon derided anti-war students as nothing more than "bums blowing up campuses."

Ohio's Kent State University was roughly twenty miles from the Church of the Risen Christ farm in Windsor. A campus demonstration was held on May 1, 1970, and another was planned for May 4. As each day passed, the crowds and anger increased and by May 2, Kent's Mayor Leroy Satrom had declared a state of emergency. Subsequently, the National Guard was sent to Kent to help maintain order.

An estimated two thousand people gathered on the university's commons on May 4 for what proved to be the final protest. A group of about one hundred National Guardsmen, with bayonets fixed on their weapons, began to advance on the hundreds of protesters. As the guardsmen pressed forward, the protestors retreated up and over a hill. It was at this point that a number of guardsmen at the top of the hill abruptly fired into the crowd. Nine students were wounded, and four were killed. The shootings led to protests on college campuses throughout the United States and the Kent State campus remained closed for six weeks.

Larry Hill would later imply that he had known the tragic event was going to occur months before it happened. The *Freedom Bell* reprinted an article in which he told reporter Jean Mlincek in the *Kent Record-Courier*:

> Four months before the May fourth shootings at Kent University, I felt real burdened to come here. I don't know, but Kent was pressed upon my mind, and there's people who can verify that. When the killings came, I wondered in my heart if I had waited too long.[6]

However, since Mlincek references James Michener's book on Kent State, *What Happened and Why* (published in April 1971) it means her article was written more than a year after the campus tragedy. So Larry had plenty of time to think up another of his "after the fact" prophecies. And who at Fortney Road would not verify he had prophesised the event?

"It was a very emotional time and everyone was angry and in shock over what had happened," Joe said. "Larry immediately felt the Lord was directing us to the streets of Kent. We started the effort with street work leading up to a concert held in one of the university's large auditoriums. I remember the meetings we held were well attended. For a short time we held Sunday services in Kent's Student Union building, but it was so crowded that we eventually moved to Joe Bujak's (JB's) bar on Water Street." Larry made an agreement that no alcohol was to be served and the church was free to use the large upstairs area for its services. More than 125 street people and college students regularly attended the meetings. The All Saved Freak Band later recorded a song "Water Street" about the events at JB's bar, and include it on their second album.

One of the Kent State protesters, Tom Miller, heard the All Saved Freak Band perform, attended one of the Sunday afternoon services at JB's, and eventually moved to Fortney Road.

Alan Canfora—one of nine students shot and wounded during the Kent State shootings—was a friend of Tom's. "He was born and raised in Smithville, Ohio," Alan told me. "We loved him as

Image 26: Tom Miller in 1970.
Photo courtesy of George Caldwell.

our brother at KSU. He was beautiful, very poetic and artistic, and he loved Bob Dylan."

"Tom was one of the sweetest, gentlest, kindest people you'd ever meet," Leon said. "He exuded strength of character and humility."

Tom Miller was born in April of 1949, one of eleven children. In his youth, he had been very active in church, choir, band, and sports. His younger brother by eighteen months, John, told me, "Up until the end of his sophomore year in high school, he was my best friend in the world. That's when he started doing drugs. He started with marijuana and eventually graduated to stronger things. During that time, his personality changed dramatically. By the time he was a senior, he had dropped out of everything.

"As young men, we often had discussions about God and the church. He cared about the Lord deeply but often struggled with his faith, and by his senior year, he had given up on the notion of God. Vietnam and the death of a cousin in that war served as proof to him that God did not exist. If by some chance He did exist, Tom had no interest in following a God who would allow such suffering. At that point in his life, God was for those foolish enough to believe."

Tom Miller eventually did graduate from high school. At Kent State, he not only used drugs, but also began bringing them back and selling them to the kids in his hometown of Smithville, Ohio. "He believed that drugs liberated a person to see the truth about our existence," John told me. "His cynicism, drug use, the political climate and probably his age combined to form one angry young man. He had a close-knit circle of druggy friends who knew him as a fun loving and caring person. He was very loyal in that regard."

One of Tom's college friends, Tom Grace, told me, "Because he was so nice and from a really religious family, everyone called Tom 'Aquinas' after Saint Thomas Aquinas. He had some saintly qualities about him."

On the day of the Kent State shootings, a bullet struck Tom Grace in his left ankle. "I had already been removed from the scene but my friends told me that Aquinas had picked up a flag and went over to where Jeff Miller had been killed." (Jeff Miller and Tom Miller were not related.)

Image 27: Tom Miller waving the blood-soaked flag. Photo courtesy of Howard Ruffner.

"There was a huge puddle of blood after Miller's body had been taken away," Tom Grace said. "Aquinas took the black flag and dipped it in the blood—really saturated it—and began jumping up and down in the blood. After that he proceeded to whip this flag around as quickly as he could, spraying blood everywhere."

According to Alan Canfora, "When Tom saw the body of Jeffrey Miller lying there, he just lost it. He just wanted to get blood on the others to make it more real for them."

Tom Miller immediately gained a great degree of notoriety after Howard Ruffner's photo of him with the flag appeared in *Life* magazine.

John Miller said, "On the Friday following May 4, 1970, I was alone in my dorm room at Wittenberg University when my phone rang. It was my brother Tom. He talked about what had happened at Kent State and was highly critical of the soldiers and the government. He told me that he was among the group that set the ROTC building on fire. He also admitted to provoking and throwing rocks at the soldiers. He was so mad that he was yelling, swearing and cursing all at the same time."

When John heard what part his brother had played, he got angry and accused him of being just as guilty as the men who pulled the triggers. "I remember his last words to me were, 'You just don't get it!'"

A few hours later, in the middle of the night, there was a knock at John's door.

"It was Tom. I didn't realize it then, but he was on the run. The police and the FBI were looking for him. He had been identified as one of the 'Kent 25.'" The Kent 25 referred to the twenty-five students and faculty indicted by a grand jury on criminal charges connected with the campus demonstration and the fire at the ROTC building.

Tom Miller recalled what happened during the shootings in an interview in the *Freedom Bell*:

> Those bullets were everywhere but in me. And I was the one that really deserved them. For previous to the shootings, only myself and two companions out of a mob of hundreds stood out in the open, taunting the guardsmen who later did the killings. I cursed them and actually invited them to shoot me, screaming at the top of my lungs, "Shoot me! I'm a helpless woman! I'm a child! Shoot me!" (I was referring to the My Lai massacre). It was then that there was a shout and something seemed to be driving the mob toward the guardsmen. When I saw one of the soldiers drop to his knees and aim, I turned and started to run like everybody else, but then I jumped behind a small tree. The bullets flew by me so close I could feel the wind from them on my left and my right. One of my companions was cut down a few feet to my right. Another close friend had squatted down behind me and his wrist, which protruded only a few inches from behind my left side, was pierced with a bullet.[6]

After a week of hiding out with his brother John, Tom Miller announced that he was going to go out west to "find himself."

"I'm not sure where he went," John said to me, "but it was during that time that he accepted Christ. He had challenged God to show Himself in a tangible way. He asked God to take away his addictions, and God did—immediately and powerfully. Tom had finally found peace. And soon after, Tom met Larry Hill, and he was attracted to this preacher who had himself claimed to have been powerfully delivered from addiction."

Tom was also attracted to the All Saved Freak Band's music. It was loud and raucous, very much of its time, and also unique since it was all about Jesus. Joe told me, "When playing live, the All Saved Freak Band were loud enough to have our electrical connections cut off on more than one occasion," by chuch groups offended by the secular sound. "Remember, we were all reared on Hendrix, Cream and Blue Cheer, so when it was time to crank it up . . . we smiled!"

John Miller told me he had two opportunities to go to the Sunday services where the All Saved Freak Band played. "It was so deafening that I had to hold my hands over my ears."

An art student and musician, Tom Miller went on to contribute greatly to the graphic look of the *Freedom Bell* and was an enthusiastic member of the Church of the Risen Christ community. Tom concluded his story in the *Freedom Bell* by stating:

> I started attending church services at JB's in Kent on Sunday afternoons. Brother Larry Hill preached, the All Saved Freak Band played and gave testimonies, and the power of God began to work stronger in my life. It was in Brother Hill's ministry that I came to realize the necessity of actually living the Christian life every day. By the grace of God I am privileged to have good teaching and to be part of the All Saved Freak Band. We continue to worship God as we sing, play, and testify under the anointing of the Holy Spirit. Brother Hill continues to preach, and souls are continually being saved. Praise God for giving the increase![6]

Larry's church services at JB's bar soon became so crowded on Sunday afternoons that a "daughter" church was started called the Kent New Generation Church. For the remainder of 1970, the community members and the All Saved Freak Band—at this point made up of Larry, Randy, Dave Bechler, and Joe—shuttled back and forth between Kent and the farm on Fortney Road.

Image 28 was taken in the alley outside Butcher Boy Meats after a Sunday meeting of the Kent New Generation Church. Larry

Image 28: The Kent New Generation Church held worship services from 2:00 p.m. to 4:30 p.m. every Sunday.

Hill is the second person from the left. Joe Markko and his wife Sandy are on the far right. Sandy is holding their son Jonathan.

A month after the Kent State shootings, the film *The Cross and the Switchblade*, based on the Teen Challenge ministry of David Wilkerson, was released. It opened strongly in nearly 300 theaters and with Pat Boone as the star, attracted a great deal of national media attention. So of course Larry Hill boasted to the *Kent Record Courier* paper that he was "a former associate with David Wilkerson's Teen Challenge."[6]

That same year, the talent pool of the All Saved Freak Band increased significantly when Pam and Kim Massmann showed up. According to the *Freedom Bell:*

> It was an especially exciting time the afternoon that the Minnesota University Orchestra Conductor's second oldest daughter, Kim Massmann, walked in to hear the All Saved Freak Band. Next week she came back and a friend asked Rev. Hill if she could sing for the group. Usually the Rev. was very strict about who he let sing before a congregation or in a concert. He said, "I don't believe in making a whole auditorium full of people miserable just to make one person happy." But there seemed to be something special about this girl. After [Kim] had sung, everybody knew why![6]

Rob Galbraith, who would later produce the All Saved Freak Band, said, "I've heard about voices like hers but I never had the privilege of being in the studio with a voice as clear as Kim Massmann's."[6]

Kim became very enthused about the All Saved Freak Band and returned several times to hear them play. She invited her older

Image 29: Kim and Pam Massmann.

sister Pam to join her. Pam's voice was as beautiful as Kim's and soon they joined the band and, with their parents' blessing, moved to Fortney Road when they were just out of high school.

Kim and Pam were the oldest of five siblings and were both trained in vocals, piano, and guitar, while Pam was also an accomplished cellist and Kim a violinist. Their father, Dr. Richard Massmann, was then the conductor of the Minnesota University Orchestra and he had trained them in classical music.

"Having a violin and cello live on stage as an integral part of rhythmic music was a brand new concept when we did it," Joe said, "and these women weren't 'schlock' musicians. They had trained, delicate voices and musical skills that matched the sound of their instruments, and they taught the rest of us music theory in classes for the band."

Kim and Pam quickly absorbed Larry's end-time teaching and the three of them frequently wrote songs together. "They often collaborated on what may be considered some of the more controversial songs we recorded," Joe said. "They were very much about the whole 'prophetic' side of things. They wrote songs about things we'd been hearing at almost every church service for years. Larry ended up being extremely conspiracy-oriented and was always warning us about groups and individuals he considered false and dangerous. They sang from their orientation, trying to warn the world with what they'd been taught."

Pam Massmann also took care of all concert dates as well as all the band's business. She wrote letters and made phone calls, and worked hard to book the band.

It was a few months after the Massmann sisters joined the band that Tom Miller's brother John remembered contacting Larry Hill to have the band play at the Springfield College campus' spiritual emphasis week. "Larry was an absolute control freak," John recalled. "He demanded that we place radio spots, newspaper ads, and posters announcing their coming. Every day, he called to make yet another demand on us."

However, just two days before the concert, John called Larry to make sure everything was in order and Larry announced that they wouldn't be coming. John said, "He gave no explanation. I contacted the newspaper and radio stations to cancel everything. I also cancelled the gymnasium with the university."

The next day, Larry called John and informed him that the band would come but only if they were sent gas money, which John wired to the farm by Western Union. "Of course, it was too late to get anything about the band's now on-again concert in the paper, and the radio station refused to do any spots for us. But we quickly put posters up around town and on campus, and I was able to secure the gymnasium again. It was a grand and glorious mess."

John lived off campus in a rented old Victorian house with thirteen other students. When Larry and the group arrived, John remembers that Larry walked into the house as if he owned the place. He informed John that the group would require something very light to eat before the concert and then a full-blown meal afterward.

"The concert went well—we had done the best we could promoting it—but the hall was only three-quarters filled due to the on-again, off-again advertising," John said. "There were probably several hundred in attendance."

After the concert was over, Larry asked to see all the students who had been involved in the promotion of the event. He called them up on the stage and had them gather behind the curtains. "Then he proceeded to ream us out royally," John told me. "He was furious that we hadn't filled the hall for him. He told us that we should have been out in the streets inviting people to come. He ranted and raved for over half an hour, informing us that it had been a waste of his time to come all that way for such a small group."

When they all returned to the house, John exchanged words with Larry, pointing out that the problem was not the students' "laziness" in promoting the event, but Larry's inability to be organized and keep a commitment. "He did not receive that word very well at all," John said. "I noticed that the group that came from the farm were entirely cowed by Larry, and I became very uncomfortable."

During supper, John observed that Larry refused to talk with the female students, and the women from the farm "were not permitted to look at any of us, and they were only permitted to speak in very soft voices. They shielded their eyes and continually looked down at the floor. And all the guys seemed exhausted and worn out."

Concerned for his brother, John managed to get Tom away from the group so that he could speak with him in private. "This was very difficult under the watchful eye of Larry. It was obvious that he did not want us to be alone together."

John asked one of his friends to chat with Larry to distract him, and John managed to get Tom out of the room without Larry noticing. "I asked Tom what was going on. He talked about how great things were at Fortney Road, how he was learning so much about himself and the Lord. I asked about his daily routine and he said he had a factory job during the day to provide much-needed cash for the farm. After he got home, there was farm work to do, and then Larry would give him a long list of things to pray about."

Larry's list included needs within the community, ministry opportunities, and then there were the personal observations that Larry would make about Tom's need to submit more fully and be more committed to Larry's vision.

"I pleaded with Tom to get away from Larry Hill and the farm," John said. "His comment, as always, was 'You just don't get it!'"

Although John tried numerous times to reach out to his brother and find out what was really going on at Fortney Road, he was always rebuffed. What little he was able to discover alarmed and terrified him. According to John, "Larry would give Tom a laundry list of 'sins' that he needed to confess. One of Tom's friends at Fortney Road told me that he would often find Tom asleep on his knees next to his bed in the morning.

"To Tom and his friends, this seemed a wonderful thing, but I was horrified."

Glenn Schwartz confirmed the story, telling me in his 2007 phone interview, "Tom Miller slept near me and he would sleep kneeling on the floor all night because he didn't feel worthy to sleep in a bed. And every morning he would wake me up by saying, 'Arise and shine, Glenn, for thy light has come!'"

Chapter 13

The Blueness
of a Wound

T hose chosen few living on Fortney Road were soldiers in God's Army, and Larry stressed that the children needed to learn to fear their parents the same way his children—and wife—feared him.

Larry wrote in the *Freedom Bell*:

> The scripture teaches, "Beat thy son with a rod, and let not your soul spare for his tears." We're so squeamish about bruises on our children's legs, but we can stand and watch their souls and emotions be mutilated.[6]

Carol Hill will never forgot the night her husband went for a walk in the woods and returned with a solid wooden board. It was about one-and-a-half inches thick and three feet long. "At the time he brought it in, he set it in the corner and said, 'Now, there's something to give a beating with.'"[7]

Larry justified his brutal abuse by teaching from Proverbs 20:30, which in the King James Version states: *The blueness of a wound cleanseth away evil: so do stripes the inward parts of the belly.*

He used the passage to convince the congregation that they were to begin beating their children until their "will was broken" and they quit crying. And he threatened the parents with punishment when he thought they weren't beating their children long or hard enough.

Joe said, "I was a kid trying to figure out who I was, where I fit into this increasingly complicated thing called 'life' and how to be a dad. I now had a 'spiritual father' or 'prophet' who taught me it's Biblically commanded for a father to discipline his children or wife in any manner necessary if they didn't toe God's line . . ."

Joe hesitated before continuing.

"It's an unending source of sadness to know I allowed myself to trust a man who used the Bible to justify my short-tempered violence against my own child. It was the easy way out, I suppose, being the predominant patriarchal model of my life. Time and healthier teaching changed my view of life and thus my approach to our younger children. Still, I sit here many decades later thinking how scary it must have been to have me as a dad."

Carole King Hough told me, "We were to get ready and prepared, so when the Great War began, we could help others survive. We were trained in the woods to be quiet. That was part of the reason the kids were beaten—to teach them not to cry. It was for their survival. Our enemies could hear us and only God could protect us, so we needed to follow the rules He gave us through Larry."

A horsewhip, a steel-shafted riding crop, or the three-foot board Larry found in the woods were always available when someone at Fortney Road violated one of Larry's "God-given" rules.[13]

"It is said by those who know him that religious leader Larry Hill has one simple rule about disciplining children of all ages—beat them until they stop crying," John Griffin wrote in the *News-Herald of Willoughby*. "And when he believed his followers were not horsewhipping their children hard enough to make them stop crying, he would show them how."[13]

One member told me, "Intellectually, my brainwashed mind was convinced that this practice was correct, but every time I saw a child or adult being beaten I was horror-struck. Child abuse was a daily occurrence, and I remember praying to God, 'God, even if it means going to hell, I will leave Fortney Road if You ask me to beat anyone.'"

"The only thing we knew about Larry Hill was what Larry Hill told us," said another member, who claimed to have received sixty lashes from a whip. "We never stopped to think, 'Hey, we don't know a thing about this guy, except for what he's told us.'"[13]

Another member told me, "We all studied Greek and Hebrew with Larry; we had *Strong's Concordance*. The truth was right in front of us, but it was all filtered and twisted by what Larry taught."

Larry's son Tim told me about his mother's desperate attempt to protect her young children from the prophet's rage. "What I have always wondered is that many times the police came knocking on the door and me and my brothers and sister had to hide upstairs. My mom had complained about her treatment and the beatings we were getting and for us kids not showing up for school but no one ever helped or investigated what was being done to us.

"And I could hear the cops talking to my dad downstairs. Whatever he said seemed to put them at ease—over and over and over again—because they never investigated or tried to help us. Never!"

The frustration of not having been able to stop the abuse makes for a painful memory for Larry's ex-wife, Carol Hill. "It is so terrible that people can't believe that it is that bad. You see, anything that bad can only happen in California," she said in an interview, referring to Jim Jones' Peoples Temple, "because things like this do not happen in Ashtabula County."[7]

She recalled a particularly horrific Christmas. Their one-year-old son Lucas, still in diapers, had been sitting in a high chair near the refrigerator. Carol Hill was serving dinner to Larry and Laura Markko. The child called out to her, hungry for his food: "Mama!" Carol Hill finished serving Larry but she wasn't quick enough.[7]

Lucas again called out for his mother. Larry threw down his napkin and made his way to the high chair. "He grabbed that baby out of the high chair and he took that [three foot long] board and started beating that baby," Carol Hill said. "He kept beating that baby, and I knew what would happen [next] because it always did."[7]

When Lucas had stopped crying, the beating ceased. Larry began to bathe his son, whose buttock was blackened and swollen from the beating. "You go lay down on the sofa, Carol, and stay quiet," he said calmly over his shoulder.[7]

Her voice trembling at the memory, Carol Hill recalled, "And I laid down on the couch. You better believe I did, and he beat me with that board and I was not supposed to make a sound and I did not make a sound." Larry grunted with exertion as he pounded the board on his wife, scarring and bruising and breaking her skin.[7]

"He beat me with that board, while I lay on the couch, while the baby was laying on the floor."[7]

While the baby had screamed and cried in terror and pain, and while Carol Hill received her own merciless pounding with the board, Laura was present, calmly taking the ornaments off the Christmas tree. [7]

Carol Hill knew she had to get her children out of there. So in the fall of 1970, she became one of the first to escape from Fortney Road and Larry's brutality.[7]

Tim Hill said, "What I remember is that the beatings of me and my siblings got so severe that my mom was planning to take us all away. Larry had just about beaten Lucas to death many times so she had to get him out of there."

Larry had told those living at Fortney Road that the Lord had spoken to him and told him that the discipline was only going to get more extreme, especially among the church's adult population.[16]

"He said that he tried everything else and that we just refused to obey. He said he didn't want to, but he didn't have any other choice other than to kick us out," one member said.[16]

Larry always told his followers they could leave Fortney Road anytime they wanted, but to do so would be to turn their backs on God. "I used to pray all the time that there'd be some way for my family to leave that wouldn't be my fault," one former female member admitted.[16]

Tim Hill, ten years old at the time, still remembers his mother's departure.

"It was daytime and she had taken the car and gone to the grocery store with my sister and brother, Rebecca and Lucas. When she returned, she wanted all of us kids to help her get the groceries out of the car and into the house and then, because we would all be together, we would slip back into the car and drive away.

"What happened was that my brothers Mark and Brett and I were on the porch when she arrived with Lucas and Rebecca. Larry was also on the porch and he was yelling at us—telling us we had done something wrong or hadn't finished a chore correctly or something. He was furious, really over the edge, and Mom could see that a major beating was going to happen so she grabbed the two kids who were already with her—Rebecca and Lucas—and put them back in the car and sped off.

"She always meant to take all of us, but she could only manage to take two."

Word spread quickly and in hushed tones the news was repeated: *Carol ran off with two of Larry's children!*

"Paralyzing shock was what we all felt," Joe recalled. "Larry accused us of knowing that it was being planned and not stopping it. He felt [we were] traitorously disloyal because we hadn't forcibly intervened, hadn't bothered to go after Carol Hill or Lucas or Rebecca. Like everyone else I simply took the insults from a heartbroken man, searching my soul, wondering what I might have done differently."

Carol Hill divorced Larry in 1971 after sixteen years of marriage. She is said to be damaged beyond understanding. Family members are very protective of her and absolutely ruled out me talking to her or having her contribute to this book. "She's tormented that she ever had the name of Hill," was all a family member would say to me.

Tim said, "After my mom left, the beatings and abuse from my dad—and Diane—seemed to increase. Diane would hit me with whatever was available—shovels and wrenches, whatever was at hand. Dad would use his fists whenever he lost his temper.

"I remember one time Brett and I were baling hay and after we loaded it in the truck, Diane was driving us to deliver it somewhere. She ran out of gas—as she frequently did—so we went to a farmer and we saw that he charged her for a gallon of gas but gave her less than that. We loved the idea that he had pulled one over on Diane but we kept it to ourselves and didn't tell her. But we couldn't contain the laughter at her expense—it felt so good to laugh and we couldn't stop once we started. This infuriated her so she pulled over next to some old barn and went to find something to beat us with. She dragged out an old car bumper; it was all she could find so she tried to lift it and hit us with it and it was so comical and she was so exhausted and mad that we just collapsed in giggles, barely able to breathe as we watched how frustrated and helpless she was.

"Finally, she gave up and we all got in the truck and drove on."

Back to Fortney Road.

Chapter 14

A Yard Sale
after a Storm

I n the summer of 1970—a few months before Carol Hill and two of her children escaped from Fortney Road—PG&E's third album, *Are You Ready?* was released. It did not fare as well as the previous album, reaching only number 101 on the charts. However, it did yield the band's only hit single in the title track.

"Are You Ready?' is a gospel-influenced rocker with background vocals by the acclaimed Blackberries. The advance single was released in the spring of 1970 and climbed to number 14 on the *Billboard* charts in June 1970 and featured a lengthy guitar solo by Glenn. The album stayed on the charts for almost three months. That album is a favorite of director Quentin Tarantino who featured the band's version of "Staggolee" in his 2007 film *Death Proof*.

Although the band was enjoying modest public success, Glenn's outspoken beliefs and growing distrust of the music business caused internal tension. "Changes in the band started to occur during the recording of the *Are You Ready?* album," is how bassist Brent Block described the beginning of the end to me. "We were playing a club called The Golden Bear in Huntington Beach when Glenn announced that he could no longer live the sinful life of a rock musician."

Shortly after *Are You Ready?* became a hit single, Glenn decided he was ready and walked away from his second band, but this one had a record deal with a major label and a hit single.

Glenn returned home to Cleveland. Perhaps he had nowhere else to go. By rejecting the overtures of national record companies, Glenn had destroyed what was once his dream. Friends said that when he showed up seeking reconciliation with his ex-wife Marlene, she was furious with him and the decisions he had made and wouldn't take him back. Glenn moved in with his parents and brother Gene. Over the years Gene had learned to play bass, so together they formed the Schwartz Brothers. They started to play weekly at a bar called Faragher's in Cleveland Heights.

By 1971, much had changed. As the late Larry Norman put it, "Jimi took an overdose, Janis followed so close." Jimi and Janis were dead and Glenn was grateful to have escaped the tragic fates of his friends and be back home again, playing guitar in a little bar with his brother. But there was still a longing in his heart to know God's will for his life.

God, there must be a bigger purpose for me, Glenn would frequently pray. *Reveal that purpose. Bring me to a place where I can be 100% dedicated to You. Lead me to where You want me to be.*

The back room of Faragher's Bar was rocking out to Glenn Schwartz's version of "Brick House" when Larry Hill entered, followed by Joe Markko, who told me he would never forget his first encounter with Glenn playing live. "Though I'd heard his work on recordings nothing quite prepared me for his live performance. He simply blisters the air!"

When the boisterous set was over, the Reverend Larry Hill introduced himself to Glenn and invited him for a cup of coffee. They talked about religion, and found they had much in common.

"He had had a huge career already," Larry said. "If you listened to him talk, the unhappiness that was in his life . . . Fame might be wonderful for the handlers, but for the musicians, their life was nothing but drugs and unhappiness."[10]

The three of them continued talking and Glenn was excited to realize that Larry and Joe had the same all-consuming fascination with the Bible that he did. While his religious passion had scared his family, friends, and bandmates, these men were nodding their heads in complete agreement with whatever he said. He felt comfortable and relaxed, able to have a conversation about things that really mattered to him.

This is like an answer to prayer, Glenn suddenly realized as he spoke with the two men. *It's like an answer to prayer is being revealed to me right at this moment!*

Larry began to tell him about life on Fortney Road at the Church of the Risen Christ farm, how they lived together and shared all things in common for the good of everyone. There was a lot of Bible study and memorizing Bible verses. They prayed for one another and were accountable in their behavior so they all lived good, Christian lives. Glenn was touched by what he heard. After the demands of the record company and the contracts and the touring and all the immorality he'd seen on the road, the simplicity of communal living with other like-minded believers and helping people get free from drugs sounded exactly like what he was looking for. And praying for.

Then Larry added the clincher: there was even a band he could play in, one that sang exclusively about Jesus. "Larry mentioned the idea of Glenn playing with us," Joe told me. "To me, there was absolutely no thought that Glenn Schwartz would play with the All Saved Freak Band! We had just gone to the bar to hear, meet and encourage another brother in Christ."

But the seeds had been sown, and Glenn started showing up occasionally to gig with the band. Glenn made some visits to the farm on Fortney Road and invited his ex-wife and sons to join him. He also introduced his parents to Reverend Hill and, while they visited the farm, neither they nor Marlene and the boys had any desire to follow Glenn's path.[22]

Glenn spent more and more time at Fortney Road. The company of other believers and the opportunity to play exclusively Christian music was a tremendous draw for him. He eventually began playing with the All Saved Freak Band on a regular basis and finally announced his decision to move to Fortney Road and join the community full-time. His parents, ex-wife, and friends were so alarmed by his decision and the changes in his behavior, that to appease them, he agreed to be committed to the Fairhill Psychiatric Hospital for observation. After six weeks, he was released. The doctors said there was nothing wrong with him.[22]

In early summer 1971, Glenn Schwartz called Larry. "Pick me up," he said, and Larry sent Joe to bring Glenn to Fortney Road and Glenn officially joined the Church of the Risen Christ community and the All Saved Freak Band.

"I went to pick Glenn up in Cleveland," Joe remembered. "He had tried several times to reconcile with his ex-wife, Marlene, but she was furious with him when he told her what he was doing. First he had left music, his only income, and now he was leaving society to live on some isolated farm. She thought he had lost his mind. When I arrived at her house, the front yard looked like a yard sale after a storm. Marlene had thrown all his personal belongings outside: his guitars and amps and his clothes. She had torn pages out of his Bible and thrown them at him."

Joe remembered that was the thing that troubled Glenn the most. "None of his possessions mattered, but his Bible was everything to him, and that was the one thing Marlene had destroyed."

Once Glenn had moved to Fortney Road and was no longer seen playing in the Schwartz Brothers, his absence was immediately noticed.

According to Rick Kalister, "Glenn's three-piece blues band stopped gigging around town. Rumor had it that Glenn had joined some type of fundamentalist Christian cult out in the rural farmlands of Ashtabula County, about seventy miles east of Cleveland.

"We heard that the cult's leader was a total wacko who disciplined those in his commune by either starving them or beating them. Guitar fans in Cleveland thought, 'Oh my God! What has happened to Glenn Schwartz? Has he lost his mind?'"

Image 30: The All Saved Freak Band in 1971: Glenn Schwartz, Randy Markko, Dave Beckler, Joe Markko and Larry Hill.

Soon posters announcing "The All Saved Freak Band with Glenn Schwartz" were plastered all over Cleveland.

Mark Jones told me, "I remember seeing advertisements in the local papers in Kent and Cleveland for the All Saved Freak Band, usually with Glenn's name prominently displayed since he was the one who was most famous. I'm sure Larry Hill used Glenn as the crown jewel in his cult for that purpose."

"What a bizarre experience it was to see the All Saved Freak Band!" Rick Kalister said. "The band was always dif-

Image 31: All Saved Freak Band poster.

ferent. It usually featured five or six amateur musicians singing songs about Christ. The whole point of the band was that they were all ex-hippie dopers who were now better off because religion had saved them.

"In the middle of the show, the cult leader, Larry Hill, would come out and threaten and insult everyone, telling us how we would burn in hell if we didn't accept Christ. After the speech, Glenn would be brought out with a big build-up that went like this: 'He could have been a millionaire rock star like Jimi Hendrix! Some have called him the greatest blues guitarist in the world! He founded the James Gang! He played to over eighty thousand screaming fans at the Miami Pop Festival! But, he gave it all up to serve Christ! Here he is, Glenn Schwartz!'"

After he joined the All Saved Freak Band, Glenn tried to explain to the public via the *Freedom Bell* where he was coming from:

> I had been deeply involved in drugs and the revolution and the peace movement. I wore freaky clothes and traveled across the country playing rock and roll and blues. I was voted star performer at the Palm Beach Rock Festival where I played in front of 80,000 people. All the great names were there, but I just wasn't satisfied and couldn't find contentment even in the midst of all that fame and glory. Then I finally found Christ! Needless to say, from then on, playing with a rock-blues group [PG&E] that was infested with drugs, there was great conflict. I still wanted to play

my guitar and it seemed like the deeper I got into Christ, the better I could play. I wanted to find a group that was Christian and creative. A group that played my kind of music. I found it in the All Saved Freak Band.[6]

Although I was unable to document any of this, Larry Hill wrote:

> The music was so unheard of that big record companies didn't know how to categorize it. No contracts could be signed for the band felt that the music was sacred and would not sell the publishing rights, even when millionaires flew to Kent from West Germany and producers from California.[23]

According to Kalister, Glenn could still play, but something had changed.

"The sweetness in his music was gone, replaced by bitterness. His hair was cut short, and he wore Amish farmers' clothes. As his philosophy got rigid, so did his music. People used to cry with emotion at Glenn's soulful blues; now, they cried out of concern for him.

"What had happened in that cult's farmhouse on Fortney Road? Brainwashing? Mind control? Beatings? The Glenn Schwartz we had known and loved was dying in front of our eyes!"

Chapter 15

Gathering the Flock

R eligious zeal—both on and off the farm—kept the community growing and flourishing through the early 1970s. Joe said, "The All Saved Freak Band—especially after Kent State—became the exclusive outreach tool for the church. It also provided a public persona that masked what was going on at Fortney Road." And now that the band featured Glenn Schwartz, it was easier to get bookings and they began to play frequently in the area.

New converts—attracted by the band's music—were then eagerly swayed by what the Prophet Hill taught. Those who were deemed worthy were recruited and moved to Fortney Road, overjoyed that they were part of God's "lasting generation."

Joe told me, "I still have to catch my spirit from slipping into some real depression when I remember how many people I helped convince to come to the farm. Guilt is the gift that keeps on giving."

The farm on Fortney Road saw its greatest growth at this time, and those who joined the community embraced Larry Hill's teaching of a coming Great War. To some extent they all knew what they were getting into. They just didn't realize how hard it would be to get out.

It was in 1971 that Leon first met Larry Hill.

"I really thought he was a prophet," he told me. Leon is a tall, lanky and thoughtful man with a quietly dry sense of humor. He told me that Larry claimed to have supernatual "words of knowledge" and he had forms provided so church members could write out and testify as to the accuracy of his prophecies. These affidavits were often published in the community's *Freedom Bell* newspaper. Leon made the following statements affirming Larry's prophetic powers:

> I had known Larry Hill less than 2 months when in September of 1971 he told me in a church meeting that the Lord had shown him that I had an uncle on the West Coast. He further stated that this uncle was my father's sister's husband, and that he was an alcoholic. At that time no one to my knowledge outside of our family knew that my uncle was an alcoholic, and none of them had ever come in contact with Larry. As early as 1972, I heard Larry Hill predict that a terrible earthquake would strike Central America. This was fulfilled this year in Guatemala. He further prophesied that California would have a terrible earthquake and much of it would eventually be under water, reaching to Arizona.[6]

"I was also really impressed by the dedication of the people that lived on Fortney Road," Leon said. "Randy and Joe conducted a Bible study in town and they talked about how earlier that day they had been up so early baling hay and how hot and sweaty the work was. I also knew they had to spend an hour driving from their farm to lead the Bible study, and after the study they would probably not get home before midnight. I was really impressed with their religious dedication."

Leon soon became a Christian and was deeply involved in the church's activities, including frequently visiting the community of believers at Fortney Road. After several weeks of close observation, Larry invited him to join the growing community and Leon accepted.

Leon told me that he invited his childhood friend Jack [not his real name] to attend one of Larry's church services. Jack was handsome and outgoing with bright, friendly eyes, always looking for a good time. He too was impressed with the prophecies Larry gave and the dedication he saw among those who attended the church services.

Margo [not her real name]—whose father would later serve in President Gerald Ford's cabinet—was invited to move to Fortney

Road around the same time Leon did. She was a serious, sober-minded woman who was organized and always punctual and expected everyone else to be, too.

In true opposites attract fashion, Jack and Margo began courting at Fortney Road. Larry later presided over their wedding ceremony and they eventually had two children.

Margo told me, "Everyone who lived at the farm was crammed into a very small space. Our bedroom was packed tightly with a double bed, a crib and a dresser—you had to walk sideways to get around the room."

Daryl Pitts, soft-spoken with wheat-blond hair, said, "I came to Christ while working as a roadie for Phil Keaggy's band, Glass Harp. Phil led me to Christ and we were close friends. Larry 'encouraged' me to terminate that friendship and convinced me that it would be better to come and be trained for the ministry at the farm, so I moved to Fortney Road soon after Margo did."

Bob Tidd remembered, "I was twenty-four-years-old and it was on a Good Friday when I first heard Larry Hill preach. I think it was an outdoor service on Public Square in Cleveland." Fit and muscular all his life, Bob was already losing his hair in his early twenties. Bob noticed that there was an "air of secrecy that surrounded the members, but I did not pay attention to that because of the quality of the people and the clarity of the preaching. Larry would really preach and pray and weep over people. He was a little rough with his preaching, very black and white with his teachings and beliefs, but I got used to it and sort of liked his no-nonsense approach."

Later that spring Bob accepted the invitation to move to Fortney Road. He told me that he was compelled to join the believers at the farm since "the structure and discipline Larry promised at the farm would be good for me. And the fellowship with people of like mind gave me security." Bob said he believed that Larry could "see right through you. It seemed that he knew your thoughts and attitudes. So it forced me to try to live an honest, transparent life."

Larry Hill promised his followers that he would teach them ways to be able to survive the coming Great War and join other pockets of true believers across the country. It was a high calling and required tremendous sacrifice and loyalty. To ensure their trustworthiness in the trying times ahead, Larry began a series of teachings known as the "Ark of Safety."

Joe said, "The Ark of Safety referred to that remnant of people, that last or lasting generation; all pretty much the same thing. Any reference to a 'lasting generation' could only be in connection with that group of people who survived everything and were alive when Jesus returns three-and-a-half-years after everything hits the fan. It all fit pretty well into the Mid-Tribulation Rapture theory that Larry was into, big time."

Some have the misconception that Larry taught that only his group would survive as a "remnant" but according to Joe, this wasn't true. "I never remember hearing that it was 'just us and nobody else.' To imply that we believed it was just us fifty who God might be pleased with in the end makes us sound more ignorant than we really deserve."

It was in the midst of this time of growth in the community, toward the end of 1971, that Larry had his fifth vision. He saw the Soviet bear stand up in the Middle East and devour much of the land, followed by a huge serpent that crawled out of Rome and also headed for the Middle East. He also saw a black line run lengthwise across California causing the shorelines to tremble. Larry Hill and a woman named Mary Barnhard drew up the original concept and sketches of Larry's five visions. Charles Hooper is credited with the finished art [image 32], which was included in

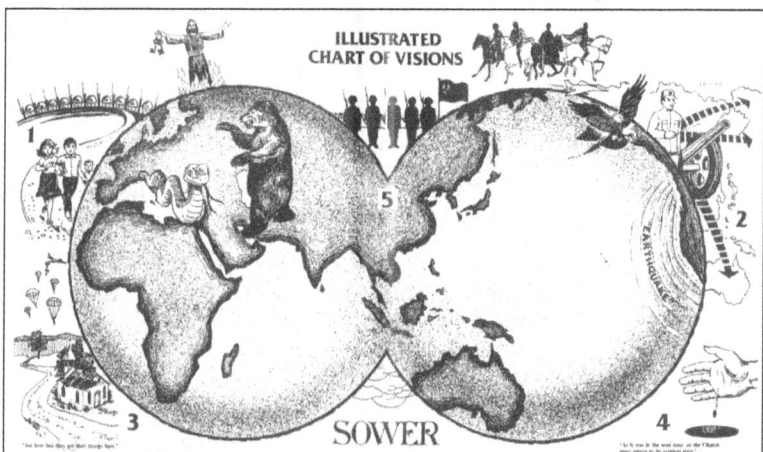

Image 32: Sketches of Larry's five visions.

copies of the *Freedom Bell* and later in the 1980 All Saved Freak Band album *Sower.* Neither Mary nor Charles were members of Larry's congregation.

"Brainwashing is a very, very, very slow process. Unless you have been there, you just don't get it. For instance, there is no way that anyone could come in and tell you to beat your kid after being at Fortney Road for only a month. No way. It took time, and Larry used the Bible, quoting the 'blueness of the wound cleanses away evil' and 'when you beat your child he will not die.'"

That was Carole King's take on life with Larry Hill. Carole was one of three siblings—John and Morgan were her brothers—who joined the community in 1972 soon after John had been arrested for drug possession.

"John had gotten into trouble for drugs," Carole told me. "He was supposed to get forty years to life because he had been involved in a huge drug bust in Summit County, Ohio. Our Dad got John off of the drug charge and put him in the care of Larry because Larry was telling everyone that he was helping kids get off drugs and he was a preacher, so the authorities released John into Larry's care to sort of rehabilitate him. And that's how John went to live on the farm.

"Of course, John soon had these Bible studies with the farm folks and they held some at Mom and Dad's apartment. Mom and Dad's feelings were that anything was better than drugs—even the Bible and a bunch of Jesus freaks!"

Larry talked a lot about helping kids get off drugs and I asked Joe about this claim. He told me, "I can't remember one person kicking drugs at the farm. Everyone had already put most of that stuff behind them by the time they got to the farm, actually showing Larry's mantra, 'We were a church trying to help young people get off drugs,' to be totally whacked. Taking credit for helping people get off drugs, when the hard work had been done before people even arrived, is an example of Larry controlling the information."

Blond-haired Carole (Image 33) had a friendly, husky voice that was always calling out for a party to begin and her welcoming arms were always ready for a hug. "My mother named me 'Miss Spontaneous' because I would grab my dog Punkin' and my VW bug and off we would go, just like that! So Miss Spontaneous was my name."

Carole's equally gregarious brother, Morgan, was disciplined and focused his energy and attention on his bass guitar and playing in as many pickup bands as he could find. A talented musician, he'd close his eyes as he played, blissfully lost in the rhythm he was creating.

Image 33: Carole King in 1969. Photo courtesy of Carole King Hough.

John King came up short on the good-natured traits of his siblings. A handsome young man, he strayed into trouble with the girls he dated, and his temper and drug use frequently drew the attention of the police.

John invited Morgan to check out life at Fortney Road, and soon Morgan joined his brother on the farm.

Morgan King told me, "No one could just show up at the farm. Before you visited, you needed an invitation from someone. And there was also the house of ministry in Kent, the Summit Street House. If you were sent to the Kent House, we'd joke that that was a demotion—that was where the 'second-class citizens' went. Fortney Road was the place to be."

After John and Morgan had moved to Fortney Road, they encouraged Carole who was working at a hair salon to join them, but she refused at first. "I loved my brothers and we were a close, close family, but I made good money and I liked my freedom. But I did begin to wonder where they lived, what this farm and community was like. So I attended some of Larry's church services, along with the rest of my family, and I did visit the

Image 34: Morgan King on the Fortney Road farm.

farm and I saw John and Morgan at the meetings and I went to the Bible studies. But there was something like fifty people crammed into that house on Fortney Road! There was no place to sleep and it was nothing I wanted to be a part of."

Then one day, Larry, Diane Sullivan, and Joe's sister Laura Markko made a trip to Atwater, Ohio where Carole was living with her parents. "They came to tell me I was going to hell if I didn't come to the farm! They argued with me and said if I was really a Christian, I wouldn't be so selfish—I'd surrender to His will. And His will, of course, was to join the community. It was real fire and brimstone stuff and with my brothers already at the farm, it sort of sounded like the right thing to do. What did they know that I didn't, right?

"So I was the last of my family to go to Fortney Road and I went totally unwillingly, never wanting to lose my freedom. It was considered a big deal to know where the farm was. I didn't really care but you were part of the inner circle if you knew. And here I was being forced to live there."

Larry also said God told him Carole should get out of the hair business so she quit her job at the salon and started cleaning houses like the other women on the farm. The first few nights at the farm were the toughest for Carole. "I slept on the floor and looked out the window the first night and just wept. Joe's sister Laura knew I sensed my own demise and tried to be somewhat friendly to me. I took her to the grocery store and she helped break me in, so to speak. She was kind to me, always was, and to this day I thank her for it. Even when things got really, really bad, she would at least be human."

And as for Larry, Carole said, "Larry and I ignored each other."

The change in Carole was profound. With no personal income and no independence, Miss Spontaneous ceased to exist. And like the other members, Carole was immediately cut off from her parents. "At the time, I never understood the part about being away from my folks. My mother's heart was broken. I was often accused of talking to my parents behind Larry's back, being a rebel, but I never did contact them."

To prevent members from maintaining a balanced worldview, cult leaders always isolate their recruits. Regardless if it's polygamist Warren Jeffs and his compound, Charles Manson and his family hidden away at the Spahn Movie Ranch, or Larry Hill and the farm at Fortney Road, separation from family and friends is key.

Donald [not his real name] told me, "Larry was always disdainful toward our parents, believing that they never raised us with any discipline or correction. Of course, he rarely if ever met any of our parents but that was his general impression and he felt God had called him to train us up, to show us discipline—both physical and mental—and if sometimes that meant beating us or forcing us to exercise or memorize or write excessive amounts of scripture, then that only reinforced his belief that if our parents had raised us correctly, then he wouldn't need to train us in this manner."

Tim Hill explained to me that this was simply another way Larry maintained control. "We were never allowed to contact any of our relatives."

Leon told me, "At the farm several obstacles always stood in the way of visiting your family: First, there was a conflicting message about family taught by Larry. While the Bible and Larry taught us to honor our parents, he constantly railed against our mostly middle-class families, said they were hung up on status and money, and, because they had not accepted our born-again variety of Christianity, they were condemned to hell unless they saw the light, specifically the light as revealed by Larry Hill.

"Second, we were given so many responsibilities for mostly physical labor around the farm—and the guilt for not completing them was so liberally applied—that even a few hours away from the farm to see your family or friends was viewed in our minds as to constitute a sin.

"Third, anything so out of the ordinary such as a trip to see one's parents required Larry's permission, and Larry was often not approachable; a great deal of fear accompanied making such a request.

"And fourth, there often was no transportation available."

These obstacles combined to make it the norm that those who lived at Fortney Road rarely saw members of their families. From what I could determine, it seemed that the most dedicated and revered members saw their families the least, even though more than seventy-five percent lived within an hour's drive of their families, and nearly all lived within two. It was not uncommon for someone who lived just a few miles from their parents to see them only once or twice a year.

Leon said, "Somehow I was inclined to let the 'honor thy father and mother' override the teaching to despise them. Given that, I still probably only saw my family four or five times a year, even though they lived about an hour from the farm."

Donald first encountered Larry Hill at a Bible study. Plump with long, frizzy brown hair and deep-set, narrow eyes, Donald always appeared to be squinting or uncertain what his next move would be.

"I remember my friend Peter invited me to a Bible study at Jack's house and that's where I met some of the people from Fortney Road. I remember there was a sense that they were really a special, spiritual and committed group of people but it wasn't easy to belong to their group. It was like they had a unique or a higher calling than the rest of us. They weren't arrogant or anything like that, but you knew being around them that they just had a deeper walk with God and that's what I wanted. But you could only be taught that deeper walk if Larry thought you were worthy and ready to receive it.

"Because the farm on Fortney Road was somewhat off the beaten track, no one knew exactly where it was unless someone told you. And you never visited the farm without an invitation. Larry and the others would closely watch you for weeks at a time to see if you were trustworthy, to see if you were serious about the things of God. I finally had my invitation and stayed at the farm a few times for the weekend and attended some services there before I eventually moved in sometime in September 1972." Donald would also go on to become Larry's right hand man, responsible for executing Larry's discipline.

Guitar player Mike Berkey and his wife also joined the community during this time of rapid growth in 1972, and Mike contributed to the music of the All Saved Freak Band. Mike had a thin face framed by black glasses and a trim goatee. Both he and rhythm guitarist Ed Durkos became fast friends and were joined like brothers in their love of the technical side of music and sound equipment. Ed had an unwieldy beard and moustache and bright, friendly eyes that could barely be seen behind his always-smudged glasses.

Mike is the one who saved all the old *Freedom Bells* and audio-tapes of church services. He told Joe, "I have no idea why I saved this stuff all these years." Mike is the reason there is written and recorded documentation of many of the events that occurred at Fortney Road.

Like everyone else on Fortney Road, Mike's wife was convinced of Larry's abilities as a prophet and testified to that in the *Freedom Bell*:

> I, Carol Berkey, affirm that I heard Larry Hill say that the volcanoes would be happening soon. These would be happening from areas that were seemingly dead to these. Following that, many earthquakes were reported as he stated there would be happening. I also affirm that I heard Larry Hill say that animals and things of nature would draw nigh to our area that are naturally unfamiliar. These animals would come close to members of our church. Since then we have seen an eagle, herons, beavers. We also have some here that were unusually close to deer and fox.[6]

Ben (not his real name) and a close friend, Ruth, whom he would later marry, also joined the community. "I really believed Larry to be a prophet of God, along with Diane Sullivan and Laura Markko," Ben told me. "We got to know about Larry Hill through Tom Miller. I grew up with Tom, he was two years older but we kicked around some and he introduced us to the All Saved Freak Band."

Short, slim and red-haired, Ruth had no-nonsense penetrating green eyes and a joyous laugh that belied her serious look. And whenever Ben was next to her, his arm would always find a way to encircle her shoulder and draw her close to him. He'd stand there content, a bemused look on his face, while she chattered away.

Most of the theology Larry preached publicly was acceptable to mainstream Christianity, and it laid the foundation that allowed him to introduce more extreme beliefs. Margo said, "I was a Christian before I ever met him. If you listen to him preach, outside of a rare occasion, it would basically be what you hear in a fundamentalist church."

Larry let it be known that he was only looking for a few good men and women, and you had to be chosen. If you expressed interest in being a more dedicated Christian and Larry felt you would be of value to his vision, you might be allowed to attend some small group Bible studies and perhaps visit the farm at Fortney Road. Then, finally, you might be invited to move in.

As his son, Tim, told me, "When Larry would meet someone or invite them to live on the farm, he'd always start by saying 'You are very important to this ministry and I'm so glad you're here.' And then it would gradually change to, 'You know, you're a great person and we love having you here but there are a few areas I think you should work on.' And then finally, 'God showed me that you need to work on these areas or you're going to go to hell and I can help you,' which is when the beatings would start.

"My brother Mark and I would sit on the front porch when new people would arrive on the farm. I remember we'd sit there with our hands across our chests, sort of fascinated in a sick way because we would watch Larry break these people down. We knew what was in the store for them."

In hindsight, Carole's brother Morgan was aware before he ever moved to Fortney Road that the residents there were not a typical group of Christians. As he told me, "I worked at JC Penney's and I knew Larry and some other people from the church—including my brother John, who joined first. I was attending some services but hadn't moved out there yet. But I heard Larry's teachings and his prophecies about this coming Great War and the need to be prepared. John and people from the farm would visit me at Penney's and ask me to use my employee discount to purchase rifles and ammunition."

In addition to whatever weapons Morgan secured for the farm, cases of Italian Army rifles had also been obtained. On one occasion, Joe actually saw them being unloaded. "I walked in on Donald who was a Vietnam vet, and he was removing the packing around the guns and de-greasing the weapons. He had served two tours with a machine gun unit of the 173rd Airborne and so he was our sergeant-at-arms and eventually carried a holstered pistol on security checks of the property."

Military training manuals were stored in the house library and dozens of loaded rifles and pistols were kept in the farmhouse for target practice and protection from outsiders.[13] Once Morgan joined the community, he became very familiar with these weapons. "You had rifle and pistol practice almost every day. You'd have archery one week, then you'd have rifle and pistol practice another week along with guerrilla warfare training."

Carole told me, "We had combat training every morning . . . the routine was to get up—*if* you had been to sleep—do calisthenics, then go to the barn for more exercises—wrestling, the pugil sticks, martial arts, bow and arrow, shooting guns, fighting techniques, rolling off the top of bales of hay and falling correctly as to not hurt oneself, climbing a rope to the top of the barn. This was my biggest accomplishment. I would pray so hard that God would help me do it. But we believed these things would help us to survive the war."

Because Larry believed that the Great War and the US invasion by foreign powers could began at any moment, he and many members of the community carried loaded, concealed weapons with them at all times.

"Dad always carried around a green book bag and rarely let it out of his sight," Tim said. "Of course, Mark and I had to find out what he kept inside that was so important. One time we looked inside the bag and found a small box of cigars, a .357 Magnum, and a flask that contained wine." On those rare occasions when Tim saw his father taking a sip from the flask of wine, Larry simply said, "wine helps soothe my stomach."

Larry would often complain about his ailments, which he claimed were caused by the pressure he was under because of his monumental spiritual responsibilities. He frequently would complain of having an upset stomach. So even though wine (and alcohol of any type) was strickly forbidden at Fortney Road, his sons accepted his explanation.

However, Larry made no excuse at all for the box of cigars or the loaded .357 revolver.

Carole recalled one time while she was performing with the All Saved Freak Band at the Smiling Dog Saloon in Cleveland. "I said something to my brother Morgan about Pam and Kim Massmann's violin and cello cases, and it turned out they had guns in them! Morgan told me that just about everyone carried loaded guns, but the way they were all positioned that night, if anyone started shooting, they would have shot one another in the crossfire!"

When I asked what an average day was like at Fortney Road, Leon told me, "When I describe a typical day at Fortney Road today, it feels—and must sound—incredible, as if it never could have happened this way, as if no one could have endured what we did, day after day, for months or years."

After reading accounts of more wildly known extremist cults like the Unification Church and the Children of God, one former member of Larry Hill's ministry said "ours was much worse."[13]

Chapter 16

Boiling
the Frog

I f you were new to the farm, demands were introduced slowly over time.

"When I first joined, life on the farm was fun and I enjoyed the environment," Leon said. "New members were well treated and not required to wake up early as most of the other members did. Often Larry would take new members on trips to the auction house to buy farm supplies, or visit bookstores."

At each church and community meeting, Larry made certain to talk about the ministry's financial concerns and the need to care for one another with Christian charity. This was Larry slowly turning up the heat, like the anecdote of placing a frog in a pan of cold water. If the temperature is increased ever so gradually, the warming will make the frog doze happily, until it eventually boils to death without ever waking up.

This is the system Larry Hill—and all cult leaders—used to "train" his converts. As a result, new members would begin to feel guilty about not pulling their share of the load and soon fell into lockstep with the grueling regimen that was to constitute their daily life.

It worked perfectly on Leon, who told me, "Gradually I began to feel guilty about sleeping in until eight or nine while everyone else—those who had now become like family to me—was up before the sun rose, doing farm chores and then off to their jobs."

The workday at Fortney Road began early—extremely early. Each morning at 4:00 members were to arise and prepare themselves for the very real possibility that the Great War might begin that day, maybe before the sun had even had a chance to rise.

If you didn't rise and shine you could expect severe punishment—or "discipline" as Larry called it. The punishment was swift and brutal for those who lingered in bed—a punch in the stomach or lashes with a whip.

"We slept so little that the average guy at the farm couldn't hear an alarm clock to wake up in the morning, he was in such deep sleep," I was told by one former member. "One time, all the men failed to awaken in the morning and as punishment, we had to run ten or fifteen times through a pond that was three feet deep—in the middle of winter!"

Immediately upon arising, Donald, the Vietnam War veteran, would lead the men and women in forty-five minutes of grueling exercises, including hundreds of push-ups, sit-ups, leg lifts, and a quick two-mile run. Some former members reported that they also had to carry a club or staff to increase the difficulty.

Following the exercise, the men rushed to feed all the animals and clean their stalls as quickly and thoroughly as possible while the women hurried to the farmhouse to prepare breakfast.

With the exception of Diane Sullivan and a few others whom Larry considered prophetesses, all the women were responsible for maintaining the farmhouse. "That house was immaculate," one woman said. "We cleaned cracks on the floor with toothbrushes. We really cleaned. We did everything in the house every day—all the woodwork. We shampooed the rugs once a week. We'd wash the curtains once a week."[13]

By 6:00 a.m., all the animals were fed and the stalls cleaned, and the men filed into the farmhouse for breakfast. But before they ate, Larry led everyone in prayer and a daily devotion to God. Many would begin to nod off as soon as they were seated, but a jab in the ribs and the fear of being caught sleeping when they should be listening or worshipping kept everyone on edge.

When the quick breakfast was over—usually 6:45 a.m.—the men would trudge out of the warm house, some to spend their day tending the animals, repairing buildings, or working the fields. The select few who owned broken-down vehicles struggled mightily to stay awake as they drove about doing errands or completing their farm duties. The rest left for jobs in the city or

Image 35: Hard at work at Fortney Road: Glenn Schwartz and Ed Durkos.

suburbs. Glenn Schwartz was not just a guitar virtuoso, he was also a skilled car mechanic so he found employment at an automobile repair shop when he wasn't working in the fields.

"Because the few vehicles we had were needed on the farm, we had to hitchhike to work," Leon remembered, "and the job was sometimes as far as forty miles one way, a real chore in the winter. So we would put in eight hours at work and then it was time to hitchhike home and start the evening chores."

Larry insisted that all the animals' stalls had to be cleaned morning and night, and at least one former member I spoke to believed that the animals lived better lives than the humans on the farm.

Dinner followed for most, but there were always some members who were fasting, either by choice or by command; they believed fasting brought them closer to God. Tim said, "We had many forced fasts that would last one to two weeks. We could eat only rice during this time or only eggs. These fasts did not apply to my dad."

Even those who were not fasting often went to bed hungry simply because there never seemed to be enough to eat.

Morgan told me, "Most of the people in the community were just young city kids trying to make a go of it by living on a farm. We often had a tough time with food, either growing the vegetables or smoking the food or even getting enough to eat. We had a smokehouse and we were always trying to preserve some meat but something would always seem to go wrong. I know at one point, about halfway through the process, someone put some pinewood in the smokehouse and that's poisonous, so we lost all that meat. Other times, food was allowed to spoil by neglect or ignorance so maggots would appear. I ate dog food at times because I was hungry, and even when I was cutting raw meat, I'd sneak some of that, too. It was simply a matter of survival."

Although it was often more famine than feast at Fortney Road, Morgan recalled one Thanksgiving that the community had a huge dinner. "We all just stuffed ourselves, it was so good to just eat and eat and eat!" Then when the meal was over and no one could move, Larry made them all run twelve miles. "We all just barfed our guts out, we were all so sick," Morgan said.

Under these conditions, it's no wonder that members of the community would often give up and leave the ministry, and if they did, they were rarely allowed to return. Larry considered those who fled as betrayers on the level of Judas and regardless of how faithful they had been while at Fortney Road, once they left, any contributions they had made were denigrated and deemed to have been worthless.

"Once I ran away from the farm and managed to hitchhike to Daytona Beach, Florida," Morgan told me. "But I felt guilty so I called Larry and said I wanted to return. I asked for some help in getting back home and he told me, 'You hitchhiked down there, hitchhike back!'"

After dinner, Larry, Diane, or Laura Markko would read carefully compiled lists of work assignments that needed to be completed that evening.

And then punishments for the previous day's infractions were handed out. These punishments were based on twenty Godly standards residents of Fortney Road were told to judge themselves against each day. For example, each person was to pray for an hour each day, maintain a certain level of cleanliness—"They would inspect your shoes, your boots, everything, even your fingernails!"[13]—and exhibit self-control ("sweetly obey").

In the two-day example published in a *Freedom Bell*, an individual had failed to pass inspection on Sunday for silence, frugality, industry, tranquility and humility. On Monday, he or she failed at memorizing scriptures, witnessing to others about the Lord, following the orders and methods of Fortney Road, resolving conflict, frugality, sincerity, justice, holiness, and evening meditation.[6]

Because it was so easy to violate these standards and cause "spiritual infractions," most of the members began to live with the sense that no matter how hard they tried or how much they sacrificed, they would continue to come up short in their relationships with God and their pastor. These feelings were enforced by Diane's diatribes and Larry's long, late-night sermons about how displeased God was with them. He would often publicly humiliate individuals, singling them out for criticism in front of the entire group. Church members felt they were continually disappointing the God who did so much for them; they couldn't seem to do anything right. And, since members of the community were also encouraged to point out failings in others to help everyone live a more godly life, spiritual finger pointing was the norm at Fortney Road.

"We always felt we were being watched," Joe said. "Not for signs of success but for failure or noncompliance. Everyone was suspicious of everyone else."

One member told me, "Meetings could last four to five hours and they always involved most of us being 'called on the carpet' for both material and spiritual infractions. Secretly, I think we all preferred the manual labor because once you got your chore done, you could go to bed."

"Sometimes [during those] all-night meetings," Margo said, "you would go through each person and say, 'Okay, what have they done?' And you got to where you felt like nobody looked at you for your achievements or what you could do, or felt there was any worthwhile thing in you at all. All anybody saw were your faults."[24]

After thinking back on her time at the farm, Margo said, "For all these years, I thought I really had no friends from the farm. I always felt like I kept my real self locked up—held back from truly connecting with anyone else because I knew that if Larry asked any one of us what someone else had said in any conversation—no matter how private—they would tell him, because he was the authority. You thought he would know if you were lying. And swift punishment would follow."

Diane Sullivan can be heard on an audiotape publicly expressing God's displeasure with Margo during a Sunday evening meeting:

Margo, for two weeks the Lord's been speaking to me about you and I got a real bad feeling when I was going to the house the other day. Margo, we didn't have the money but we sent [some] to Chicago. And we begged you, and Jack called you on the phone and begged you to come here and do a job for God. And we paid you money that we didn't have to pay you and a lot of times we got behind because we truly believed before God [that you belonged here].

We trusted and we believed that you'd go out on the streets and you'd witness every day. And you were supposed to do it every day for eight hours and every day for one year Larry had to push you and push you and beg you and we have absolutely no record of no souls that really got through to God for all that year.

And Margo, you stand before God and you'll never be right before God until you go back to that place and start all over again and I really feel that's right. You'll never be right with God until you go back to that place where you didn't surrender to God. You didn't want to do that job but you came anyway but you never quite surrendered your heart and you know what? You never did do that job for God and God is still holding that against you and He's holding all those souls until you get yourself right with God on that one point. [25]

It was usually after midnight by the time the list of spiritual infractions had been read aloud, discussed, and the punishments announced.

"You never knew what the punishment would be or how horrible it would be," one former member told me. "One person might be told to run ten miles for the crime of not washing the goats properly before milking, while another person was told to run five miles for failing to wake up on time or someone could be told to write Bible verses over and over while someone else would receive a beating with a riding crop or a bullwhip."

Leon told me that he was beaten thirteen times with a bullwhip, up to forty lashes at a time. "While we might have believed we deserved the public dressing downs," he said, "they brought absolute dread."

The community was always relieved when the meeting was over because if it ended at one in the morning, it meant they could get three hours of sleep. But before they could retire, another sleep robber—the watch list—was posted, and eight unlucky men would draw guard duty.

"The watch listed consisted of teams of two who were assigned to go on a rotating twenty-minute patrol to check the animals," Leon told me. "This meant what little sleep you did manage was interrupted if you had watch that night." The watch was required because the Great War could start at any moment and Larry didn't want to be caught unaware or unprepared and didn't want the animals harmed.

Carole recalled a particularly memorable event that illustrated Larry's obsession with an invasion by the Chinese. "At one point, Larry had told the men on the watch list to be on the lookout because he sensed the Chinese were doing some 'takeover maneuvers' of some sort, like a practice run for when they invaded the United States. Of course, the Chinese had singled out the farm on Fortney Road to use as a rehearsal for the big invasion!

"We had quite a few caged rabbits and one night Larry secretly told a few of the men to cut off the rabbits' heads but to tell no one. In the morning, the dead rabbits were discovered and Larry told Darryl Pitts and Norris McClure that *the Chinese had done it*. He told [them] to be on high alert and watch for the Chinese and kill them when they showed up. Of course, the men who had killed the rabbits didn't speak up."

Not all the men had weapons so Norris went off to purchase a gun to protect himself and to kill the Chinese when they arrived. Norris, a talented bass player, had recently moved to Fortney Road and was willing and eager to show Larry how dedicated he was.

Darryl and Norris "were all riled up and Norris was eager right then and there to hunt down the Chinese who had killed all our rabbits," Carole continued. "So off they all went, intent on finding the Chinese. Of course, they didn't find anything. To think Larry sent those guys out there in the middle of the night for absolutely nothing but silly war games! It's a wonder no one got hurt or shot by another member. Norris told me that to have so little sleep and then to be all riled up to get the Chinese, there was no telling what he might have done!"

But during the hunt for the Chinese invaders—or perhaps some other invasion that Larry concocted—the men on watch did find something. One night at the far end of the farm the men reported seeing a flickering light and they thought for sure this time someone was trying to sneak into the farm and attack them. They all got down on their bellies and crawled across the dirt in military fashion just like they had been trained. And when they got to the end of the property, they discovered that it was just the fence warning light that had illuminated, indicating low or intermittent voltages.

No Satan-led invaders—that time, anyway.

It seemed that bedtime was always many, many hours away because nighttime was when the work began in earnest. In addition to the watch list, the tunnels also needed to be dug.

The community of believers at Fortney Road were so exhausted that they often went to sleep immediately upon sitting down. This was a challenge when trying to stay awake for three- and four-hour church services, and a life-threatening problem when driving.

"We employed creative solutions for staying awake," Joe said. "Beyond the 'stick your head out the window into the winter blast' kind of therapy, some carried a cup of coffee in their hand and held it high enough to create a problem should they start to drift off. My brother Randy used to hold a small ball-peen hammer in one hand, handle up, directly above his crotch. It worked."

Leon said, "I had narrowly escaped three near fatal auto accidents while I was living at Fortney Road. In one I woke up in the opposing lane with a tractor trailer filling the view in my windshield and his horn blaring away at me; in another I nearly drove over a cliff; and in still another I drifted into the opposing lane and forced another driver into a field. Once I fell asleep at work and nearly fell into a large piece of moving machinery. Another member fell asleep at the wheel and plowed into an Amish buggy. There were many demolished vehicles and near accidents."

Margo told me, "I remember that when I was preparing for the children's Sunday school class, I'd lay on the floor with my legs propped up against the closed door to plan my lessons. That way I could get some much needed sleep but in case anyone knocked on the door or pushed on it, I'd wake up and could pretend to have been studying."

Another former member said, "There were many times when I went to my job in the fields and I fell asleep walking."[24]

In an audiotape of a Sunday evening meeting at the farm-house, Joe's sister Laura exhorted the people who had been complaining of being so tired:

> You know, it seems like everyone is real tired all the time, and you'll see that every one of the [Bible] verses I just read talked about life. If you believe in God, then you will have life and you won't be tired and you won't be dragged down and you won't be disgusted about things and you won't be depressed all the time. And by not being depressed and not being dragged down and stuff, you'll find yourself being more joyful.[25]

Although every night was a late night at Fortney Road, Sunday evenings were a bit different since they were reserved for Bible memorization.

"We committed ourselves to a program of Bible memorization in case the scriptures were not conveniently available during the Great War." Joe said. "Larry believed the writings of Stalin specified the physical liquidation of every Bible. So each person was assigned several books of each testament so that the entire Bible might be resident in our collective memory.

"I was given Galatians and Ephesians from the New Testament and the Old Testament books of First and Second Chronicles. After worship and a sermon, every Sunday night we each, in turn, recited the verses we'd memorized that week. One chapter from each testament was expected from everyone. Each succeeding week, we rehearsed everything memorized to date. It made for some very long nights . . ."

During one late night meeting, Larry can be heard on an audiotape berating the members of the community:

> Sometimes you think, "We need more of the Word." [Shouts.] You're gettin' the word! Obey! You have received the Word. OBEY! You know the truth. Will you stand with it, or will you stand by yourself and rebel? Your attitude, your attitude, your attitude! Because you love the idle god of youth so much! I used to wonder why I had to go through the things I went through. I can put a CLAIM on you because I ask you to do only what I have done. And TENFOLD MORE! Have you gone so long without food that you've paced the floor in PAIN night after night? God, who loves to be gentle, God, who loves to speak in peaceful wisdom, SENDS HIS ROD! You say, this can't be Christian, the

way we're sent and directed. I want you to know, friend, that that rod is God's LAST mercy to save your soul and if you kick against that, you don't have NOTHING![26]

After hearing from so many former members what a typical day was like at Fortney Road, I wondered if there was ever anything to look forward to. Only Carole responded, saying, "I am going to try to think of a good time and I guess that would be if we were going to have band practice. That made everything else at least bearable. I can't say it was 'fun'—maybe 'relief' is a better word, but it all depended on the mood Larry was in."

During this time, the Church of the Risen Christ community at Fortney Road and the Kent New Generation Church ministries grew and flourished and Reverend Larry Hill continued to preach his revelations based on his 1965 and 1971 visions. He was frequently asked to appear on local religious television programs such as *Scene on Sunday* and *Dialogue* to talk about his "work in the youth movement and drug rehabilitation programs," which is how the TV programs listed his appearances. The hosts of these programs had no idea what was actually occurring at Fortney Road.

And while everyone struggled at Fortney Road, it was the women who had the most difficult time pleasing God and Larry.

"The women were always dominated," one former member said. "You had no say-so in anything. You did what you were told or you got slammed up against the wall. I have scars to prove it. You were to keep your eyes down at all times. You were not permitted to look up."[13]

Keep their eyes down? It was back in the mid 1970s when I was at Keith and Melody Green's house, asking Glenn Kaiser what he knew about the All Saved Freak Band. All that he could recall about the band was that the women couldn't look the men in the eye. He didn't really know why. More than thirty years later, I was about to find out the reason.

Chapter 17

With
Downcast Eyes

B eing a woman in Reverend Larry Hill's congregation meant that you were considered responsible for most everything that had gone wrong with the world. Because Eve looked at Satan and listened to him in the Garden of Eden and led Adam into deception, she was the cause of the Fall of Man. If she had kept her eyes averted from Satan, all would have been well.

Larry derived his downcast eyes doctrine from 1 Timothy 2:9 in the King James translation: *In like manner also, that women adorn themselves in modest apparel, with shamefacedness and sobriety.* The Greek word for "shamefacedness" is *aidos*, which is defined in *Strong's Concordance* as "a sense of shame or honor, modesty, bashfulness, reverence, regard for others, respect." But digging much deeper, Larry went to the word's origin and discovered an obscure definition, "the idea of downcast eyes."

He also believed that lust was in the women's eyes and if they didn't look at any of the men, it would keep temptation far from them. So he decreed that all the woman at Fortney Road were to always have "downcast eyes," which required that they look at the ground at all times.

Bob Tidd told me that for him, "there were no problems with sexual temptations. The women were very reserved and did not even look into the eyes of the men."

Carole King Hough recalled that when she first moved to Fortney Road, "I thought there was something wrong with the women, especially Diane. Like a mental problem or something.

The girls would walk around staring at the ground, never looking up. I think Laura Markko looked up occasionally, but never Diane."

A few years later when the All Saved Freak Band recorded their albums, producer Rob Galbraith told me about the long, seventy-mile drives to and from the recording studio. "Diane would drive and Larry insisted she drive with these downcast eyes, so she couldn't look at the road! We were weaving and swerving and other cars were honking at us, it was ridiculous! She had to avert her eyes from the road! I remember yelling at Larry to tell Diane to look at the road when she was driving and Larry gave her permission. It was just incredible."

Joan Dolch Marks told me, "I remember when I went to my first Bible study and I brought a friend, Bonnie, with me and we had smoked up before we came. We got the giggles during the study. Larry was hopping around on his one leg and preaching like crazy. I'm surprised now that he didn't hit us with his crutch. Bonnie never came back after that, but I did.

"I started going to the Kent New Generation Church in July 1972. I was a young girl looking for truth in my life. I had been into drugs and alcohol. I went to the church regularly and also to the Bible studies held during the week at the home of John and Georgia King. Carole was like a big sister to me. One time we were at John's apartment and they had a birthday cake with candles for that Diane Sullivan woman. I remember Diane wouldn't look up and even Larry said, 'Look up, Diane!' and then she saw the candles. I asked Carole what was wrong with Diane. Carole took me into the kitchen and explained that she was a prophetess and the whole thing about downcast eyes."

When Dick Feagler, a reporter for the *Cleveland Press,* visited Fortney Road, he witnessed this phenomenon firsthand. "There is no pearly gate leading to Larry Hill's religious paradise-on-earth. In fact, a 'Road Closed' sign blocks the rutted dirt lane leading to Hill's commune." Describing the young woman who answered his knock on the door as "meek," he wrote that she gasped, "Excuse me!" and then lowered her head. "For, in the heavenly haven of Larry Hill, women are forbidden to look men full in the face. Eyes downcast, the girl ushered us into the house," and after Larry called for some coffee to be brought in, "another younger woman brought it, apologized for passing between us and set the cup down, keeping her eyes averted."[27]

Dick has never forgotten that interview with Larry Hill, which occurred almost forty years ago. He told me, "I've written a lot of stories over the years but Larry left me with a real impression of something; he was creepy, spooky, and all the women crept around in long dresses and wouldn't look you in the eye. I've never forgotten that."

Tim Hill said, "It was actually kinda funny. My brother Mark and I would crack up as we watched the women cover their eyes with their hands and keep their heads down. They'd rush from room to room if there were any men around, mumbling, 'Excuse me! Excuse me!' and they'd bang into furniture or bump into each other because they couldn't see where they were going!"

In addition to keeping their eyes downcast, the women had to dress modestly at all times. Their plain, calf-length, long-sleeved farm dresses were designed to avoid calling attention to the wearer by cut, color, or any other feature, and their head scarves served as symbols of their reverence and submission to man and to God.

Since their clothing and the requirement to maintain downcast eyes were outward expressions of their commitment to Christ, the women ignored any puzzled glances or derisive comments they might receive from people they encountered in town.

They were doing the Lord's work and He was pleased with them, and that was all that mattered.

If Larry Hill had been a true prophet, he would have foreseen the tremendous grief and despair that would be visited on Fortney Road in 1972. Three members of the community would die and one of his most dedicated followers would flee the ministry. But it was only after these tragic events occurred that he was able to muster God's perspective.

Chapter 18

In the Middle
of the Night

O
n Friday, December 31, 1971, the Church of the Risen Christ joined with the Kent New Generation Church and held their annual "Watch Night Service" in Kent. It was a godly alternative to a typical New Year's Eve party and the congregations honored God by giving Him first place in the events of 1972. The All Saved Freak Band played, there were praise and worship songs, testimonies, and much prayer for the coming year.

"I saw the band playing in the Jaycee Hall in Kent that night," Leon recalled. "I had bought a light blue 1955 Chevy pickup truck and the band used it to haul their gear. It was no gem—it burned

Image 36: The All Saved Freak Band in 1972: Randy Markko, Kim Massmann, Larry Hill, Glenn Schwartz, Pam Massmann and Ed Durkos.

oil and the driver's side door didn't stay latched properly, but it ran okay."

By the time the Watch Night service was over and the band had packed up, it was two o'clock in the morning on January 1, 1972 and most of the group was functioning on only a couple of hours of sleep each night, so they were beyond exhausted.

Tom Miller used Leon's pickup to transport the band's equipment back to Fortney Road. Larry's seventeen-year-old son Brett was his only passenger. Brett soon fell asleep, leaning against the door of the truck.

Tom struggled to keep awake. It had been a very long day. He kept nodding off, jerking himself awake, and realigning the truck on the road. Even frigid winter air blowing in from the open window wasn't enough to keep him alert.

He dozed.

For a few seconds, the truck stayed on the road. But as Tom slumped over the steering wheel, the Chevy drifted off the north-bound lane of Route 44. The truck was going fast enough to make it over a shallow ditch. Then it bumped its way into a cornfield and over a few rock-hard rows of cornstalk stubble. The truck bounced and swayed violently.

Brett's door popped open and he fell out.

Before Tom registered what had happened, the truck's wheels rolled over Brett's head.

After Tom was able to flag down a car, Brett Hill was taken to Robinson Memorial Hospital in Ravenna, Ohio, where he was declared dead. Tom, banged up, scratched, bruised, shaken and dreadfully guilty, survived.

"I was awakened by a phone call with the news that Brett had been killed in an accident with my truck," Leon told me. "A prayer meeting was called at the hall and we prayed that God would raise Brett from the dead. We really believed this was possible."

Joe remembered entering the intensive care room after Brett had been pronounced dead. "I stood beside Larry who was staring at the wall. Speaking softly, Larry said, 'I knew the instant he was gone. I felt his spirit get up out of his body and just drift away.'" With extended arm and finger, Larry kept pointing at something that only he could see, tracking it as it rose higher and higher. Finally, it was gone and Larry broke into sobs. "We were devastated." Joe said. "Larry was our pastor and friend. Brett had been our bandmate and younger brother in Christ. And he was gone."

According to Leon and Joe, Larry said that the Lord had shown him that one member of the church would not make it home that night. "Apparently he was smart enough to be able to talk to God and hear from God, but not smart enough to heed God's advice," Leon said.

Joe added, "If that were the case, why didn't Larry see that timely warning as a wonderful bit of good luck and just have everyone stay home that night? After the fact, anyone can look like a seer."

Larry claimed that Leon had told him before the Watch Night concert that he had fixed the loose door on the truck, and tried to use his son's death to further cement Leon's dedication to him. Leon said, "In a church meeting Larry stood face-to-face with me, and, poking me in the chest, said: 'You owe me for the rest of your life! If you had listened to me and repaired your truck like I told you to, my son would be alive today!'"

Leon told me, "Normally I would have gone to the junkyard and purchased another driver's side door, but it seemed the demands of work at the farm never allowed me or anyone else a spare moment."

During a phone interview in 2005 with Shelley Terry of the *Ashtabula Star Beacon*, Larry said, "He [Leon] lied to me," adding that after his son was killed, "I had him sell the truck immediately."[28]

Leon told me, "Fortunately, I never accepted the blame for Brett's death. I told myself that until I came to the farm, I had always maintained my vehicles. The lack of money and time to do so were Larry's fault, not mine. Further, I didn't think he had ever warned me about fixing my truck. And it is only now, more than thirty years later, that I realized that while Larry had tried to blame me for not fixing the driver's side door on the truck, it was from the passenger side door that Brett fell."

When Tim Hill spoke to me of his brother's death, he said, "It became all about Larry—a new source of anger he could nurse. He would say to all of us, 'See what I've done for you? I've lost my son for the gospel! And my wife, I had to give her up, too. If God was going to take one of my sons, why did it have to be Brett?' Of course, my mom was contacted when Brett was killed but I wasn't allowed to speak to her on the phone. And even at the funeral for Brett, Larry wouldn't allow Mark or me to get near her."

Tom Miller was left to deal with the guilt of falling asleep at the wheel. Leon told me, "I can only imagine the guilt he probably felt over this accident. But the person who actually caused the accident was Larry, who drove people to go without sleep until their every action posed a danger to themselves and others. Larry lost his oldest son to sleep deprivation. One would think that he would have decided that this practice had become tragically expensive, but the long hours and sleep interruptions would increase to even higher levels in the coming years."

Joe agreed, adding, "We were sleep deprived over a long period of time and then sent out on cross-country drives in the middle of the night."[28]

But at the time, there was no blame. Everyone at Fortney Road was in shock and felt only compassion for Larry.

"Our pastor, friend, teacher and confidant was now severely damaged and we ached for him more than ourselves," Joe said. "Youthful band of idealists that we were, his tragedy-wounded spirit served only to bind our hearts closer to him. Our love for him made us willing to forgive his ugliness."

Within six months of his son's death, two more members of the community would die, but first one of Larry's most dedicated followers—overwhelmed by the grinding, day-to-day workload and sleep deprivation—would flee the ministry.

Chapter 19

Dark Clouds

J oe said, "Early in 1972 I couldn't take any more and I ran away, leaving behind my wife and children. For months I wandered around, tending bar at a Geneva-on-the-Lake nightclub and selling marijuana to get by. But the Fourth of July was coming, which was my daughter Shannon's birthday, and I had to see my daughter."

He returned to Fortney Road during the early morning of the Fourth. He reconciled with his wife Sandy and his five children, and although Larry might have preached about forgiveness, he didn't model it. Joe had been with Larry from the beginning, and Larry and many of the members considered Joe to be an elder in the church. Not only did he assist in leading Bible studies and counseling, he worked with the jail ministry and led other outreaches. And Larry had known Joe the longest of anyone and perhaps trusted him more than the others.

But now Larry knew Joe was no longer as loyal or committed as he once was, so he banished him. "We could no longer stay at the farm," Joe said. "We were too much trouble and I had totally broken Larry's trust by running off."

One member told me, "Joe was excommunicated from the farm and had to live offsite with his family. He and his wife and family were expected to be at the meetings like everyone else. But it was just a known thing that we were to give him the cold shoulder. What a Christian thing to do, right? Larry would prophesy that Joe would have an accident, that it would be God's judgment on him. Larry did not say how it would happen, just that Joe was in rebellion."

Joe found an apartment for his family about two miles away and they walked back and forth to church activities. They were now viewed as second-class citizens among those in the community.

To leave Fortney Road for good meant eternal damnation. To leave and return meant you were in limbo.

Leon said, "We were indoctrinated to believe that if we left the all-important mission that God had assigned to us personally—helping fulfill the mission of the Church of the Risen Christ —then we not only had failed God but our eternal souls would be lost in hell."

Larry had more faith and trust in Tom Miller, and in June of 1972 Tom was given permission to leave the farm to attend his brother John's wedding. "I was surprised that Larry let him come by himself," John told me. "Our wedding was on June 17, 1972. We only talked briefly, and I again pleaded with Tom to get out of Larry's group."

John's wedding was the last time he and his family would ever see Tom Miller.

In mid-July of 1972, Joe arrived at Fortney Road one evening and discovered a small group getting ready to leave for a rock festival in Bull Island, Illinois. They were off to do what they always did: witness and live off the land. After thousands of pieces of Christian literature had been packed in the Chevy Blazer, Peter, the driver, settled himself behind the wheel. Larry's son Mark, Carole's brother, John, and Tom Miller squeezed into the back seat, and Joe's brother Randy rode shotgun.

Randy rolled down his window and kissed his wife, Cookie, goodbye. Their three children scampered over to the car to get a hug and kiss from their dad, then dashed off to continue playing. Joe squatted beside the car as they all prayed for a safe journey and many souls won. With a final hearty "Amen!" the five passengers waved their arms out the windows and the Chevy turned up the gravel road, kicking up stone and dust. Soon the taillights were just pinpoints and then vanished in the gathering darkness.

The next morning, Diane Sullivan sought out Joe. She had Cookie with her. "I knew right away that whatever this was, it wasn't good," Joe said. Cookie, her eyes red-rimmed and wide with shock, could only stand there numbly as Diane spoke. "I knew she was talking because I could see her lips moving but I couldn't comprehend what was being said."

Shortly after crossing into Kentucky, the driver and everyone else in the car had fallen asleep. The car had been speeding down the interstate. It veered off the highway like a torpedo and exploded into a concrete abutment. The impact slammed the engine through the firewall and into Randy's chest, killing him instantly. The force was so great it snapped the bolts holding Randy's seat, driving him back into Tom Miller, trapping Tom in the rear of the Chevy. Peter, Mark, and John were severely injured, with John's back broken when he was thrown from the vehicle.

Tim told me, "Mark was pinned under the truck and Peter was able to drag him to safety." The surviving men tried to help free their two companions but the vehicle burst into flames and they barely managed to escape. The fire had almost burned itself out by the time the highway patrol arrived.

Left with nothing but a brass buckle from the melted, nylon belt Randy wore, his funeral, like Tom Miller's, was closed casket. "We buried Randy next to Brett in the Mennonite cemetery behind their church house. Larry performed the ceremony using my brother's casket as the altar for an altar call," Joe remembered.

Randy's wife Cookie was now left with three children. "Raising these babies with any hope of normalcy under conditions as oppressively abnormal as these was fantasy," Joe said.

By email in 2007, Cookie wrote, "My husband believed so much in Larry's ministry and Larry took advantage of him. I hardly ever even saw my husband, he was always working trying to put food on the table, then working for Larry and he thought it was for the Lord. It was Larry that took advantage of all of us. Randy loved saving souls so much, that is all he wanted to do. He would of been a great minister if he had a better pastor."

Image 37: Randy Markko in 1971 with one of his three children. Photo courtesy of Joe Markko.

Tom Miller's brother, John, told me, "The pastor at my folks' Lutheran church graciously allowed Larry to preach at the church and at the graveside. Larry gave an impassioned plea for the people in attendance to get right with God. He invited the young people to come forward and stare down into Tom's grave. He gave solemn warning of their fate if they continued in their sinful ways. Several of the kids that Tom had introduced to drugs knelt at the grave and prayed with Larry to receive Jesus. Tom had tried over and over to persuade these young people to turn away from the drugs and accept Christ. Most of them mocked him to his face. He carried that burden of guilt to his grave."

Alan Canfora—a close friend of Tom's and one of the wounded students from the Kent State shootings—and some of Tom's KSU friends attended his funeral and didn't take kindly to Larry's altar call. They remembered only as, "Larry Hill openly berating us during his eulogy in the church."

Larry's son Tim said, "It always freaked Mark and I out that this horrible accident happened so soon—just six months—after Brett had died. We wondered if Dad had somehow caused the accident because Tom and Randy were in the car and maybe it was his way of getting back at Tom who had survived the first accident that had killed Brett."

Larry Hill managed to profit from the accident. John recalled, "My folks had purchased a $10,000 life insurance policy on Tom during his years of rebellion. It was primarily meant to be a funeral policy and to cover any debts he might have. It offered double indemnity in case of an accident." Larry had found out about the policy and had Tom make him the primary beneficiary, receiving a check for $20,000 when Tom died. "Larry didn't offer to help with the funeral expenses or anything," John told me. "He kept the full amount, and my parents were stuck paying for the funeral out of their own personal funds."

According to Tim, the tragic events of the year were so devastating that Glenn Schwartz expressed the grief of the community by composing "Dark Clouds Rollin' Over 1972."

But there was more to come in the following year, and this time the storm would rage against Joe.

Chapter 20

A Blue Flame
in the Sky

A short distance from Fortney Road, the village of North Madison was in the process of building a water filtration plant for their community. Cleveland Electric and Illuminating ran new 27,000-volt electric lines into the plant.

On May 3, 1973, Joe Markko—four days from his twenty-fifth birthday—was across the road from the plant, doing construction work for a small company that specialized in the prevention of soil erosion for lakefront properties. It was a gray spring day and the clouds kept piling up. Soon a mist began, followed by a steady drizzle. The soil grew soft from the moisture.

Joe took a truck to the area where the concrete materials were stockpiled and began loading. He spent a few minutes searching for ground solid enough to deploy the truck's stabilizing pontoons. This prevented the truck from tipping despite the heavy cargo. In order to load the parts properly, Joe had to manipulate the boom of the truck between the high-tension lines using remote controls at the end of a twenty-five-foot safety cable.

Because Joe was paying attention to the stability of the load, he momentarily lost sight of the end of the boom. It snapped a high-tension line. The broken cable whipped around the boom and the electrical current did what electricity does: it traveled. The surge flowed looking for the most natural ground: Joe holding the boom controls in both hands, standing on damp earth.

"Twenty-seven thousand volts of electricity arced to the metal buttons on my Levi jacket." Joe said. Electricity travels through the human body at the speed of a single heartbeat. It burns everything. One of the workers from the water filtration plant was an

147

eyewitness. He said, "I heard a noise, loud like a shotgun. I looked up and saw what looked like a blue flame in the sky."

Running over to see what happened, he found Joe's feet sticking up out of the grass. The worker ran to the nearest house to call an emergency vehicle.

While the man was gone Joe heard a voice in his head repeat, *"Get up and keep walking. Get up and keep walking."* Whether this was the voice of God or survival instinct kicking, Joe can't say. "I do know this: specialists at Cleveland's Metro General Hospital speculated the only thing that kept my heart beating after such a massive shock was the fact that my body stayed in motion."

When the worker returned, Joe was standing in the middle of the road as if waiting for someone. Having been electrocuted with 27,000 volts of electricity, both of Joe's hands had already turned black. Smoke from burning flesh was escaping through the top of his shirt, and skin was hanging from the back of his neck.

"The emergency vehicle arrived and I got in under my own power," Joe remembered. "I was taken to the emergency room at the hospital in Painesville, Ohio, where they needed only remove my shirt to uncover the extent of the devastation."

Realizing their hospital was unequipped to deal with such a massive injury, Joe was immediately loaded back into the ambulance and sent to Cleveland's Metro General Hospital.

Within an hour and forty-five minutes Joe was under a surgeon's knife.

"Fifty-five percent of my body suffered third degree burns," Joe said. "There was no skin on my back. My breastbone, chest muscles and rib cage literally exploded from my chest."

The damage was so severe and widespread, some of the medical staff predicted Joe wouldn't live more than four or five days. Time stretched on, however, and Joe spent the next six weeks either unconscious or semi-conscious. He couldn't be turned onto his chest for obvious reasons and every night, his body fluids seeped from his skinless back, causing him to stick to the sheets.

Larry wrote about Joe's devastating accident, stating that:

Immediately the group formed a 24-hour prayer chain and set aside certain days for prayer and fasting. For several weeks, Laura and I went to the hospital at night and sat in Joe's room praying with him. I remember the night of crisis when I was at the hospital praying and it did not look like Joe was going to make it. As prayer and supplication went up before God that this young man would not die before some of his music could get to the public and that God would have mercy and let him live for the sake of his family, a quiet voice spoke, "I will give him his life."[20]

"There was certainly fasting and prayer," Joe told me, "but reading this material, I am reminded of Larry's normal pattern of taking the credit for all the stuff God was doing. What Larry didn't mention is that, at the farm, Larry used my accident to instill more fear in everyone and make him look more the 'prophet.' He told people that he prophesied the event years before, he declared it God's punishment, the price for my rebellion and disobedience to God, the result of my running away from the farm . . ."

Tim Hill agreed, telling me, "My dad took me to the hospital to see Joe and he said to me, 'You see, this is what happens when you defy me!'"

In this this taped meeting from the July 15, 1973, Sunday service at the Kent New Generation Church, Larry preaches to the congregation:

> You better humble yourself. You better humble yourself before YOU find yourself in a car accident! You better humble yourself before YOU get ahold of a hot wire. That's the way it is with all God's children. You don't play with God. God will have mercy on you for a while. God will send a warning, saying if you don't do so and so, this and this is going to happen, and that's just the way it's happened. We better take God's warning before we wind up in a hospital.[29]

Altogether Joe spent nine months in the hospital. The permanent, deforming scars on the outside of his body were nothing compared to damage done inside. "In many ways I never fully recovered and my opinion

Image 38: Joe playing with one of his children, two years after his accident. Photo courtesy of Joe Markko.

of myself is forever damaged," Joe said. "I was transformed from a 185-pound construction worker, convinced the entire world was waiting to hear what I had to say, to 120 pounds of raw meat with the bones sticking out the ends."

"Following Randy's death and my accident, Randy's widow, Cookie, was made to live under deplorable conditions," Joe said. "She was in Ohio because of her husband and, when there was no one to look after her welfare, she was treated shamefully."

Larry took advantage of Joe being in the hospital and "borrowed" $10,000 from the meager insurance settlement Cookie received following Randy's death. He used the money to purchase new equipment for the All Saved Freak Band. "He never paid it back," Joe said.

"Her relatives came from Chicago to get her, taking her and the children in the middle of the night to reduce the potential for any ugly scenes. No one even told me she had left. They didn't want to upset me," Joe said. "The news didn't reach me until I came home from the hospital. I'm still saddened to this day that I wasn't there for her and the children."

When asked about her time on the farm, Cookie emailed me: "I have gone through a lot back then and I don't like digging into my brain about facts on Larry. I really dedicated myself to the Lord and Larry took it all away from me. It has taken me a lot of pain and suffering to get where I am today. I have not talked to anyone besides my therapist about the time I spent at Fortney Road. I was so young and after Randy died I should have just taken my family and left after my daughter was born in 1972. I suffered such mental abuse, and it was all because of Larry. He kept me on some land away from my own husband, with small children, on cold freezing nights in a log cabin, alone.

"I have been silent about the past, but I do not even like to say the name 'Larry.' I know inside I want people to know what we've all been through but it is so hard for me to go back. I never wanted my children near Larry. I left the farm early and it was not early enough for me. I have really blocked out so much . . ."

In Larry Hill's mind, the death of three members of his flock—his son, Brett Hill, Tom Miller and Randy Markko—combined with Joe's horrific injury could only mean that God was not pleased with his ministry and He was judging Larry's congregation.

Larry claimed he didn't want any of his followers to perish due to lack of obedience, so out of a love for them and God, he introduced a new form of discipline: The White Judge.

Chapter 21

The White Judge

L arry's love for God and his flock came in the form of a six-foot white buggy whip fashioned from strips of pure white leather bound onto a flexible plastic rod.

It became known as the "White Judge."

"That whip ripped the clothes right off of your body," one woman said. "It ripped the skin out of you completely." Larry's favorite room in the farmhouse to use for beatings was Tim's room. "In Timmy's room, all the women got it," she said. "I was beat in the study. I was beaten on the front porch. I was beat in Timmy's room."[16]

Bob Tidd told me, "As time went on things got worse, discipline got heavier. I was a fortunate one. I only got three whippings. The most painful was when I got twenty lashes two days in a row. The second day was hard and put a real fear of the whip in me."

A former member told me, "You see how it started out: first pushups, then running miles, then a whip, finally the riding crop with a metal shaft—the White Judge. It would literally rip your clothes off of your back. And it dug into your flesh, the tail end would rip at your thigh. It had some fringy thing on it. I remember just seeing it was a terror for me. It would be lying up against the wall in the corner. I wonder if there was anyone that did not get it? I saw Pam, Laura, Diane and Kim, all with black eyes. I think back now and know why people think we were crazy to put up with it. But all I can say is that you had to be there to understand what it was like."

Larry was especially brutal in his treatment of Glenn Schwartz, snidely calling him "Star." In 2007, Glenn told me, "The Preacher

Man would say to me, 'You think too much of yourself, don't you, Star? You need a good beating and I'm the one to do it! There are no stars in this ministry!'" And then Larry would lose himself in a rage.

Glenn said, "The Preacher Man would beat me if I didn't memorize the scriptures like he wanted. He smacks you around and beats you. He taught me with the rod, with the White Judge. I've seen the rod of His wrath and have been beaten with it."

Donald told me, "I remember once I needed a ride to Fortney Road and I asked my mom to drop me off. Of course, I didn't realize until it was too late that I was breaking one of Larry's rules—never tell anyone the location of the farm. After my mom dropped me off, Larry was furious that I had disclosed the location and I had my first encounter with the White Judge. That beating with the White Judge was sort of an initiation or a rite of passage I guess; it was a sign you were accepted—that God accepted you—and you could be trusted to learn and experience these inner truths that Larry taught. The wisdom and insight and visions that he had could now be imparted to you."

And Larry showed no mercy when it came to using the White Judge.

Joe said, "During one Sunday service I told Larry I believed God spoke to me about the direction of the church, and Larry replied to me, 'I don't think that's God. He would've told me first.'"

Sitting in a rocker crafted from grapevines and covered with a handmade quilt, Larry stopped rocking. Joe stood nervously before him. Larry leaned forward in his chair. Lost in thought for a moment, he seemed to be listening for God-given instructions. Then, having apparently heard them, he reached up and grabbed Joe by the beard.

Pulling Joe down and toward him until they were face to face, Larry glared into his eyes and in steely, measured tones, demanded, "Why do you always gravitate toward my enemies?!"

Joe was dumbfounded at Larry's accusation. "I had been with him from the very beginning, and he now publicly labeled me as untrustworthy? If I'm gravitating toward his enemies, I knew no one was going to associate with me. They didn't want such criticism attached to them. Anything other than absolute obedience to Larry was viewed as total betrayal and no one escaped scrutiny as a potential Judas."

Sensing Joe was on the verge of betraying him again like he did back in 1972 when he ran away for a few months, Larry decreed Joe's punishment. Clearly, being shot through with twenty-seven thousand volts of electricity wasn't enough.

Joe said, "I stood against the wall in the barn and received ten lashes from Donald because I made a mistake, believing God would speak to me. Ten lashes across a backside reconstructed with grafted skin. Ten lashes from the White Judge."

And nobody provided comfort after the discipline was meted out. Bob said, "It was felt you deserved the beating, you had missed the mark and the discipline was needed. How you felt, physically or emotionally, didn't matter."

Larry's son Tim said, "This whip—this White Judge—it was the same one he had been using on his own children for years without a single member of the community objecting. It didn't seem to bother anyone on the farm until it was them or their children being beaten and not just Larry's kids."

Another former member recalled, "I don't know how Kim Massmann lived. Three of us women listened through the wall as Larry beat her near death and then told Laura and Dee Dee to take her to the bus station."

"And Kim would beg to be allowed to stay," another woman recalled, "and the violence would continue, and it seemed to go on for weeks."

But not everyone begged to stay. Some people refused to accept the brutal discipline and fled the cult. "It was very difficult to see people that I loved and worked with, and lived with, leave," Bob explained to me. "Larry always said, 'If you leave here Satan will turn your mind in twenty-four hours!' To me it was beyond terrifying to see some who were so committed just turn and question all Larry had taught us and just discard fundamental truths."

And if the whip wasn't handy, Larry used his fists.

"Larry punched me in the face once, really hard," Leon told me. "He knew how to throw a punch, that's for certain. And he may have had one leg but if he wanted to beat on you, there was power behind him."

As an outsider hearing of such relentless brutality many years after the fact, it was hard to comprehend what these people had told me. It is a simple, mechanical function to transcribe notes from interviews, no matter how repulsive the content. But I needed an answer to the why—Why didn't they just run away? It wasn't like they were locked away in a compound somewhere. Many of them were off the property alone during the day at jobs or in town doing errands. The answers that came back by email, phone call or in-person interviews all had the same underlying reason: They stayed out of fear.

Leon and several others had an identical answer: "Larry said if you left the farm, you'd go to hell. It was as simple as that. So no matter how bad or hard things were on the farm, at least it wasn't hell. When I would be beaten, I would repeat to myself, 'Hell will be worse than this, hell is much worse than this,' and when I was whipped, because the lashes burned in my skin, I'd repeat over and over, 'Hell will burn more than this.' It was the only way I could endure the beating. If you left the farm, you'd go to hell, so there was no escape, no plan to escape, and no reason to escape. Who would want to go to hell?"

One woman sighed deeply when I asked her why she had stayed at Fortney Road for more than three years. It was clear it was a question she'd heard many times. She shrugged her shoulders, tears in her eyes, and said quietly, "I don't know why. I don't know. My husband can't understand any of it. I don't talk to him about it anymore. He can't believe anyone would go through what we did. I understand how he feels. I can't believe it myself."

Morgan King told me, "I felt bad for the others when they had been beaten but you couldn't go and comfort them. You couldn't talk to them about it or touch them, so we all learned to say a lot with our looks, with our eyes. We'd joke a bit to keep from crying. Not often, but sometimes." He learned the best way to avoid a beating was to "keep my nose clean. I learned if you kept your mouth shut, you didn't get into trouble."[16]

"People really will think that we were losers to let those things happen to us," one man admitted, "but they don't know how strong we really had to be. I don't think that we even realize it."

Another woman told me, "I can't believe I was there for all those years. Nobody would believe that a person would go through that willingly. There were so many times when I was pregnant when I would go to Akron for a doctor check up and I would almost not go back to the farm. But I was afraid of what would happen to us—to my husband and children—if I didn't return."

"You want to know how crazy it all was, and how did we all fall for it all, right?" one woman asked me over the phone. "I think I just lost my mind for a while. That's about the only way I can explain it."

Now divorced, one woman told me, "When I met Larry Hill, I never liked him. I was always afraid of him. I should have gone with my conscience and left there a long time before I did. My husband was totally caught up in it. I knew there was something weird—I just didn't have the tools at the time to figure it out."

When I asked if anyone had reached out for help locally while they were living at Fortney Road, a few said they had. But at the time, all that anyone in town knew was that Larry Hill was helping kids get off drugs and he was frequently seen on the Sunday morning religious television programs. At that time, no one would believe a minister was other than what he appeared to be. "No one had any good advice for me," one woman said. "Even a college professor I knew at the time said he didn't see anything wrong with it. I had asked him what he thought about my life on the farm and all he said was, 'It's not for me, but I think Reverend Hill has a valid ministry.'"

One woman I interviewed by phone said, "It has been so long since everything happened. I used to have nightmares all the time. I feel like a fool when I think of what I let myself go through. Does anyone else feel that way?" I assured her that they did. Then she said, "I saw Larry's face on one of the album covers and I got sick to my stomach.

Because in his own mind he was such a powerful and indispensable prophet, Larry Hill saw enemies around every corner and believed there were powerful forces—including the Mafia, the Illuminati, the Communists, the National Council of Churches, and the Roman Catholic Church—who were determined to silence and destroy him. He regularly raged against all of them in the *Freedom Bell.*

But his greatest fear and enemy was not an organization, it was a semi-truck.

Carole told me, "If you were the person driving with Larry in the car, it was an absolute horror to pass by one of those semi-trucks, because he would get so agitated and nervous. He thought it was a conspiracy and that 'they' planned to run us off the road, just to kill him, God's Messenger. He believed the semi-trucks were coming to get him."

Larry's paranoia enlarged its borders until he no longer felt safe at Fortney Road. Convinced that his enemies would eventually infiltrate the farm, he prepared for that day by finding a place in Tidioute, Pennsylvania, where he could hide and no one—not even his closest followers—would be able to reach him. Since it was less than 300 miles away, he often disappeared at a moment's notice for days at a time, usually accompanied by Diane Sullivan and Laura Markko.

As Tim Hill told me, "We were always so relieved when he was out of town, hiding. It meant there were no beatings, no abuse."

In addition to the horrific physical, emotional and spiritual abuse, sexual abuse had also begun to occur at Fortney Road. Many cults tend to follow a pathway that ends in the objectification of the cult member, and this is achieved through sexual dominance. By enforcing sexual submission, the follower is now merely an object

Image 39: A rare photo of Larry Hill from the early 1970s

that the cult leader uses however he sees fit to fulfill his or God's plan.

Bethy Goodenough was being physically and sexually abused on a regular basis, sometimes several times a day. Because she was so young, Bethy doesn't remember how long this abuse went on but said she "felt like the most alone person in the whole world." Larry Hill was a sexual predator and Bethy was being eaten alive. He was devouring the young girl right in front of everyone's eyes, and as he consumed her, she seemed to grow smaller and quieter and on some days, she seemed on the verge of disappearing all together.

I found it hard to believe that not one of the adults who lived at Fortney Road was aware of what was happening to Bethy. Did they not see changes in her behavior or appearance? Did they not hear or see things that raised any suspicions?

The former members I spoke to said they weren't aware of the sexual abuse but also admitted that if they questioned anything, they risked being labeled a Judas and severe punishment would certainly follow. Several also reminded me that life at Fortney Road was a matter of survival and they were looking out for themselves and simply didn't have the strength or awareness to see if someone else was worse off.

Margo finally admitted to me, "When I heard Bethy's story, it affected me deeply. I had no idea all this was going on and yet, looking back I'm absolutely amazed at our naiveté. How could we not know? Or at least suspect? How could any sane, caring person allow any of the horrendous things that went on at Fortney Road to continue? I'm so sorry for all she suffered."

Carole told me, "I do think Larry had sex, of some sort, with everyone he could. After hearing about Larry's sexual abuse of Bethy, I feel I must be honest about what happened to my dear friend, Anne."

Anne was Carole's age and joined the farm soon after Carole. They became immediate friends, and years after leaving the farm, Anne confided to Carole what had happened to her at Fortney Road. One afternoon, Larry had beckoned Anne into the den, and she recalled him telling her, "I know you have needs, and you have to keep them here."

"He proceeded to kiss me, tongue and all," Anne said. "He slid his hand down into my dress and masturbated me. I hated it but I was paralyzed. I was in shock. I couldn't process what was happening to me. Was this even real? Was it really happening to me? I couldn't do anything. I couldn't move. Then he laughed and, thank God, finally stopped."

She left the room and they never discussed it, pretended it never happened. But he continued to abuse Anne, Bethy, and some of the other women. Anne told Carole, "Some days, when I was headed out to work, he'd be sitting in the kitchen by the sink. He'd call me over to feel me up as I was going out the door. It's too much to bear."

At times Larry would have too many sips from his wine flask and wouldn't bother to hide his abusive behavior. In 2007, Glenn told me that he had seen Larry touching the women. "The Preacher Man had his wine back then and I seen him with his hands all over the women at the farm."

Larry's son Mark confided in Leon about some of the sexual acts he witnessed. He said that Diane would often perform fellatio on Larry while Mark was in the room. And Joe told me Larry once said to his son, "Mark, this could all be yours one day," meaning the farm, the community, the people. It was as if it was all just property to Larry, especially the women.

Leon said, "Larry incorporated what I've learned is called a war against self, or a war against one's own ego."

One manifestation of this war or struggle was Larry's treatment of women and sexuality, by both demanding that the women have downcast eyes and secretly using them for his sexual depravities.

"There was a considerable amount of preaching advocating the suppression of sexual thoughts for unmarried believers," Leon said, "not an easy task for a group of people who were mostly in their early twenties. In retrospect, I believe nearly every person there failed at this task of suppression, and they probably experienced the same requisite guilt, fear, sense of failure, and self-loathing that I did. The game is to convince people their natural impulses are sinful and then set them at war against their own personality and nature."

The victim then continually works at suppressing his or her own "unholy" personality, and then self-doubt drives the person to further surrender his or her will and judgment to the leader. And once someone has surrendered to the leader, he or she is at his mercy.

Unfortunately, cult leaders like Larry Hill have no mercy.

Although Larry had privately achieved sexual dominance over his congregation, he continued to seek public acceptance and some form of acclaim from the mainstream Christian churches and ministries in the surrounding area. In an effort to come across as just another member of the local clergy who were outraged by the moral decay he saw in society and culture in the early 1970s, he wrote in the *Freedom Bell*:

> We are living in an age when purity is a joke, and high moral standards are continually being destroyed by Hollywood, modern novels, television, magazines, lewd stories, advertising techniques, and community practices. A committee of the U.S. Senate investigating juvenile delinquency reported that the moral fiber of the country is being undermined by a deluge of vile and filthy books, pictures, and other pornographic material. The worst part of it is, up to 75% of it falls into the hands of minors. In high schools across America, students are required to read such trash as J.D. Salinger's The Catcher in the Rye, which has four letter words sprinkled on nearly every page. On college campuses students are being exposed to unbelievable filth.[6]

With powerful rhetoric like that, it's no wonder the local clergy continued to invite Reverend Larry Hill to speak to their congregations and television hosts eagerly booked him for their Sunday morning religious programs.

Although Larry relentlessly brutalized his congregation in private, in public he praised them. In 1972, Larry used the *Freedom Bell* to boast that he and members of his Kent New Generation Church were leaders of a new work that God was doing:

> [They are the] leaders of the new day dawning. They are the prophets of the new government that will be established by Jesus when He returns before the year 2000. They are a main line of purity and faith established by Christ in this day when everything

has gone stale and corrupt. They are the New Generation Church![6]

Larry, like almost every cult leader before and after, could not resist letting slip a prediction of when Christ would return. And like every other cult leader and self-proclaimed prophet, Larry Hill was wrong

And while he privately trampled over and degraded the physical, sexual and spiritual lives of his congregation, he delighted in the public acclaim that Glenn Schwartz and the All Saved Freak Band were attracting. So, based on the success of their live performances, in 1973 Larry decided it was time to take the next logical step and record an album.

Chapter 22

My Poor Generation

"**T**hat was a big deal, Larry deciding it was time to record an album," Joe explained to me. The financial demands of Fortney Road were very challenging at this time since more than fifty adults and children were in the community. So the idea of recording an album involved much soul searching. Was it too much of a financial commitment? Could the money be raised?

In 1972, with the notable exceptions of Larry Norman's *Upon This Rock* (1969) and Agape's *Gospel Hard Rock* (1971), there was very little recorded Christian rock or folk music, so it was a relatively unknown and uncharted territory.

Joe said, "I remember Larry and I sat down to listen to Larry Norman's album, *Upon This Rock*. We were astonished by the fact that this musical 'thing' [i.e. Jesus Music, now known as Contemporary Christian Music or CCM] seemed to be happening simultaneously in pockets across America. While his album provided great encouragement and validation for what we were doing musically, it actually discouraged

Image 40: Larry Hill composing a song at the piano for the All Saved Freak Band.

me a bit as a musician. It made me think, 'Man, have we got a long way to go!' *Upon This Rock* was so good and we were so amateurish."

The band had met their eventual producer, Rob Galbraith, while on tour in Nashville in 1971. He was a studio producer for Columbia, and Glenn, Larry, Randy and Joe had taped a demo of a few songs and sent them to Rob who appreciated their unique sound.

Rob recalled, "We kept in touch off and on, and then one day Larry called and said they were ready to cut their own album. Having found a studio in Cleveland where they could record, they asked me if I would come up and help with production and studio work."[23]

He agreed but expressed some reservations as to how good an album could be done in as short a time as they had allotted and could afford. "They recorded that first album very quickly, in just three to four days, I think," Rob told me. "From start to finish, including the overdubbing and final mix, I think we were done within a week."

Adding to his concern was his unfamiliarity with the studio—Cleveland Recording Company—and its sound. But Rob had nothing to worry about when it came to the studio, which was a state-of-the-art recording and mastering facility. The engineer and owner, Ken Hamann, had worked with some of the biggest rock bands to come out of Cleveland including Grand Funk Railroad and the James Gang.

"But let me just say now that I couldn't have been more pleased with the album or the studio," Rob said. "Ken Hamann is one fine engineer. I was already high on [the group] from earlier days, but they had recently added these two girls who just ruined me with the way they played, what they wrote, and how they sang. I found the time spent, the music, and the people to be a very special blessing and, as Pam says, 'Praise God!'"[23]

In 2007, I met Rob in Manhattan when he was visiting from Nashville. We did the interview over lunch on the West Side in a diner. He told me, "I considered producing them like a tithe or offering to the Lord. They were a good-hearted bunch of people. Glenn was just such a sweet and gentle man. Joe was a quality guy and he had a wonderful voice. I remember how nice his sister, Laura, was, too. And Morgan and his sister, Carole, were also great people to be around."

To record the band's first album, Larry flew Rob up from Nashville and paid for him to stay in a motel. There was a distance of seventy miles from Rob's motel to Cleveland Recording and Rob remembers that he dreaded those early morning and evening drives.

"Larry would talk pretty much the entire time, both ways. And he had an opinion about everything. I remember there was a billboard advertising a bunch of bananas and he would point at it and say, 'See! That's Communism! *Join the bunch*!' And the poor people that lived with him had to put up with his crazy talk all the time. He never influenced me about politics or the Lord. He knew I had been a Christian longer than he so he sort of left that topic alone."

Rob wasn't alone in his disdain over Larry Hill. Joe said, "About two years before his death in 2003, Ken Hamann confided in me that he could never stand Larry, but, being a local boy, he'd long known and loved Glenn Schwartz so he wanted to be involved in our recording, even if it meant putting up with Larry."

When it came time to record their album, Rob recalled, "None of them were really what I would consider 'trained musicians' but I think their roughness worked to their advantage, although they certainly learned and improved from album to album."

For their debut album, the band consisted of Larry Hill (piano, vocals), Kim Massmann (cello, vocals), Joe Markko (guitar, vocals), Ed Durkos (rhythm guitar), Pam Massmann (violin, vocals), Morgan King (bass), and, of course, Glenn Schwartz (lead guitar).

"If it weren't for Ed Durkos, my participation in the band would have been over following my accident," Joe said. His right hand had been replaced by a hook and he had three fingers on the left hand but they lacked nerves and tendons. "Ed learned all of my songs and helped me write others by playing the chords I called out to him."

Rob has gone on to produce a variety of artists including Ronnie Milsap and Kenny Rogers, contributed vocals to the

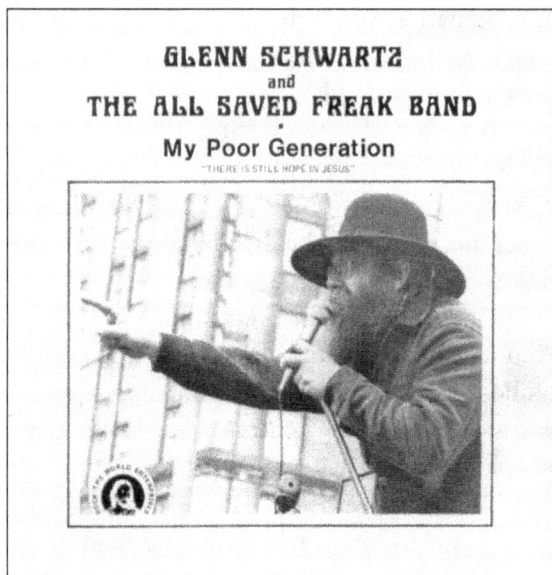

GLENN SCHWARTZ
and
THE ALL SAVED FREAK BAND

My Poor Generation

"THERE IS STILL HOPE IN JESUS"

Image 41: My Poor
Generation cover

Finding Nemo soundtrack, and produced actor Kevin Bacon's band, the Bacon Brothers, with Michael Bacon.

Rob and Ken made a great team, recording and mastering all of the band's albums. During the making of *My Poor Generation*, Rob also recorded an impromptu version of "Old Rugged Cross" on the piano. "They heard me playing 'Old Rugged Cross'—I was just playing it for myself—but they liked it, asked me to play it again and decided to record it." Larry would hold on to Rob's track for eight years before putting it on *Sower*, the final All Saved Freak Band album.

When it came to the final selection of songs to be recorded for the band's debut, personal experience played a major role. "Remembering those in our community—Tom Miller, Brett Hill and my brother, Randy—who had been recently killed, our hearts needed the sense of pervading gentleness that comes with many of those songs," Joe told me. "They ended up being songs that ministered to us on a number of levels."

Larry made the choices for the album covers and provided the content for the liner notes. The picture of Larry on the *My Poor Generation* album cover was taken while the band performed on a street corner somewhere in downtown Cleveland.

Joe said, "I was surprised and actually a bit uneasy when I saw Glenn's name on the cover as 'Glenn Schwartz and the All Saved Freak Band.' No one had ever discussed that prominent use of Glenn's name. Larry took it on himself to do that."

The first track on the album—and the listener's first exposure to the All Saved Freak Band—was not a raucous blues number as one might expect from a group that featured one of the nation's leading guitarists. Instead, over some very subdued, somewhat menacing guitar picking, "Elder White" is introduced via Larry Hill's rough and raspy voice.

New York-based *Fusetronsound* online music reviews wrote:

First album by apocalyptic Ohio contingent of talented drug addicts, pastors, activists (Tom Miller of the Kent State 25), and famous musicians turned Jesus Rock band; the main interest in this band is the lead and rhythm guitar playing by Glenn Schwartz; when the first words of an album are "out of the backwoods of the Mississippi Delta," you know you're in for something that's not just for Sunday school classes.[30]

My Poor Generation was ranked as number 228 in "Contemporary Christian Music's 500 Best Albums of All Time":

The opening track, "Elder White" is reminiscent of the bluesier side of *Creedence Clearwater* Revival. The song never kicks in to a full fledged rocker and that is what is so compelling. The listener keeps waiting for the big chorus that never comes, just a plodding, mesmerizing blues tune tribute to the civil rights movement.

This is about as essential "Jesus Music" as has ever been released. It not only is a great artistic achievement, it so defines a generation musically and ministerially that any true fan or historian of Jesus Music can not be without this classic album.

One can also read of the tragedy and controversy surrounding this amazing band, a collection of misfits that somehow formed one of the great Jesus Music bands of the 1970's.[31]

Joe said, "Those early experiences with the black churches were drawn on for the song 'Elder White.' It was the first song on our first album and it sets a mood as much as anything else and we wanted people to approach this music thoughtfully."

The popularity of the song "Elder White" led to Larry forming an important relationship with former top-rated celebrity disc jockey and new Christian convert, Scott Ross.

Ross' career began in the 1960s as a DJ and assistant music director for WINS radio in New York City where he gained access to popular acts of the day such as the Rolling Stones, Jimi Hendrix and Bob Dylan. He also was the master of ceremonies for one of the Beatles' concerts at Shea Stadium and later married Nedra Talley of the Ronettes.

Following his conversion to Christianity, Ross approached Christian Broadcasting Network owner Pat Robertson with a vision for the first Jesus Music radio program and Robertson gave the go ahead and funding for the program. *The Scott Ross Show* grew to a syndication aired on 200 stations across the United States, eventually winning five *Billboard* awards.

Scott Ross not only liked the music of the All Saved Freak Band, he played it and actively promoted it on his nationally broadcast radio program. It was an enormous promotional boost for the band's debut album. (Scott Ross had no knowledge of the abuses occurring on Fortney Road.)

At this time in the Jesus Movement, Ross's radio program and the burgeoning Jesus Music genre were all experiencing significant growth. In the same way Larry would mention his affiliation with the now well known David Wilkerson, he frequently mentioned that the All Saved Freak Band was often featured on *The Scott Ross Show,* and the show was benefiting greatly. "They are using 'Elder White' on their demonstration tape that they send out to all the stations and they picked up seven new stations and we know it's all because of 'Elder White!' and we just really praise the Lord!" Larry boasted during a service.[32]

However, when I reached Scott Ross at CBN in the spring of 2007 and asked him to comment on this quote, it was much like the response I received from David Wilkerson. Although Larry would boast for years in the *Freedom Bell* and during concerts and from the pulpit about his relationship with the radio program, Scott Ross told me, "My memories of any specifics in regard to the All Saved Freak Band are vague at best. I do not think I can contribute anything meaningful at this time."

Regardless of the role Scott Ross did or did not play, the *My Poor Generation* album did garner a good deal of interest when it was released. "I think we had five hundred albums pressed," Joe said, "and because there was no distribution deal in place, the band gave six LPs to local DJs, and word got around."

Larry Morrow, a disc jockey for WWWE, remembers Larry's attempt to convince him to plug the album. "He was pushing the fact that he had Glenn Schwartz on lead guitar. Schwartz was one of the best but the music was not of interest to a general audience. He had made the album at Cleveland Recording and when he was trying to sell it to me, he had some chick with him who kept her head down the whole time."[27]

The disc jockey may not have been a fan, but the group continued to aggressively promote the album. According to Larry, who was prone to exaggeration:

> Most bands think that the way they are going to sell their album is by selling themselves through big record companies. God's ways are different than ours. His ways are higher. The circumstances of our first album wasn't a case of trying to sell the album to the public—it sold itself. We had no distributors. We had an original number of albums made up and gave six of them to DJs. By some mystical communication between DJs that we don't understand, the word got around.
>
> Letters came from disc jockeys from all over the country asking for the album. Soon letters started coming in from record shops, bookstores, and private individuals from almost every state in the nation, asking for the album. The album was played on over four hundred stations and in about ten different countries, and requests for the album continued to roll in.[33]

There was nothing lyrically on the album that expounded Larry's paranoid worldview or belief in a soon-coming Great War. That would all come later.

Instead, Tom Miller was eulogized in a song written by Morgan King and sung by Morgan and the Massmann sisters:

> O Tom Miller can you see
> I'm doing all I can?
> O Tom Miller, wait for me
> At the gate to the Promised Land.

You went on ahead of me
Now I must go alone
And so did Christ on Calvary
It will be worth it once we get home.[34]

On the back of the album jacket there is a graphic reminder of the Kent State shootings combined with a dedication to Tom Miller, "the burning brand of the Kent-25 . . . [he was] singing with the group when he and the bass player, Randy Markko, were killed on a journey to spread the Gospel at a rock festival."[23]

The *My Poor Generation* recording project was entirely self-financed and the All Saved Freak Band created their own record label for their debut, Rock the World Enterprises. With the release of *My Poor Generation* in 1973, the All Saved Freak Band increased their visibility beyond Cleveland thanks to radio airplay. According to the *Freedom Bell*:

> The first album, *My Poor Generation*, began to take hold across the country. Noted disc jockeys began to play it, even WMMS, rated as one of the high ranking underground radio stations at that time, played the cut "Daughter of Zion" from the album for over a year and a half.[6]

Early reviews of the album are difficult to find due to the limited number of publications reviewing Christian music at the time. Ken Scott, archivist and writer of *Vintage Vinyl Jesus Music (1965–1980)* wrote:

> One of the more fascinating chapters in Jesus music history is that of Ohio's commune-bred All Saved Freak Band . . . Lead guitarist Glenn Schwartz is the person primarily responsible for the blues angle, his high-powered talented licks having done previous service within the James Gang and Pacific Gas & Electric. "Great Victory" and "Daughter Of Zion" are first-rate heavy blues/boogie rockers that give plenty of room for Schwartz's extended sizzling workouts. Sisters Kim and Pam Massmann add artful folk and classical textures through use of violin, cello, acoustic guitars and piano. In between are slow mysterious psychy electric moods like the haunting minor-key "Ancient Of Days" and the eerie opener "Elder White."[35]

Bob Felberg of *New Creation Radio* wrote:

[*My Poor Generation* is the] totally essential Jesus rock album. Some prog baroque chamber folk with harpsichord, strings, piano, and woodwinds. Some other-worldly smoky dream psych. Some stripped-down electric boogie blues. And that's just side one![36]

The *Cleveland Plain Dealer* reported that, "Guitarist Glenn Schwartz is featured with the All Saved Freak Band in an album now in stores. Proceeds from sales of the album will go to the nonprofit organization, the Kent New Generation Church, to help drug addicts and other street people with problems." (By 1974, Larry disbanded the Kent New Generation Church and focused his attention on the community at Fortney Road and his trips to Pennsylvania.)

The success of the All Saved Freak Band and their album seemed to imply that the community at Fortney Road was a thriving, healthy spiritual community with a popular Jesus Music group. But the family and friends of Glenn Schwartz were still suspicious as to why the talented guitarist had given up such a promising career in music to live on an isolated farm. What exactly was going on at Fortney Road?

In 2014, Glenn's son Bob told me, "I remember we were allowed to visit my dad while he was at Fortney Road, but he was never left alone with us. We always had to visit him inside the house. We'd go into this big living room and people were always around him. He could never come outside and see us by himself."

Image 42: Glenn Schwartz at Fortney Road.

At the time, Glenn's family was certain he was being brain-washed. His mother, Anne, was convinced that Larry had "taken over Glenn's mind" and the brainwashing had caused Glenn to forsake his career.[37]

Was there any evidence that Larry was controlling Glenn's life?

Glenn's son recalls one event. "I know once when I was a child and my dad was at the farm, Larry wanted him to come and force my mom to move out there with him. My mom and dad were still married at the time and Larry taught that men were the head of the house and women needed to obey their husbands. So Larry told Glenn to come and get my mom and discipline her until she agreed to move to the farm. My brother and I were just kids and were taking a bath when Dad showed up.

"At first, he and my mom talked quietly but soon I heard some yelling and me and my brother went out to see what was going on. My dad had his belt off and was beating my mom with it and she was screaming at him to get out of the house and leave her alone. She told us to get back in the bathtub but the screaming and yelling continued and the neighbors called the police. When they arrived, they had to smash down the door to get in and they led my dad away in handcuffs. I remember seeing the door was all busted in, torn off its hinges. My dad never hurt me or my brother, but he really went after my mom that night, just like Larry told him to."

"My son's mind has been broken down by that man," Glenn's mother insisted. "Larry Hill wanted him for his guitar talent. We will continue to try to get him back."[27] Anne had tried personally to talk to Glenn and then sought assistance from the courts, but both efforts were fruitless.[37]

Glenn's mother was right to be concerned. Anyone who was recruited to Fortney Road was rarely seen and those who lived at the farm were cut off from society.

One member told me just how isolated they were. "I didn't even know who the president was. I didn't know when Elvis died. We were so consumed with our chores and survival, nothing else mattered, it wasn't really relevant. Sounds weird now but I know I am not the only one that felt that way. After I left Fortney Road, the Jim Jones thing came out and I just couldn't watch it on TV.

I thought to myself, 'They were like us!' And I could so relate to Patty Hearst. That is how my brain was anyway."

Joe agreed, adding, "Since our commitment to Christ included separating ourselves from anything having to do with 'the world' and because we lived in an isolated community, we didn't know anything about anybody until long after things happened. We didn't even have T.V. sets."

In April of 1973, Glenn's mother tried another approach: she attempted to have him forcibly removed from Fortney Road and committed to a mental institution. Judge Calvin W. Hutchins of the Ashtabula Country Probate Court presided over the case. Anne appealed to Judge Hutchins and received a letter back from him dated April 18, 1973:

> I am in receipt of your letter concerning your son, Glenn, and wish to report to you that I can be quite sympathetic to you as this boy's mother, but wish to advise you that we are helpless to act upon the facts and conditions as they presently exist.
>
> I would feel that if I were in you shoes I would whisk my own son away from such an environment as you report though my own forces and main strength. However, until we have a medical report that he is presently mentally ill, this court cannot act.[37]

"I tried to have her son removed from Hill's commune," Judge Hutchins said. "Unfortunately, I couldn't grant her request because I had no statement from a psychiatrist to back it up."[27]

It was a small town and Larry and the others at Fortney Road were now well aware of the impression the community had about them, and Mrs. Schwartz's very vocal and public opposition only angered the Prophet. "There is a judge," Larry said, "Judge Hutchins. He hates the ground I walk on."[27]

Judge Hutchins didn't deny the fact that he loathed Larry Hill. "I presided when Glenn Schwartz's mother tried to have her son removed from Hill's commune. I told him that if I saw his face in my courtroom again, I'd throw the book at him."[27]

"My relationship with the press has not been a happy one," Larry admitted. "What we do here has been twisted and distorted. Glenn Schwartz is here because he has found Christ. I am thirty-eight. I found Christ when I was nineteen. Glenn Schwartz has found Christ. Now he plays for Christ. He tried and tried to get his wife and sons to join us here but they refused. They refused to follow his way of life. Glenn Schwartz is afraid to go back to his parents. He is afraid they may try to commit him, to give him electric shock treatments."[27]

Judge Hutchins was able to briefly remove one of Larry's sons from Fortney Road and place him in a foster home, and a second case was held involving Larry's youngest son who had failed to attend school.[27]

Tim Hill said, "I was the son who had failed to attend school—because I had run away from the farm! I ran away when I was thirteen and was sent back to the farm by a social worker!"

"The authorities have harassed us," Larry said bitterly. "They think I am running a house of prostitution here. They think I am engaging in drug activities. The fact is that most of the people here neither drink nor smoke."[27]

The local legal and medical authorities may have failed her, but Anne Schwartz was not about to give up on her son. She and her husband had a plan to help Glenn escape from Fortney Road and the brainwashing efforts of Larry Hill, and what they attempted would make headlines in all the local papers.

Chapter 23

Black Lightning at the Gateway Motel

I n February 1975 Glenn Schwartz was thirty-four years old, and while he knew that none of his family approved of his life at Fortney Road, he was a grown man and he wanted another chance to explain to them that he was happy and at peace. Even though his parents thought he was crazy, had tried to have him committed, and had publically said terrible things about Reverend Larry Hill and his other friends, Glenn wouldn't give up on them.

With the goal of seeking reconciliation, he contacted his family and asked them to meet him for dinner.[22] When they readily accepted, he praised God; maybe the Lord had set up this time together over a meal so Glenn could get through to them about his love of Jesus and their need for Him.

In February 1975, the average temperature was in the low 20s in Euclid, Ohio. Life at Fortney Road was not only exhausting mentally and spiritually, it was also cold, so Glenn relished the idea of a warm restaurant meal. Although there was usually food of one sort or another at the farm, there never seemed to be enough. And Glenn found he was more tired and clumsy than usual because in addition to his work and duties at the farm and car shop and rehearsals with the All Saved Freak Band, he had a job at the Middlefield meatpacking house. So he was looking forward to sitting down for a couple hours with his family and eating as much as he could.

They met at the Howard Johnson in Euclid.[37]

Things started well. Glenn hugged his parents and brother Gene and they enjoyed a pleasant meal together. Glenn focused on telling them about Jesus and how good his life was and all that was being accomplished at the farm. He ordered up a big dinner and enjoyed every mouthful. His family seemed a bit distracted and didn't ask many questions so Glenn continued to talk and eat, sharing as many Bible verses as he could with them, desperate to convince them of the saving power of Jesus.

When the meal was over, the family put on their hats, scarves, coats and gloves and braced for the blast of Ohio winter as they left the restaurant. Glenn was in the middle of a sentence when someone stumbled into him, nearly knocking him over. Before he could recover his footing, he was grabbed from behind and found himself surrounded.

"What?" he cried confused and scared. "What's happening?"

He looked to see if his family was all right, and then he noticed that they had moved away to the side and were watching him. Glenn stopped struggling and turned to look at his captors. He was shocked that he recognized them.

They were friends of his brother Gene, hot rod pals and guys that Glenn had known around town for years. He counted six of them holding him tightly.[38] He started to smile, thinking it was some joke. He looked over at his mother for an explanation; she turned away.

Glenn's father, William, came over to Glenn and without saying a word moved behind him and after fumbling with Glenn's hands and wrists, snapped on a pair of handcuffs.[22]

"Oh, Dad," Glenn groaned, realizing that it had all been planned, all a set-up to kidnap him. His family was going to take him away from Fortney Road, from the people he loved.

Glenn began to pray quietly to himself as his parents, brother and six friends gently maneuvered him into the car. His father drove a few blocks in silence so grimly preoccupied, he didn't think to turn on the heater. Glenn stared out the window at the cold, black winter night, praying to himself, wishing he were back home at the farm.

William turned the car into the Gateway Motel.[22] Everyone got out, still not speaking, and the men in the other car surrounded Glenn but didn't touch him. Glenn noticed that no one went to the front desk to check in so obviously everything had been carefully planned out ahead of time. His father fished a motel room key out of his pocket, glanced at the room number, and led the way.

Once Glenn was settled in the room, his parents and Gene departed, leaving behind a few of Gene's friends to be sure Glenn didn't escape. He continued praying and reciting scriptures while the other men settled in for the night.

Glenn was scared and had no idea what was going to happen next.

Back at Fortney Road, the evening meeting had gone on until almost one in the morning. Since Glenn was in town trying to reconcile with his family, and might have to hitchhike home, there was no immediate concern over his absence. By the time the unlucky men had received their night watch assignments, the rest of the community had already fallen into an exhausted sleep, minds too worn-out to wonder why Glenn wasn't yet home.

The next morning—about twelve hours after Glenn had been abducted[37]—the motel room door burst open and two people Glenn had never seen before entered as Gene's friends hurriedly left.

A forty-five-year-old African-American man approached while a woman hovered at his side.[37] The man brusquely introduced himself, and Glenn recoiled at the man's name and his presence.

Ted Patrick, or "Black Lightning" as he was known in the media, had made front-page headlines for his daring daylight kidnappings and "deprogramming" of cult members. He had told *Time* magazine that he had successfully deprogrammed 600 people.[37] The network news had featured his interstate car chases to elude both cult leaders and state troopers.[39]

And now he stood before Glenn with his assistant, Sondra Sacks, at his side.[37] Glenn had heard stories from Larry and others about Ted Patrick, and he was terrified.

"The cults tell them that I rape the women and beat them," Ted said. "They say I lock them in closets and stuff bones down their throats. What they don't know is that they're making my job easier. They come in here frightened to death of me, and then because of all the stuff they've been told, I can just sit there and look at them and I'll deprogram them just like that! They'll be thinking, 'What the hell is he going to do now?' They're waiting for me to slap them or beat them and already their minds are working."[39]

Ted began to question Glenn and based on his answers, Ted said he could determine exactly how Glenn had been programmed.[39]

"From then on, it's all a matter of language," Ted said. "It's talking and knowing what to talk about. I start moving his mind, slowly, pushing it with questions, and I watch every move that his mind makes. I know everything it is going to do, and when I hit on that one certain point that strikes home, I push it. I stay with that question whether it's about God, the Devil or the person's rejection of his parents. I keep pushing and pushing. I don't let him get around it with the lies he's been told. It's like turning on the light in a dark room. They're in an almost unconscious state of mind, and then I switch the mind from unconsciousness to consciousness and it snaps, just like that!"[39]

For two days, Glenn Schwartz was held captive at the Gateway Motel. During that time, Glenn's ex-wife Marlene and their two sons were brought to the room. "Glenn had no reaction to seeing his former wife," Sondra said, "and displayed only a little emotion when he saw his sons."[37]

Glenn's son Bob told me, "When Dad was kidnapped, Mom was asked to see him along with me and my brother. When we arrived at the motel room, we saw that Dad was tied to the bedpost. He was glad to see us it but as a kid, it was awful seeing him tied up like that and we didn't really understand what was going on."

Glenn's mother visited him, too. "I sat on the bed next to him," she said, "and I put my arm around him. He recoiled from me and then he suddenly jumped up and ran for the door. It was the only time he tried to escape."[37]

They caught him at the door and forced him to return to the bed. Glenn resisted all attempts at conversation. He closed his eyes and rapidly began chanting, "Praise the Lord! Praise the Lord! PRAISE THE LORD!" while he rocked back and forth on the bed.[37]

While Glenn was facing his ordeal in the motel room, Larry and members of the community were frantically looking for him.

"We were on the phones and streets night and day trying to find him," Joe said. Knowing how Glenn's parents and family felt about the farm, Larry assumed Glenn had been kidnapped, so he sent Laura, Pam, and Kim into town to contact the police.

Frank Payne, the Euclid chief of police, recalled that three women with long flowing hair and ankle-length dresses had approached him and wanted to report a missing person. "They looked a little grimy," Payne said, finding it odd that only Laura would occasionally meet his gaze while the other two focused on the floor. "They said they were from a commune and they had some reason to believe that Glenn Schwartz had been kidnapped."[37]

While the three women waited, the police chief called Mrs. Schwartz and she assured him that her son was not being harmed in any way. He turned to the women and told them not to worry and said it was not a matter that required police involvement.[37]

After forty-eight hours, Glenn was finally released from the Gateway Motel.

Carole recalled the day Glenn returned to the farm. "I was in the kitchen and he just walked in the door like it was a normal day. Larry was so happy to have him back and kept asking him what they had done to him. And Glenn was laughing and trying to answer in his soft-spoken way. Finally, he said 'They tried to deprogram me, but it didn't work.'"

"There were days like that," Carole said. "Sometimes, there were days like that when things weren't as bad as they got at the end. And this was one of them. A good day. Glenn had come home."

To celebrate Glenn's homecoming, Carole remembered baking him a special cake.

"I made him a life-size guitar cake, making it up as I went along. I used Tootsie Rolls for the tuning knobs at the top and licorice strips for the frets. An oatmeal cookie was made for the hole in the guitar. It was really cool!"

When Larry wrote about the event in the *Freedom Bell*, he attributed different motivations to the family and changed some of the facts:

> The pressure from family and former friends to return to his
> former way of life and music was very great. In March of 1975,
> Glenn met his father for dinner in Euclid, Ohio. His father

informed him that they were going to eat in another restaurant. Upon leaving the restaurant, Glenn was accosted by two men who shoved him into a car. He was later imprisoned in a nearby Wickliff hotel. When he failed to return home, members of the band and friends began a search for him.

The local police were in cooperation with the kidnappers, and Glenn's whereabouts remained unknown for several days. The kidnappers were members of Glenn's family and a man who has received national news coverage—Ted Patrick. Glenn's parents had hired Patrick for the fee of $1400 to "deprogram" Glenn, or, in other words, convince him that his way of Christian faith was foolish. Glenn withstood these days of threats, questioning and verbal abuse from Patrick.

Although the news media has pictured Patrick as a sincere Christian freeing youth from the grips of religious communism, Glenn says that Patrick is far from a Christian. The first thing he did was to take Glenn's Bible. Glenn says that Patrick swears, smokes a big cigar, and has contempt for the Bible. After three days of trying to "break" Glenn, Patrick gave up and released him.[6]

As reported in the *Freedom Bell*, the community followed the teachings of Christ and "turned the other cheek," taking no action against those who had abducted Glenn. However, "Several weeks later, the *Cleveland Press* printed a series of articles that were outright lies and distortions . . . the articles were simply attacks on Schwartz and his pastor, as if Schwartz had done something wrong by being kidnapped."[6]

William Schwartz, deeply disturbed by having to kidnap his own son, checked into the Euclid Glenville Hospital for medical care.[37] Glenn's mother, Anne, went to Mass each Sunday to pray for her son.[27]

Larry had been correct about one thing: the $1400 his parents had reportedly paid to Ted Patrick to de-program their son, but to no avail. Glenn had immediately returned to Fortney Road.

For the most part, the local papers sided with Glenn and the idea of religious freedom.

In the *Cleveland Press*, Dick Feagler wrote:

The Glenn Schwartz story had no neat ending. What right does anyone have to interfere with Larry Hill? Did Ted Patrick have any right to interfere with Glenn Schwartz's life at all? Schwartz is not a minor and an attempt to deprive him of his rights borders, perhaps, on the unconstitutional. How many people are there who have drifted into the kind of life Schwartz leads? Communes are commonplace today and the people in them cannot be pigeons for a form of legalized kidnap.[27]

At the time, most people in the community only thought of the Fortney Road ministry as a place where the youth were being helped to kick drugs. What kind of mother would kidnap her own son from something like that? Was she not a religious woman?

So Glenn's mother found herself in the awkward position of having to defend her extreme actions, claiming that she was desperate to save her son from what she believed was a "commune of Jesus freaks." This anti-religious statement didn't sit well in the small community, so she then went on to claim that Judge Calvin W. Hutchins of Ashtabula County Probate Court suggested she kidnap Glenn. "He told me to use my own forces," she insisted, and presented his April 18, 1973, letter as proof. When reached by the paper, the judge said that he "did not recall the letter but acknowledged that 'it sounds like my verbiage.'" He went on to say that he "would let the letter stand on its own interpretation and would have no further comment."[38]

Headlines about the kidnapping dominated the local papers and residents sent in letters to the editor, expressing their opinions both for and against the kidnapping of Glenn.

Roger Bohn, manager of the Smiling Dog Saloon where the band played three or four times a year, had a great deal of respect for the ministry at Fortney Road. "They seem to be helping many people who were on drugs. They don't come in here with their hands out, they are self-sufficient. How can you criticize that?" [22]

Bohn was quick to point out that when the band played at the bar, no liquor was served and the women made bread and brought honey, and a cup was left for contributions. (In appreciation for his public support of the ministry, Larry and Glenn would write the sprightly blues tune "Having a Ball at the Smiling Dog" for the *Brainwashed* album, with Kim singing lead vocals.)

Curious about Mrs. Schwartz's claims about her son's treatment, two reporters for *The Plain Dealer* decided to visit Fortney Road to see what all the fuss was about. Larry warmly welcomed them and gave them a personal tour, and the result was a glowing article:

> The house where Hill's congregation meets is a white frame building with red shutters, one of the better looking homes in the neighborhood. Likenesses of Jesus adorn the walls. Services are held twice on Sunday and once in midweek. Members pledge to abstain from adultery, fornication, alcohol and tobacco. The central idea is to help people find Jesus, said Hill. The men wear work clothing, much of it made by the women. The women wear ankle-length dresses. Their All Saved Freak Band plays at schools, churches and prisons, mixing in an exhortation for salvation with the rhythms.[22]

Only a few people in town were beginning to suspect something wasn't right about the ministry.

John Hansen, a Cleveland Recording executive, was no fan of Larry Hill and said, "He gives bad vibes. He comes in here with his girls and they hold prayer meetings. It's a big con. Look, I see a lot of freaks. Some of them I suspect come in and smoke pot and I wish they'd get out of here. But this guy is weird."[27]

Rock concert critic Anastasia Pantsios agreed, writing in *The Plain Dealer*, "Larry Hill is an opportunist. He turns the people in his congregation into zombies, with no minds of their own."[22]

The local papers gave Glenn the last word, calling him articulate, clear-eyed, and ruddy-cheeked. He was said to speak thoughtfully and clearly about his experiences, concluding that his desire was simple. "I want to be a full-time Christian."[22]

Larry only hinted at the turmoil the kidnapping had caused himself and those who lived at Fortney Road, writing in the *Freedom Bell* that, "Due to personal circumstances and circumstances concerning our church, we have been made more aware than ever before of the preciousness of freedom and liberty."[6]

With that ordeal behind him and the community feeling they had been persecuted for righteousness sake, they prepared to record a second album that would be a response to those who criticized their beliefs. It would address their communal life and Glenn's kidnapping.

Unlike *My Poor Generation*, their quiet and somewhat hesitant debut, this was going to be a rock-and-roll album.

And Glenn and his guitar were to be front and center.

His kidnapping served to bind the community together more tightly. It was clear to them that the ministry at Fortney Road was being persecuted for its beliefs, so the All Saved Freak Band decided to title their new album with the one word that had been hurled at them for so many years—*Brainwashed.*

Chapter 24

Brainwashed

J oe said, "*Brainwashed* was one of those projects that just seemed to come together. Generally, album titles evolved after we decided to record. 'What are we going to do and what are we going to call it?' was the general order of things. If a theme developed, it was generally by accident. But *Brainwashed* was named as an intentional response to our critics. They had said that our conversions were nothing more than being brainwashed so the entire album was dedicated to that issue."

Larry wrote in the *Freedom Bell*:

> The attack prompted Glenn and the Band to write and collect material already written on their experienes. The album will be called "Brainwashed" because, as the group says, they have had their minds cleansed by the forgiving power of Jesus Christ.[6]

Image 43: Brainwashed cover

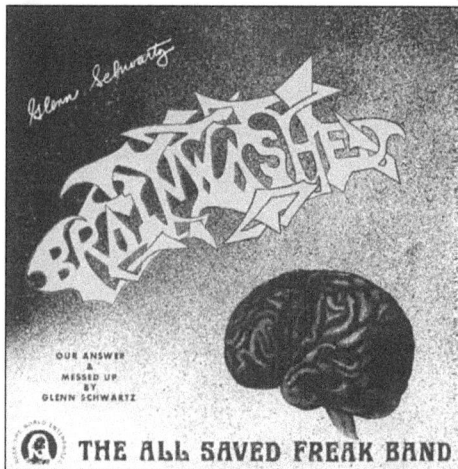

Producer Rob Galbraith told me that when the band booked time to record, they came prepared and they came to work. "I would focus on the arrangements but the songs themselves were more or less set. They would spend a lot of time before I arrived rehearsing and then when they had the money for the studio, they would give me a call and we'd schedule the sessions. I think we spent a couple weeks working on *Brainwashed* sometime early in 1975 and the sessions probably started about nine a.m. and lasted until the evening. Of course, we had that seventy-mile drive to and from the studio, so they were long, intensive days of recording."

For the *Brainwashed* project, more musicians were involved than the debut and the band consisted of Larry Hill (piano, vocals), Kim Massmann (cello, acoustic guitar, vocals), Joe Markko (vocals), Ed Durkos (rhythm guitar), Pam Massmann (violin, keyboards, vocals), Morgan King and Norris McClure (bass), Carole King (keyboads, vocals), Tim Hill (percussion), Tom Eritano (drums, percussion) Mike Berkey (acoustic guitar, vocals) and Glenn Schwartz (lead guitar, harmonica, vocals).

Joe wrote the music and lyrics to the second track on *Brainwashed*, "Ode To Glenn Schwartz" which featured an electric guitar and bass playing the same riff, joined by the cello after the lead break. A sound like no other, it is heightened and distinctively enhanced when Larry Hill's hoarse vocals whisper along with some of the last verses. Joe said, "It was actually Rob Galbraith who suggested the whispers and it worked well with Larry's raspy voice."

Fell on my knees once, it hurt so I rose
My woman, my woman dressed me up in white clothes.
She took off her ring and put it in my nose
And I follow her now wherever she goes.

But the great King of glory is calling my name
If I don't give my all soon I won't be the same.
I know what I must do, Lord kill my pride
I got no place to run to, no place to hide.
My sins are before me, on the altar they lay
I know they'll destroy me—let us pray[40]

"Those words were designed to describe what was happening in Glenn's life," Joe explained. "He contemplated abandoning his faith after all the rejection from his family and friends. They committed him to a mental institution before joining the farm to prove that he wasn't crazy, that his faith was sincere. That's where the 'dressed me up in white clothes' and other comments came from. They were sadly a description of the way he was treated, the kidnapping, the time in court, everything he had gone through."

Today, Glenn still plays the song and audience members request it, frequently thinking its title is "Images, Images" and usually having no idea as to the origin of the song or the meaning of the words.

The centerpiece to *Brainwashed* and the song that gives Glenn his greatest workout is the seven-minute track, "Don't Look Back."

Joe said, "The song is intensely personal and involves my relationship with Larry Hill. He led me to Christ in Chicago when I was fourteen. He later came to believe that God was going to judge America for her sins and that the cities, including Chicago, were going up in flames."

"Don't Look Back" features some of Glenn's longest and most fluid leads. When asked if Glenn simply showed up and jammed to such a complicatedly structured song or sat down and broke it out, section-by-section, Joe said, "Glenn had to do a lot of practicing for some of his parts due to the unusual chord progressions taking place behind him."

Perhaps the brilliance of Glenn's performance distracted listeners from Larry's ominous lyrics:

If I can't get to your body I'll get to your mind.
I'll think of some way to leave you behind.
One day I'll leave you wallowin' in the ditch,
In the meantime I'll use you to get all my kicks.

(spoken)
When the vulture gobbles up what's left by the dove
And we say we did it all in the name of love
And you crawl out from your small narrow crack,
Screamin,' "Forgive me, baby,
Some way I'll make up the slack!"
While a foreign spy's gun points at your back!

Realized I got too far behind
A speedin' bullet tore open my spine.

My fadin', dyin' eyes asked for a sign
I couldn't understand it, it was really too much
I saw movin' toward me a white, rattlin' crutch.[41]

Joe said, "Larry used a pair of white, Canadian crutches that rattled when he walked. It suggested that his presence was a precursor to judgment, and that's what that last line is referring to."

But so much guitar fire and power etched in vinyl must have concerned Larry. Joe recalled, "Upon leaving the studio when we'd finalized the *Brainwashed* album, Larry told me, 'This is as far as we go,' meaning this is as far as we're taking the rock or contemporary sound. That's why the following recording has a different edge."

Recorded in 1975, *Brainwashed* wasn't released until 1976, and even then it wasn't made available until after another, quieter All Saved Freak Band album was created.

Chapter 25

For Christians,
Elves, and Lovers

B efore the third album was recorded, Larry Hill's second oldest son, Mark, ran away from the farm after more than a decade of beatings.

Tim Hill was fourteen years old at time. "Mark went straight to Phoenix, Arizona, where my Mom was living. With Mark gone, I was basically a kid all alone on the farm. My Mom had fled with two of my siblings, and my brother Brett was dead."

Some time after Mark left, Tim remembers becoming very ill with the flu, confined to his bed for almost a week. "Larry came into my bedroom to sleep one night and then Diane showed up and they started to have sex in Mark's bed. I tried to pretend to be asleep, I was feeling so sick, but they just kept at it and I felt nauseous at what they were doing in Mark's bed. I remember finally just throwing up."

This type of repulsive conduct indicates that Larry Hill was incredibly adept at compartmentalizing his behavior. When he was functioning in one role—the pastor, prophet or leader of a popular Jesus Music band—was he consciously or subconsciously suppressing his opposing personality state, his sexually sadist behavior and his abuse of children?

When I asked Tim if he had any insights into his father's behavior, he said, "Is Larry an evil con man? Is it a mental disease or the result of the trauma from the car accident where he lost his leg? Did he ever really believe, ever really convert to Christianity? I don't know; I don't have any answers."

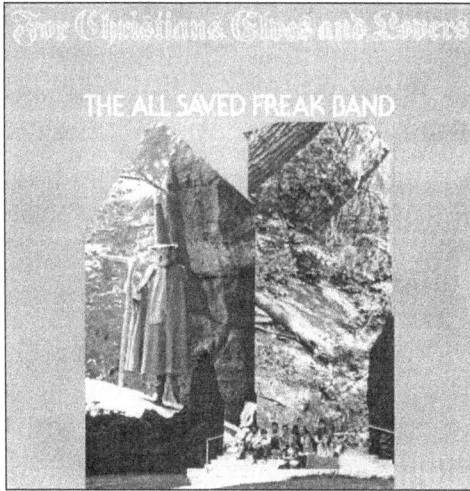

Image 44: For Christians, Elves, and Lovers cover.

Over the years, Larry's obsession with J.R.R. Tolkien's *Lord Of The Rings* trilogy grew and he talked about the books constantly. In 1975 he decided that the All Saved Freak Bank should record something gentler than *Brainwashed*.

The Massmann sisters came up with the title—*For Christians, Elves, and Lovers*—reflecting Larry's Tolkien obsession.

Both the title and the cover of the album would prove problematic. The front of the album is a photo collage divided into three sections. On the left, Larry is dressed as a one-legged wizard in a blue cape with a tall, pointed, blue Dumbledore hat. On the right, some trees and branches, and below, band members sitting on some steps.

Larry Hill dressed as a wizard?

Joe said, "Yeah, that's Larry dressed as a wizard. He put three pictures together for that cover. The background was actually a church building, the outline of which Larry filled with pictures of rocks and trees. The group is pictured sitting on the steps of the church building. I always felt something was lost in translation."

With the exception of Norris McClure, the same band members who participated in the *Brainwashed* recording played on the *Elves* album. "The Lord is my Shepherd" and "Great Victory" were carried over from the debut, and the only genuine rock song on the album was "Water Street," which was written about the band when they played at JB's bar on Water Street after the Kent State Shootings.

The *Elves* album included what's become a classic of the Jesus Movement, guitar player Mike Berkey's "Stephen" which begins the album.

Joe said. "We responded very enthusiastically when he first played 'Stephen' for us. That song was completely molded by Rob Galbraith; chimes, voices, strings, everything."

Like many All Saved Freak Band songs, the music was gentle but the message was not. For example, the instantly memorable and somewhat melancholy acoustic guitar melody for "Stephen" actually laid a foundation for dire warnings about End Times, the appearance of the Antichrist, the Great Tribulation and the believers' coming martyrdom:

> Time is wasting away, I gotta get moving
> Brothers and sisters, hey,
> Look at the hours we're losing
> We are chosen people to do a task
> And we're gonna meet the devil someday
> When he takes off his mask.[42]

When *Brainwashed* and *Elves* were recorded, producer Rob Galbraith had been invited to stay at the farm and forego the expense of a motel room. "They gave me a nice room and the farm itself was well cared for," he told me. "They had fixed it up quite a bit, even made themselves a sauna. I guess I stayed with them about three weeks while we recorded *Elves*.

"I know when I stayed at Fortney Road with them that something just didn't seem right—I remember people were up really early, roaming around at four or four-thirty. And people kept disappearing from album to album. I know that Morgan left before I quit working on *Elves*. I liked Morgan a lot, and suddenly, in the middle of recording, he was no longer there. And I asked where he was and they never really answered. 'He just left' is all they would say. They refused to discuss it."

Rob told me he enjoyed the recording process and working again with the owner and engineer of the studio, Ken Hamann. The only drawback to the recording experience—once again—

was Larry Hill. "Often, Ken and I would sit in the recording booth and one or the other of us would mutter about how crazy Larry was, just wishing he'd shut up and go away."

But Larry never went away and never stopped speaking, and finally his behavior drove Rob from the project.

"I left about halfway through the recording of the *Elves* album. I think all the basic tracks were recorded, we were getting ready for the overdubbing and the final mix, but I simply had to get out of there. I couldn't take Larry's behavior any longer. I stayed as long as I could because I really loved those people, they were good folks, but I had had enough of Larry Hill."

Even though Rob had stayed at Fortney Road for weeks at a time, he had no idea what was happening. Other than people getting up very early or abruptly leaving the farm, no one had ever privately asked for his help, no one had ever given any clue that anything was remotely wrong or out of the ordinary.

After we had finished lunch and the interview portion about his producing the band's albums, I told Rob what really happened at Fortney Road, and the full extent of the physical, sexual and mental abuse that Larry Hill and Diane Sullivan were inflicting on those who lived at the farm.

He was stunned. "I had no idea what was going on at the farm," he finally said after processing what he had just learned. "No idea at all. No one ever pulled me aside and told me the truth. If they had, I would have called the police immediately, I would have confronted Larry, I would have done anything necessary to help them. I loved those people and the music we were making."

Rob didn't listen to the completed *Elves* album until 2007, when I gave him a copy of the CD after our interview in Manhattan. I called him later that week to see what he thought of the recording, and he said that of course it had all been colored by what I had told him.

Unable to give an objective opinion, all he managed to say was, "Thinking back about all of this, it's amazing how much I have repressed."

Chapter 26

Jumping Off a Burning Bridge

"**I** don't tell many people about my years at Fortney Road because most people think we were ignorant to have put up with all of that," Morgan King told me. He was a member of the Church of the Risen Christ since November 1972 and one of two bass players for the All Saved Freak Band. As Rob Galbraith said, Morgan abruptly left Fortney Road in the summer of 1975 before the band's third album, *For Christians, Elves, and Lovers,* was completed.

"I know myself and the others, and our intentions were pure and single focused: *Serve God,*" Morgan said. "That was our only desire. I hate that I went through it and I had a very hard time for a few years after I got out. I was always just in it for the Lord. And things had gone horribly wrong so the question is, at what point do you jump off a burning bridge?"

Because of the coming Great War, Larry wanted everyone who lived at Fortney Road to have practical survival trades. So after Morgan joined the farm, Larry sent him to Mesopotamia, Ohio, where he lived next door to the bishop of an Amish sect.

"I trained there as an apprentice harness maker. I lived there and would return to the farm a few times a week," Morgan said. "The man who trained me was very nice and it was a peaceful and pleasant time for me. Even though we were supposed to keep to ourselves, I was learning a trade so it was okay to be with them."

Morgan also worked for a time in Cleveland, hitchhiking back and forth to Fortney Road, and also in Orwell, where he worked at a steel company. Another paying job was at a machine shop. But Morgan, like the others who lived at Fortney Road, was never allowed to cash his paychecks. "I would just sign the check and give it over to Larry. I never had a dime the whole time I was there.[16]

"In addition to the barn at Fortney Road, we had another barn miles from the farm and we had to spend the night there to guard the animals because the cows tended to get loose and wander off. I remember one Christmas Eve I had to spend the night alone at that barn, far away from everyone else. But I can recall thinking, 'This is just like You, Jesus, born in a manger.' I remember I really felt close to Him that night."

Morgan recalled that Diane Sullivan was always busy ordering people around and he never had much to do with her. "Laura Markko was second or third in command and she had a way of doing things that was just nice," he told me. "She was pleasant, showed a lot of kindness. Acted like a human being. Laura did what Diane did, only with kindness."

Although the beatings and other forms of abuse were common, Morgan said, "I was only beaten once and what they had accused me of—giving away the location of the farm to someone—I was innocent of, and I swore right then that I would never be beaten again. It would never happen to me again."

He promised himself that he would leave before it happened again and to accomplish this, he needed to quickly find someone he could trust and that meant someone who didn't live on the farm.

"I was working at a grocery store and had gradually began to trust a woman who worked there. So I told her a little about what was going on and my desire to get away. She agreed to give me a place to stay so I planned to leave the next day. I did have to go back to the farm to get a couple things. I didn't have much. I went back the next morning and I just picked up my bass guitar and a couple things, then I headed out across the field."

Unbeknownst to Morgan, Laura Markko had seen him and watched him as he started walking away. She didn't know what he was up to or where he was going. He simply never stopped walking and before she thought to call out to him or alert anyone, she could no longer see him. He had disappeared into the horizon.

His plan had come together so quickly that Morgan wasn't able to say goodbye to his sister, Carole, or brother, John.

Carole told me, "The day Morgan left, I came home and Laura told me that he had gone. She had watched him, not sure what he was doing, but all at once, he was just gone. I cried and cried. I did not understand what was going on or what had happened. How could he just leave like that? How could he leave me and John behind?"

Morgan told me, "After I got out, Carole found the lady who had befriended me and Carole yelled at her for helping me escape."

"I found out only recently that he had gotten a beating," Carole said. "He said it only took one, and he was gone."

Carole soon experienced another great loss. "My brother John had married my best friend Georgia in April of 1972 and they lived on the farm for several years but they soon left after Morgan did. To lose such close family and friends was devastating to me."

To keep Carole and the other members in check in the midst of such departures, Larry would warn them, "If your relatives come to the door beggin' to come back in, you must not let them in! No matter how they plead, even to save their own lives, they are granted no mercy!"

"That had a profound affect on me," Carole said. "I loved my brothers and Georgia with all my heart. I remember thinking to myself, 'I can't do this—I can't treat them that way.' To have my own thoughts, that was one of my first steps to my freedom. I've often thought that that was a real turning point for me."

Morgan said, "After I left the farm, I always felt like they were following me and I felt like I was going to hell. Larry was very good at making that clear that if you left Fortney Road, you were bound for hell."

And Morgan had terrible dreams about Fortney Road. "I had nightmares, three or four a week, either of being beaten or about the rough treatment you would get there, or just going through a normal day there. I had nightmares about that."[13]

For a short time, Morgan lived with the woman from the grocery store but after that ended, he had no place to stay so he lived in his car. "My folks were in the area but I was too ashamed to go back to them or ask for help. It was a very lonely time for me. I finally got enough money together to get a room in a boarding house and then my Dad helped me to get settled and I sort of moved on from there, step by step, day after day."

Morgan admitted to me, "I carried a gun around with me after I left and I am not a gun person. That tells you how paranoid I was after I left Fortney Road."

Chapter 27

The Public Face

A fter the departure of Morgan King—the latest Judas— Larry was shaken. He reminded his congregation that they were in a spiritual battle and things would only get more intense as the time of the Great War approached.

A week after Morgan left, a handful of people did not show up at breakfast. They had slipped away sometime during the night.

Furious, Larry knew he needed to tighten his grip so that even the youngest followers would not find a way out of his grasp. Satan not only wanted to steal the adults in the ministry, the enemy also wanted the children. In the *Freedom Bell*, Larry wrote:

> As Christians, we believe in living separately, in obedience with God's commands. In public schools, our girls were laughed at for the way they dress (modestly in long dresses) and the kind of conversation in which they engaged. We teach them to keep their minds on Christ and the simple tasks in life rather than on silly junk that young girls' heads are full of. [6]

"Our kids didn't belong in public schools since we believed witches and warlocks were becoming educators," Joe said.

After much prayer about how to best protect the children, Larry applied to the state to establish a private religious school for the children at Fortney Road. At this time, a religious school in Ohio did not have a charter. Since the small school would not receive state funding and only had to meet safety and health requirements and a few minimal educational standards, it was simply a matter of completing some paperwork and passing an inspection. Although the State Department of Education had the authority to ask for basic information about religious schools, at that time it was difficult to keep track of them and to maintain accurate enrollment figures.

Larry quickly received approval for the Church of the Risen Christ School and easily passed inspection since the farm was always kept remarkably clean. Five children, all members of the community, were the first students and the school opened in September 1975.

In the *Freedom Bell,* one of the teachers from the farm wrote:

> I love our school. I love our kids and I think they deserve the best. I feel good knowing that God's ways are being taught not only in the home but in the school and that our kids can grow up without the drugs, sex and perversion that we had to live with to get our education. Some kids weren't as fortunate as I, they got hooked.[6]

A few months after the school was started, Larry finally went ahead and incorporated the name the Church of the Risen Christ on December 30, 1975. Laura Markko is listed as the registering agent, with C. Larry Hill, Diane Sullivan, Laura Markko, and M. Goodenough identified as the incorporators. M. Goodenough is Bethy's father.

Once the school had been established and the church incorporated, Larry turned his attention to the All Saved Freak Band. It was time to determine which album to release. He finally settled on the gentler and non-confrontational *For Christians, Elves, and Lovers.*

In *Vintage Vinyl Jesus Music (1965–1980),* Ken Scott wrote of the *Elves* album:

> The Freaks discover that J R R Tolkien was a Christian, inspiring the album title and some of the songs on this their sophomore release. The Massmann sisters' voices are frequently highlighted, and they've never sounded sweeter. "Water Street" serves some fine lead electric guitar within its minor-key folk-rock groove. Good progressive folk-rock from the States is hard to come by—I wish that other works were even half as creative as this.[35]

Patrick "The Lama" Lundborg wrote in the *Acid Archives:*

Somewhat unexpected move from the Christian mainstream rockers as they go on a British folk/folk-rock bender here, complete with sparse guitar arrangements, some tasteful chamber music orchestration, and female vocal harmonies.[43]

Russ Proctor wrote in *Harmony* magazine:

An absolutely incredible album which might well become a classic in the annals of Jesus music. Because of their talent and versatility, the 14 cuts never suffer from being repetitious or boring. This belongs on the shelf of every Jesus music fan.[44]

The liner notes of the *Elves* album make mention that Tom Miller and Randy Markko "were killed on a journey to speak the Gospel at a rock festival" with no mention of the cause of the accident, which was the sleep depravation brought on by Larry Hill.

When *Elves* was released in the fall of 1975, it did not garner the acclaim or sales that Larry or the band had expected. "It was not as strong as our debut because the Christian community wasn't sure what to make of the album title," Joe said. And Larry Hill on the cover dressed as a one-legged wizard didn't help either.

Because there wasn't much response to the *Elves* folk album, Larry put out a DJ-only 45 single with two rock tracks from *Brainwashed*, "Ode to Glenn Schwartz" and "Seek Him." Before incurring the costs of pressing and promoting the album, he wanted to see what the reaction was to the more rock-oriented material.

The response was immediate and very enthusiastic from the radio stations and their listeners; everyone wanted to hear music like this, so Larry gave the go ahead for *Brainwashed*, the hard rock album it seemed the public was waiting for.

Ken Scott wrote in *Vintage Vinyl Jesus Music (1965–1980)* of *Brainwashed*:

If *For Christians, Elves, and Lovers* is the mellower side of ASFB, *Brainwashed* is the flip side of the coin. All those blues rockers they'd been saving up get released here full force. Plenty of heavy organ, harmonica, and of course Glenn Schwartz's searing guitar fireworks. This in an incredible album folks. Several different vocalists and lots of new participants; it's hard to tell from the credits who was in the band and who was just hanging around for the session. So much variety here, too—it never gets boring. Get your brain washed now![35]

Ken Scott had no idea of the dark echo behind the words in that last sentence.

The Acid Archives editor and founder Patrick "The Lama" Lundborg wrote of *Brainwashed:*

> At best their music is stunningly powerful (check out "Ode to Glenn Schwartz" on *Brainwashed),* with a dark, creeping psych-rock menace achieved via songwriting and guitar/organ arrangements that spell big league all the way. Apart from the incredibly strange testimonies the All Saved Freak Band have a mainstream, upmarket 70s sound.[43]

Russ Proctor wrote in *Harmony* magazine:

> Glenn Schwartz is in fine guitar-picking form once again on this LP, and his musical testimony entitled *Messed Up* is a humorous lesson in speed speaking. The ASFB seems to be particulary adept at composing haunting (if not eerie) songs . . . It should be interesting to see what the All Saved Freak Band comes up with next.[45]

By the time *Brainwashed* was released, a Daytona, Florida, newspaper reported that tracks from the band's three albums were being played on approximately 1,000 radio stations in the U.S. and in several different countries. Those are extraordinary results because for the most part, the band was distributing the records themselves.

At this time, the demand for their sold-out debut *My Poor Generation* required they re-press the album, so it was re-released in 1976 as a "collector's album." The ad for the 1976 collector's album was what first brought the band to my attention and became the catalyst for the writing of this book.

The back of the *Brainwashed* album proclaims that the "whole group stands free," when in reality, several band members had already left or were desperate to leave Fortney Road. A 1976 ad for the album appeared in *Harmony* magazine with the headline, "Did you get *Brainwashed* yet?" Knowing what was occurring at Fortney Road, the headline is unsettling.

Brainwashed joined *My Poor Generation* as being voted one of the Top 50 Collectible Jesus Music Albums of All Time.[46]

With three albums now available, Larry wanted the group to perform as much as possible, so Pam got on the phones and scheduled a high profile tour for the All Saved Freak Band.

The busy year of 1976 started with an invitation to perform at the New Orleans' March 2nd Mardi Gras at Jackson Square. After appearing before thousands of people, the band played later that evening for 500 invited guests at Mayor "Moon" Landrieu's private reception held at the City Hall. The *Freedom Bell* reported that senators, congressmen and celebrities were in attendance:

> So not quite knowing how these city officials and social stars would react to our music, we opened up with some songs that rocked on. And to our surprise, they cheered us on for more! I never thought I'd see the day when people would dance to the music, but they danced on merrily. I think a picture of our faces would have won a prize! Even the police liked us! As we were packing up to go home, they came over and asked us to stay. "You're the best group we've ever had play here!" Everyone enjoyed themselves immensely. Mayor Landrieu came over and thanked us and had our picture taken [Image 45]. Though the parade and decorations were brilliant and entertaining, his wife told us that the Band was the highlight of the ball![6]

In 1976, the commemoration of the Bicentennial of the United States of America went on for months. The All Saved Freak Band performed for numerous television and radio shows,

Image 45: The All Saved Freak Band posing with Mayor "Moon" Landrieu, who is third from left. Larry Hill is sixth from left.

Image 46: Larry Hill conducts the All Saved Freak Band at the International Bandshell in Montreal during the 1976 Olympics.

and the media exposure brought them more invitations to play, a highlight being their appearance in Philadelphia where they met General George Smith Patton, the son of World War II General George Patton. "Larry was invited by the general to come to Camp Hood and preach from the pulpit in his church."[6]

The All Saved Freak Band also performed at the 1976 Summer Olympics in Montreal as headliners at the Man and His World pavilion.

Bookings in Chicago followed, including an appearance at a telethon, and more invitations arrived from around the United States. Pam kept the The All Saved Freak Band on the road for weeks at a time and they played throughout the eastern portion of North America and Canada. The band's flexibility in number of players and style of music allowed them to present a variety of musical expressions regardless of the age of the audience. The band always put evangelism first and members gave testimonies between songs about their Christian faith. Larry held an altar call at the end where concertgoers had the opportunity to convert to Christianity.

Like many of the Jesus Music bands of that time, for most of its existence, the All Saved Freak Band charged little or nothing to travel, perform or minister. "We traveled using our own vehicles," Joe said. "What we couldn't get in my Volkswagen van got jammed into the trunks of cars. It was a convoy. Since we paid for everything, there were many times when the only thing we had to eat as we traveled were sardines and crackers. Hotels and restaurants were generally out of the question."

Although they eventually sent contracts asking for $200 per concert, none of the band members ever received any payment for their appearances or recordings; it all went to the community. And they always played, whether they were paid or not.

It was clear to me that their public image on the road was simply that of another travelling Jesus Music band, but I wondered if the mask ever slipped, just a bit, exposing what was underneath. Did other Jesus bands or concert promoters ever have any suspicions that something wasn't quite right with Larry Hill's ministry?

Glenn Kaiser, a Chicago-based blues musician, singer-songwriter and pastor, was the leader of the Jesus Music group Resurrection Band and now heads up the Glenn Kaiser Band. One of the long-time leaders of the Jesus People USA (JPUSA) Christian community in Chicago, I had first met him at Keith and Melody Green's home in the mid-70s where he mentioned to me that the women from Fortney Road all had "downcast eyes."

In 2007, he told me about encountering the All Saved Freak Band. "Most of what I know is hearsay as I only met Glenn Schwartz once that I can remember. We did attend a couple of their concerts way back when, but I don't really recall much except that Larry simply seemed a wild dude with—in my view—extreme Pentecostalism mixed in with his own oddness. It was just a gut feeling and hearing and seeing him onstage, that's really all I recall, but the band was cool, some of the tunes pretty cool, that's about it."

Jon Trott, also of the JPUSA community, told me, "We became aware fairly early on that they had issues. The depth of those negative internal issues we did not know until later, but early brushes with the All Saved Freak Band folks left those of us in JPUSA a little weirded out."

According to Trott, some JPUSA members tried to converse with some members of the Fortney Road community after an All Saved Freak Band concert. "I was told that when our people spoke to them, the women all looked down at the ground and the men behaved in a manner just this side of surly. It seemed to us they were pretty sure they were some sort of spiritual elite, which of course did get taught and believed in some Jesus communes, and which all Jesus communards—us included—were accused of teaching, whether we really did or not, and JPUSA didn't."

Eric Pement, also of JPUSA, told me in 2007, "Glenn Schwartz visited the JPUSA community after he left Fortney Road and I was his buddy while he was there. I showed him around, introduce him to people in our community, and generally helped him get settled while he visited. Glenn at that time was one of the most wounded persons I have met. I interviewed him and he told me some things that I'm not sure anyone knew before. Glenn talked to me for hours, and my opinions of ASFB really changed. I still love their music, though, especially the first three albums. I have a tender place in my heart for him and I really think someone needs to do a testimony book just of Glenn Schwartz."

During this time, Dale Yancy was a cartoonist for the Jesus paper, the *Hollywood Free Paper* and was living in a Christian commune in Vermont. He met the members of the All Saved Freak Band when they came to Burlington, Vermont, and he promoted several concerts with them at the University of Vermont.

When I spoke with him in April 2007, he vaguely recalled that, "Larry was like the head of the family—and the father figure with his long beard and he did most of the speaking. They seemed a bit cultish, but then, this was the '70s and our own

Image 47: The All Saved Freak Band from their summer 1976 tour, dressed in Colonial costumes for the 1976 Bicentennial. Larry Hill is at the far left playing piano and Glenn Schwartz is in front with the guitar.

group in Burlington, Vermont, might've seemed cultish to others as well. We didn't do a full-on doctrine check, but we sensed that they were brothers and sisters in the Lord who loved Jesus. Larry did most of the talking. Everyone else was very quiet and kept to themselves."

During 1976, the spotlight was focused solely on the All Saved Freak Band and their very public ministry. It was clearly their year. Joe said, "Aside from personal witnessing, the All Saved Freak Band became the exclusive outreach tool for the church. It also provided a public persona that masked what was going on at the farm. Publicly, we were an energetic group of young adults attempting to win our generation for Christ.

"What we ran out of was time. 1976 was the high point in the band's history. We traveled extensively and gained our greatest momentum in that year. That was also the year all of us began to realize we might be doing something of value. But we didn't know our time was about over."

Chapter 28

The Exodus

F ortunately, some of the public goodwill the All Saved Freak Band had achieved from their very well received appearances throughout 1976 rubbed off a bit on Larry Hill. After the high profile kidnapping of Glenn in 1975 and all the disparaging things the press and some of the locals had said about him and his ministry, Larry knew his public image needed some shoring up. Once the tour was over and everyone was back at Fortney Road, he decided to aggressively advertise their Morgan horse stud service.

The flyer Larry posted around town announced: "Moro Hills Magician, one of the most beloved Morgan sires on the East Coast, has moved to Ohio." The farm asked a stud fee of $750 and assured customers that Moro Hills Magician would only be bred to five outside mares for the rest of his career.

Joe said, "We had developed a breeding and training program for horses because, when the war came, there would be no other means of transportation. Morgan horses were selected as the primary breed as they could double as saddle horses and pull plows or wagons."

Of course, this was not mentioned overtly to the community. Larry's goal was simply to become a more involved member of the local horse community and raise some much needed cash for his ministry. He was certain that once people got to know him as a horse breeder, there was no way anyone would believe the lies and rumors being whispered about him.

However, buried at the end of the flyer, in the final paragraph, was a disquieting explanation for the farm's interest in endurance horses: "We have prophesied for many, many years that horses were going to become important to the American public and the United States Army again. We still believe and maintain this. Just keep watching the magazines and the headlines."

The Song of Solomon 2:15 says, "The little foxes ruin the vineyard." In other words, it's the small, insignificant things you barely notice or remember that can cause more destruction than you ever imagined possible.

For Larry Hill and Diane Sullivan, their little fox appeared the night of Wednesday, February 16, 1977. That was the evening that Diane Sullivan began the vicious beating of Bethy Goodenough, the thrashing that Larry continued with until Bethy was completely still and silent.

No one I've talked to remembers what little fox set Diane off. What had Bethy done that had so enraged Diane? Because whatever it was, Diane's reaction to it resulted in a chain of events that brought down the entire ministry and began the exodus of almost everyone who lived at Fortney Road.

After Millie and Carole witnessed the beating of little Bethy, Larry kept a sharp eye on both of them, wary that they may betray him or Diane.

"You weren't allowed to talk about it," Carole told me. "It was just a known thing that it had happened. It was totally unheard of to talk openly about the beatings any of us received; it would have been like a death sentence to say anything."

But as the weeks passed, neither woman could get the sights or sounds out of their minds. It might help to talk about it with someone, so they each cautiously confided in a few others about what they had witnessed—about how brutally Diane and Larry had beaten Bethy. Others carefully—and at great risk—began to share what they had seen or experienced firsthand. Secrets long kept were now being quietly divulged.

And the more people confided to one another in hushed, fearful tones, the more Millie knew she needed to escape for the sake of her family and her own sanity. She had heard so much about what was going on that now it seemed that everything was wrong at Fortney Road—it was truly a wicked and vile place, the very foundation was corrupt and rotten. She had to leave. She and her husband had no plan other than to leave the farm immediately. They had reached the tipping point where it was more terrifying to stay than it was to leave. If hell awaited those who left Fortney Road, could it really be any worse than what they were already experiencing every moment they remained?

Holding tightly to their children's hands, she and her husband simply hurried off the property one late afternoon when Larry was in town. She remembers how loud their shoes sounded as they crunched down the gravel road. No one knew what they were up to but no one said a word to them. She and her husband took only what they could carry, told their children to speak to no one as they left, only to look ahead, keep their eyes up and look at what was before them.

It was at the end of 1977 that Margo and her family joined those who made an exodus from Fortney Road. Jack and Margo had been members of the Church of the Risen Christ since 1971 and their departure greatly impacted Leon, since he had been friends with Jack for a long time.

Ultimately, it was one of their children who provided the means of escape that Margo and Jack had been desperately searching for. "One night our fourteen-month-old daughter Emily had a terrible fever," Margo told me. "We took her to the doctor and he thought it was serious enough that she be treated overnight at the children's hospital."

Jack and Margo visited the hospital the next day and were relieved to see that Emily was better and responding to treatment. They hugged their little girl, grateful that she was well again. They barely noticed the social worker that entered the room and quietly announced, "I know what's going on at Fortney Road."

"I was shocked," Margo said, "because he really did know things that were supposed to be kept secret."

Margo later found out that a few of the people who had recently left Fortney Road had held a meeting with some of the parents of those who were still in the community. Margo and Jack's fathers were both at that meeting and had expressed their concerns to the hospital social worker when they heard Emily had been admitted.

The social worker did not want Emily to return to the farm so it was agreed that Jack's mother would assume custody of the child. In addition, Jack and Margo were asked to attend a meeting with ex-members who wanted to share some of the information about Larry they didn't think Jack and Margo knew.

Margo and Jack met in secret with the former members and they were told about things that they had never actually seen but had sensed or suspected were going on: The beatings that Bethy and others endured, the guns that were either hidden away or being stockpiled, and other information that was brand new to them.

"There was so much that it was overwhelming," Margo recalled, "and it made you numb after a certain point, but we knew in our gut that it was all true." She called her father and he flew in from New York. Jack and his brother rented a U-Haul and went to the farm the next day to collect his and Margo's things.

When Larry saw the men arrive, he hobbled straight to Jack, his crutches squeaking and creaking. He insisted Jack, Margo, and her dad join him in the house. He had something to show them.

The three of them followed Larry into his office. He opened a file cabinet, dug around inside for a moment, and then triumphantly pulled out a dusty, moldy Playtex baby's bottle containing old, sour milk. Larry held the filthy object up to them and said in a bitter, stern voice, "If any of you say anything against me or this ministry, this will be evidence that Margo is an unfit mother!" He shook the bottle at them for a moment and waited for a response.

After several seconds of uneasy silence, Margo's father glanced at his watch and said, "Look, that's all well and good but I have a plane back to New York and I need to catch that flight." Because Margo's father had been the assistant secretary of commerce in a previous White House administration, Larry was intimidated by the man.

Breathing heavily out of fear and frustration, Larry maneuvered his crutches out of the way as Margo's father moved past him. Larry, Margo and Jack followed Margo's father outside. Jack and Margo hurried over to the U-Haul where Jack's brother was rapidly filling it with their belongings. Larry leaned on his crutches, watching. He wanted to be there, making his presence known in case anyone else thought about leaving.

The remaining members of the Fortney Road community, busy with their unending list of chores, stole glances as they wondered about the U-Haul and the presence of Margo's father. It appeared to them that Jack and Margo were abandoning the farm, betraying the ministry like another pair of Judases. Some berated them silently for their treachery, others yearned desperately to go with them.

Fifteen minutes later, Jack and his brother slammed the trailer door shut. The sound echoed about them. It was as if the entire property was in a vacuum or holding its breath.

Were they really doing this?

Jack climbed in front and started the U-Haul, with Margo and their children squished beside him. His brother took Margo's dad to the airport.

Larry had returned to the house so the other members of the community were able to steal glances at their departing friends or turn their backs on the latest group of traitors.

Jack and Margo took one more look around.

Are we really doing this?

Fear, elation, uncertainty and a dozen other emotions flittered about inside them.

Jack steered the truck down Fortney Road for the last time, the truck rolled and swayed side to side.

"Where are we going?" one of the children asked.

Margo didn't really know. She knew where they were staying for the time being, but where were they going? Was it really God leading them away? Or were they confused and headed straight to hell, too deceived to know until it was too late? Reverend Larry Hill—their Prophet and leader for six years—had warned them many, many times about a Great Falling Away, right before the Great War.

Are we really leaving Fortney Road?

"I know I was driving a bit erratically because I was terrified they were right behind me," Jack told me "I thought Larry and some others would follow me and I was really concerned for the safety of my wife and family."

Jack glanced frequently in the rearview mirror as the house and barn on Fortney Road grew smaller and smaller. But no one pursued them. For some reason, he expected to see people with pitchforks and flames, like the villagers in the old *Frankenstein* movies. But who was the monster they would be chasing? It wasn't anyone leaving Fortney Road.

The only monster was the prophet who remained

Jack glanced back again but he could no longer see the house or barn.

Just like that, in the blink of an eye, both were gone.

Later, when Larry discovered Margo and Jack had attended a meeting with former members and they had all openly discussed what had gone on at Fortney Road, he was furious and terrified. Then he learned that social workers and the police had been alerted.

The lies about him were beginning all over again.

Knowing that Margo's father had tremendous political connections and would use them against him, Larry grew even more anxious and his paranoia went into overdrive. He wanted to be certain there was no evidence of his teachings or his survival plans for the coming Great War. Those revelations were only for those in his Ark of Safety.

If the authorities invaded the farm, nothing should be available to them. He wanted it all destroyed. And it was time for him to prepare to go into hiding.

Carole recalled the night Larry left for his hideout in Pennsylvania.

"He was terrified that the police were coming any day to follow up on what had happened with Jack and Margo's child so he had us burn all of our information—all of our notes from his teachings and whatever he had written about the Great War. He wanted it all destroyed before he left. He was so agitated that night, barely making sense, and shouting and yelling at us to hurry, hurry, hurry! We were all rushing back and forth from our rooms and taking armloads of things and throwing them into this huge fire.

"It was a scramble to get everything—we had to think for ourselves to gather our things. It was like a bunch of mice scurrying and in a total panic. Get the guns, the books, the notes and burn or hide things."

Larry hobbled and swung about on his crutches, checking and double-checking that the fire was consuming whatever he felt needed to be destroyed. When the bonfire had done its work, it was time for him to go.

It was all in God's hands now.

By the glow of the dying fire, Larry climbed into the backseat of his car. He told the women to cover him with blankets. Diane and Laura were in the front seat with Laura behind the wheel. Even though it was the dead of night and they would take the back roads to Pennsylvania, which were neither well illuminated nor well-traveled, he didn't want to take a chance of being seen if the car was stopped.

In his panicked, apprehensive state, Larry most likely believed that Margo's father would use his White House connections to get the Pentagon, the CIA and the FBI involved in finding him. In his mind, every shadow government agency available was probably going to be involved in the manhunt.

There was the additional and overriding concern of the semi-trucks; it was so easy for those drivers to look down on the cars they passed, and he knew they would be out in full-force looking for him as they always were, eager to run him off the road and murder him, kill and silence God's prophet. And the police would only smile slyly and say it was just a tragic "accident" like the ones that had killed his son Brett and later Tom Miller and Randy Markko.

The car started and lurched off into the darkness, gradually picking up speed as it headed North on Route 534 for Pennsylvania. In the backseat, Reverend Larry Hill, God's end-time prophet, lay huddled under some musty blankets, drawing measured, terrified breaths.

"It all does seem so cowardly now doesn't it?" Carole wondered.

Although Larry had always preached that people should simply trust the Lord to protect them, on that February night, he was putting his faith in crossing state lines.

He wouldn't know until years later what a mistake it was to leave his flock untended.

Chapter 29

Stopping By Hell
on the Way Home

W ith Larry, Diane and Laura in Pennsylvania, it was as if a spell had been broken, and more and more people at Fortney Road were waking up to the reality of what they'd been unwilling or unable to recognize while Larry had them in his thrall.

In June of 1977, Leon, who had been a member of the Church of the Risen Christ for over six years, planned a trip to see his elderly grandfather who was in a nursing home. "He was not expected to live much longer," he said. Leon left the farm, went to work, and that afternoon he caught a ride to his parents' house.

"When I walked in I was surprised to see a female ex-member who I was very fond of sitting at my parents' dinner table. Dinner passed with some pleasantries and she then suggested we go for a walk. It was clear she had something important to say to me."

During the walk, in halting, embarrassed tones, the woman told Leon about the times Larry would have her drive to a deserted location so they could have sex near the roadside.

Stunned at what she was saying, Leon couldn't respond. He only stared at her, studying her as if she was speaking a different language.

She's talking about my pastor, a prophet of God. I should walk away.

The woman broke down several times but would brush the tears away and when Leon would try to comfort her and tell her he didn't need to know every detail, that she should really stop talking, she suddenly cried out, "No! It isn't just me! Don't you understand? I'm one of many!"

Shocked, Leon said, "The whole story seemed absolutely incredible, given that Larry repeatedly preached against adultery and premarital sex. And here was this woman accusing the most powerful man of God I knew of being a complete hypocrite, abusing her and other women."

They continued their walk and Leon was in a daze, like it was all a waking dream. The woman took the opportunity to tell him everything she and others had experienced at Fortney Road. He noticed that, out of habit, she kept averting her gaze, keeping her eyes downcast. It was almost an act of defiance when she would look him in the eye.

When they reached Leon's parents' home, she pleaded with him, saying, "Jack and Margo have some important things to say to you. You must go see them before you return to the farm."

She departed, leaving Leon in a serious quandary.

Leon knew it was, if anything, a passive offense for him to be present at his parents' house if some ex-members just happened to stop by to talk to him. In fact, Larry might even praise him for resisting their traitorous influences.

But for Leon to deliberately contact or visit ex-members, that was an offense that would surely merit forty lashes with the White Judge.

Or something worse if Larry wanted to make Leon an example for others.

After what his friend told him about the times Larry had sexually abused her and other women, Leon had to know what else was occurring at Fortney Road. And he trusted Jack and Margo to tell him the truth. He and Jack had been very close friends since high school.

Leon borrowed his father's car. On the way over, he was apprehensive, not sure if he wanted to hear anything else about Reverend Larry Hill.

It was all lies, he thought suddenly. *These people have all left the ministry, they are all* traitors, *I should* not *be listening to them.*

He slowed the car down, tried to make sense of his thoughts. But he couldn't forget what his friend said to him earlier that afternoon: "It isn't just me! Don't you understand? I'm one of many."

Leon arrived at Jack and Margo's five minutes later.

He embraced his friends warmly, realizing immediately that he thought of them as friends, not as traitors or deceived or misguided people bound for hell. He had a history with them, had known Jack for years before he ever heard the name Larry Hill.

"They both proceeded to tell me the truth about the farm and everything that was going on at Fortney Road," Leon said. "I listened intently but everything seemed too incredible to believe. But then the thought came: *This is my friend. He would not lie.*"

It was at that moment that a veil seemed to lift and Leon recognized the hideous psychological chains Larry had used to entrap him.

"A light went on that illuminated the pieces of the puzzle for me, and my first words were, 'I don't have to go back there!' My next words were, 'I am going to buy a pizza with my next paycheck!'"

Leon returned late that night to his parents' house and the next morning announced: "I have decided to leave Fortney Road. Would it be possible for me to stay here for a few months until I got on my feet financially?"

Elated, his mother and father both sighed with relief, their eyes teared up and they rushed to embrace their son. Their answer was, "Yes!"

On Sunday, Leon's parents went to Fortney Road with him to collect his belongings. "Looking back, I would later realize this was roughly akin to saying 'Let's stop by hell on the way home so I can get my work clothes.'"

Leon spent the first few weeks of June 1977 eagerly meeting daily with other ex-members of the farm. For hours and hours they talked about their traumatic experiences in the cult.

They met at restaurants, homes, parks, libraries, and diners and would occasionally, daringly, meet at a bar. Over a beer or something stronger, something that was forbidden by Larry Hill, they talked openly about the forbidden things he had done to them and was most likely doing to others.

Talking seemed to help. It was like oxygen, something that they needed or else they couldn't survive. It was like a healing balm that could be placed on the sore spots. And there were many sore spots, places of decay and rot that needed to be exposed and rubbed clean, allowed to scab over, heal and, hopefully, be forgotten. Over time, only a scar would be left, a reminder of an injury.

When they talked about what they had experienced at Fortney Road, it made what had happened bigger and smaller at the same time, like the crazy mirrors at a fun house. There was a reality there somewhere, it really had happened, but it was distorted and warped and almost unrecognizable.

"Did you know that . . ."

"Was it true that . . ."

"Do you remember when . . ."

The revelations and the secrets and the suspicions and the questions and, ultimately, the silences kept drawing them back together again and again. By phone or face to face, they had to talk it out, as if speaking about it would get it out of their lives, their minds, their souls, their spirits.

Leon noticed that everyone had such nervous energy; was that the way he came across, so jittery? The men and women were so anxious, and they all complained of horrific nightmares. A few admitted to depression and spiritual confusion. What happens when someone tells you he knows The Way but turns out to be as lost as you are? Or worse, was intentionally pointing you in the wrong direction?

"I'm kind of messed up right now, sort of at a loss as to what exactly happened," one former member said. "I'm not stupid, but I just can't seem to figure out what went so wrong. How'd I end up there?"

Leon sensed they were all in overwhelming psychological pain. Each of his friends had difficulty sleeping and had high startle responses. If the phone rang, a car horn sounded or someone rang the doorbell, they admitted they jumped, flinched or sometimes gasped in alarm.

And everyone seemed to always be looking over his or her shoulders.

"I can't go to church," one woman admitted. "Before I knew Larry, I used to go to church. I was Catholic. But now any Christian symbolism reminds me of Larry and what he taught."

Another man nodded. "Yeah, I know what you mean. Even driving by a church or seeing the congregation mingling outside . . ." He shudders. "It just brings back memories."

And there was tremendous guilt for the adults and children left behind.

"Do you think he's beating them because of us?"

"Because we left? Punish them because we got out?"

Silence followed, a pondering of what had once been such a normal part of life.

The ability or inability to eat came up frequently.

"I have no appetite. Isn't that weird? For so many years, I was always, always so hungry at the farm, but now that I can eat what I want and when I want, I can barely finish a sandwich."

Although many of them were in their mid-twenties, emotionally some of them acted as if they were adolescents again. Their emotions were frayed and they easily overreacted to situations or events, admitting to crying or weeping uncontrollably for no reason. Some said they would start out the day fine but fall into a dark gloom by the afternoon. Mood swings were the norm.

They all admitted they woke up at 4 a.m. even though they knew they didn't have to.

While living at Fortney Road, they had learned to suppress doubt but now they were all constantly overwhelmed by doubt. Was leaving Larry Hill the wrong decision? Were they all damned, each one bound for hell? Does God hate them? Will He kill them the way He killed Brett Hill, Tom Miller and Randy Markko? Will He strike them down and harm them like He did to Joe Markko? Was there even a God? If so, why had He let them go through all of that?

The meetings and phone calls were a blur to Leon, who still was in shock over all that he was learning from his friends. As the days piled up into weeks, he heard more and more former members express feelings of shame, low self-esteem, and anger. So much anger and rage at themselves for letting it happen and rage at Larry and Diane and anyone who had beaten or abused them.

It seemed as if every story had been told, every memory or event picked over until there simply was nothing left to talk about. It was as if they had all awakened from a bad dream, talked it over, and now needed to get dressed and begin the day.

But none of them really had anywhere to go. They all felt alienated from just about everybody around them who hadn't lived at Fortney Road. Having left behind the only people they'd known for several years—their Ark of Safety—they had no one to replace them with. Many of their friends have left the area or when then did come across an acquaintance, they were too embarrassed to answer the question, "So where have you been keeping yourself for the past few years?"

I wasn't keeping myself, I was kept.

They found that they viewed most people with distrust, afraid they'd be taken advantage of. And it was easy—so easy—to judge other people. Larry had very high standards and even if they weren't necessarily real or true standards, at least there was a goal, something to aim for. You had to jump, even if it was impossibly high.

Now, there was really nothing. No point to the day. No purpose.

In July 1977, Jack and Margo moved to Wisconsin. Some of the other former members of the community eventually relocated and Leon found himself feeling alone, lacking any social network. He was often depressed and had thoughts of suicide, though he fantasized about going out with a purpose by taking Larry with him.

"I counted the years he stole from all of us collectively at nearly four hundred, the equivalent of several more lives destroyed. I felt the lingering impact of all those beatings with a bullwhip and years of terrible sleep deprivation and twenty-hour workdays. But worst of all was what Larry had done to the children at the farm. I thought about how these children were beaten at least every week, if not more. And I thought about how much more vulnerable, helpless, and traumatized they had to feel than I."

Another former member who escaped when Leon did summed it up best.

"I remember I once saw a movie about an African tribe and these heathen people would take a kid, a baby, and they'd carve these lines on its stomach and put dirt in it. I just remember that baby in the film was in so much pain that he covered his eyes. And I remember one time one of the mothers at the church farm had given her child a whipping and that child had covered her eyes, just like the baby in the film."[5]

For the most part, Larry, Diane and Laura and a few others stayed away from Fortney Road, living most of the time in Pennsylvania where Larry worked the phones and focused on promoting the All Saved Freak Band and his Morgan horse-breeding business. With Larry absent so much of the time, the remaining members of the community found they had more time to reflect.

"Whenever Larry was around, it was like I couldn't think," Carole told me, "and when he was away, my mind was freed up to think for itself. When Jack and Margo left, I wondered why I was so happy inside for them, knowing that I wasn't being loyal, that I should be sad that they had left this Ark of Safety. But I was glad for them, and that was not the way Larry had trained me to feel."

With her brothers John and Morgan gone, along with many of her closest friends, Carole's days at the farm had been dreary and lonely. Taking a risk—and really, why not? What did she have to lose?—Carole began to open up and talk with her friend Janice while they cleaned houses. But as not to raise suspicion, Carole continued to be a docile and obedient member of the community

"She and I started to talk more and admitted we both wanted to leave and we started to talk about it openly with one another which was so risky but we trusted each other and it felt so good to talk about leaving! In an odd way, it was like planning a dream vacation," Carole said. "I remember looking her in the eye one day and saying, 'I'll be seeing you,' and Janice had just nodded and said, 'Okay.' I repeated myself to her because what I meant was that I'd be seeing her on the *outside*, away from the farm. It was like I was planning a prison break, which I guess I was! And it was a code with her and it also meant that I was really leaving and would not be back."

But it was also Larry's promise of three beatings that confirmed Carole's decision to leave the cult. That, and a brand of furniture polish.

"I remember Larry and Diane were back at the farm for a day, checking up on everyone. We were all busy cleaning. I went to Diane and told her that I believed the Pledge brand of furniture polish did a better job than the one we were using. Diane had already told me not to use Pledge for some reason. I wasn't being smart or anything, I just repeated my opinion that Pledge was better. But Larry overheard me, he was sitting right there, and he told me I had three beatings coming for sassing back to Diane. I had contemplated for a while that if I was going to get another beating, I would not take it."[16]

And she didn't, finally leaving Fortney Road in November 1977. At that point, Carole had been part of the ministry for five long years.

On the day before Diane was to return to the farm and administer Carole's beating, she went to work as usual. "I was back working at the hair salon and I remember I paced the floor I was so nervous about what I was planning to do!" Carole took all the money out of the cash register and asked her last customer to give her a ride to her old friend Patty's house. When she was dropped off, Carole broke down sobbing with relief and liberation.

She had done it.

Miss Spontaneous was alive again.

"My brother John showed up with a ferocious Doberman Pinscher who was trained by the police to attack people. That dog was ready to kill! And John told me not to worry, he had a gun in the car! This was all in case Larry heard about my escape and tracked me down. You see now the fear we were all under, even when we had gotten out?"

Because Larry, Diane and Laura were spending most of their time in Pennsylvania, they weren't aware of how those who remained at Fortney Road were spending their unsupervised time. Larry would make a surprise visit every few days, sort of a spot check, and spend a few hours at the farm, but he really had no idea what was going on with his flock.

For example, Daryl Pitts had been walking between two worlds for several months, slowly gathering the courage to leave the ministry. It was the local Baptist church that had begun to plant the seeds that eventually freed Daryl from Fortney Road.

"In the fall of 1977, Larry just wasn't around much so I went to work for a Baptist deacon," Daryl told me. "We hit it off immediately. He introduced me to mainstream Christian radio, books, and other publications."

When the deacon asked Daryl about his beliefs and where Larry's more outlandish claims were in the Bible, Daryl said, "I started to feel quite foolish. When this kind man gently questioned the Biblical support for some of my beliefs, the best verification I could give was, 'Larry saw a hawk,'" referring to Larry's "Parable of the Hawks" vision.

Daryl continued to go to Sunday church at the farm but spent his Sunday evenings at the Baptist service. "I invited Norris to go with me and the contrast between the services was amazing!" he said. "It was so good to hear someone teach who actually took a serious attitude toward the scripture!"

News of Daryl Pitts and Norris McClure attending the Baptist church made its way to Larry, who would not tolerate such "double-mindedness." Soon after Larry had been informed, the pair of men was given some shocking news.

"Diane arrived from Pennsylvania one afternoon to tell Norris and me that we had two weeks to clear out from the farm," Daryl said. "And she and Larry were actually disturbed that I kept my paychecks during those last two weeks! I praise God that Norris and I were kicked out of a cult! I learned then—and continue to realize—that God is faithful even when I am foolish. He was present, waiting for me to be ready for freedom."

But while Daryl and Norris and others gradually mustered the courage to leave, many simply fled whenever they had the chance and were immediately embraced by ex-members in the community.

Liberated and finally able to talk freely about their experiences, several of them went to the authorities to stop what Larry was doing. With their help, the local police and the county's Children's Services agency prepared to break into Larry Hill's private world.

His Great War was about to begin.

Chapter 30

The Great War Begins

W hen Leon had left Fortney Road in 1977 he told me, "I wasn't leaving just for myself, I wanted to be certain Larry would not get away with abusing any more children. Back then the local child social services wouldn't get involved so I decided to try my luck first with the FBI office in Akron, Ohio.

"The agent I spoke to spent a considerable length of time with me and at the end of the interview said, 'What you have told me is incredible. Do you have anyone who can corroborate your story?' I told him I could deliver as many people as he liked who would confirm that I was telling the truth. I gave him Jack and Margo's phone number and they went in for an interview."

Carole told me, "By the time I left the farm, my brother John—like Leon—had already been talking to the FBI."

The bureau had also managed to track down Millie. She had moved out of the area with her husband and children. Carole called her and convinced her to return to town and meet with the investigators. Once the two women were alone with the FBI agents, the questions came rapidly and were very specific.

Carole said, "They asked about child abuse and Millie and I just looked at each other because they wanted a specific instance. We shrugged our shoulders like, 'There were so many instances, which one to choose?' We had so many stories to tell, so much abuse, and I know we were both babbling to them, not making a lot of sense."

She remembered that one of the agents had a peculiar habit of rolling bullets in his pants pockets. *Clickedy, clickedy, clickedy.* He would walk the floor and do that as he and his partner questioned the women in the trailer.

Finally, one of the agents asked them to pick just one incident of child abuse.

"Of course, we knew immediately what it would be, the beating of Bethy," Carole said. "Millie and I had both seen it, both eyewitnesses, which was what they wanted. Looking back now, I think it was an answer to Bethy's prayers. Now that I know the end of the story. So the FBI talked to Millie and me separately and asked us to tell them what happened. And the story we told was identical."

The day after the interview, the FBI agent called Leon and told him that he believed him. "Although the FBI seemed highly interested in the details of life at the community, their main focus was on whether there were any illegal weapons," Leon said. "So I told them that Larry carried a green book bag with him all the time, and inside was a loaded gun."

Following up on that warning, the FBI asked Carole many follow up questions about the guns and ammunition that Larry kept hidden on the farm. There was concern over the safety of those on the farm and for the arresting officers should the community be raided.

"Larry was bold—very bold—in his threats," Carole said, "and I knew he could back them up." She told me that just before she had spoken to the FBI, a friend had called to see if she was okay. The woman sounded so relieved when Carole had answered the phone, breathlessly telling Carole that she had heard it whispered in the horse sales community that Larry said he had "had Carole killed."

Because it had been rumored for years that Larry was not above giving a poor person in the area a chicken and a bottle of wine to do him "a favor" and hurt or even kill one of his enemies, the implied threat against Carole was taken seriously.

"When the FBI was asking me about the weapons I told them what the woman had said. They told all of us to get guns to protect ourselves, so they believed us and knew how dangerous Larry was. So I bought a .380 automatic with hollow points. And all the time I was wondering, *Am I able to do this? It's him or me, kill or be killed. Can I?* And my frame of mind finally settled on the fact that, *Yes, I can do this.*"

But while it may have been relatively easy to physically leave Fortney Road, Larry Hill could maintain residence in the minds of former members for a long time.

Carole gave me an example of this when she visited the FBI building in downtown Akron to verify some things. "I remember that it was a big square building and the elevator was in the middle of it. When the elevator doors opened on the floor they told me to go to, I got off and almost immediately I heard this creaking noise—it was the sound of Larry's crutches!

"I totally freaked out because the elevator doors had closed behind me and I had no idea which room to go to or where I could hide. I'm frantically looking to the left and right. And the sound of his squeaky crutches was getting closer and closer! I thought they had tricked me, that Larry had somehow fooled even the FBI and they were now on his side!

"Larry had taught us to always have a way out, to never be trapped in a room or situation. But here I was, trapped in an unfamiliar building and I could hear Larry getting closer and closer to me. I just froze up and next thing I knew, I saw a woman pushing a cleaning cart with squeaky wheels! The relief that swept through me . . . I had been so terrified, and to go from one extreme to the other . . ."

In April 1978—more than a year after the beating of Bethy Goodenough—the police arrived at Fortney Road and served arrest warrants to Diane Sullivan and Larry Hill. The charge was alleged child abuse.

But they were unable to locate Larry since he was hiding in Pennsylvania.

Bethy, now twelve years old, was removed from the farm by the authorities and subjected to an examination by the county medical doctor. It was now fourteen months since she had had the vicious beating from Larry and Diane. The results showed that "she did have several narrow scars on her upper back, at the waist and behind her legs."[5]

Because the medical report indicated clear signs of abuse, all of the children of the Church of the Risen Christ community were removed to Children's Services and stripped and examined for signs of possible mistreatment.

Since Joe and his family had been banished from living on Fortney Road, they had been spared the twenty-four-hour exposure to physical, psychological and emotional damage that Larry and Diane meted out to community members.

"Sandy and I were unaware of any arrest warrants until heavily armed SWAT team members, in flak jackets, surrounded our home in April of 1978," Joe said. Even though the Markkos did not live on the farm, the authorities considered them to be very much a part of the commune so the Children's Services visited their home. And because former members had told stories of stockpiled weapons and ammunition, social services and local authorities did not know what to expect when they arrived at the farm, or what sort of weapons Joe had hidden away to protect his own family.

Joe and Sandy's five children were removed at gunpoint. "The authorities' justification for such extreme and frightening measures lay in their information," he said. "They were told we were all heavily armed and dangerous."

The complaint filed against Joe and Sandy alleged that their children had been "neglected and reared in an environment detrimental to their emotional and physical well-being, allowing persons outside the family to exercise control regarding discipline and education. The children were forced to live in an atmosphere of fear and violence and exposed to abuse of siblings and friends who are whipped and beaten to extremes by other than the parents."[47]

At the same time the Markkos' children were being examined and questioned, Bethy's father had charges filed against him, stating that he had failed to cooperate in the investigation of his seven children by the Children's Services board. Remaining loyal to Larry, he said that he would only allow his children to be interrogated in his presence.[47]

Bethy's father was held in contempt of court.[47] Eventually, he changed his mind and soon after they testified before Children's Services, Bethy's parents thought it best if they resigned from the

Church of the Risen Christ. After notifying the authorities, they took Bethy and their other children and finally left Fortney Road.

"The reason that my family finally left the farm as far as I know is because of the law coming around and trying to take the children," Bethy told me.

Larry kept a few of his most trusted followers in Pennsylvania and left the majority of the group to carry on at Fortney Road. Since he was no longer around to closely supervise their behavior, members continued to talk more openly among themselves. With the leadership absent, fearful and preoccupied with the charges against them, Mark 14:27 was proving true: *Strike the shepherd, and the sheep will be scattered.*

Leon told me, "The group fractured and I believed at that time, only about a dozen adults and children remained at Fortney Road."

Larry's son, Tim Hill, celebrated his eighteenth birthday in May and gave himself the best gift of his life—his freedom.

"In May of 1978 I ran away. I had been working with Donald at a sawmill and I told him that I had to work late so he left without me. I hitchhiked to a barn where my dad had hidden a phone and like a dummy, I called my dad and told him that I was okay but I was now eighteen and I had left the farm. Browns Hospitality Stables offered me a job if I ever wanted one so I took them up on the offer and told my dad about it. I told him that if I could work there and be left alone I'd be okay. We would talk on the phone every once in a while and he kept telling me to get back to Fortney Road but I told him I wouldn't."

Months passed and one night in October, Larry showed up and surprised Tim.

"He put a gun in my mouth and threatened to pull the trigger if I didn't swear to quit the job and return to the farm!"

Shaken but knowing he'd never return to Fortney Road, the next day Tim moved in with his grandparents in Ohio. This time, he didn't tell his father where he was.

Soon after Daryl, Norris, and Tim departed, All Saved Freak Band songwriter Mike Berkey and his wife left the community they had been a part of since 1971.

The Great Falling Away as prophesized by Larry Hill was now happening, and what was left of his ministry was about to stand trial. The very public trial was scheduled to begin in August 1978.

Joe said, "During the August hearing, Diane was confined in the Ashtabula County Jail while Larry remained in hiding across the border in Pennsylvania."

John Griffith wrote about the unfolding events for *The News-Herald of Willoughby*. When recalling this story, he told me, "This was the first investigative piece I did. *The News-Herald* was a tiny paper back then and it was always looking for a good story. I had gotten to know some federal agents and they were investigating Larry Hill and his Church of the Risen Christ group for child slavery. They told me that Larry had this saying that you beat children until they are silent—that really infuriated me. The agents wanted to stop him and they encouraged me to write the story.

"The federal officers gave me Leon's number and I remember we met in a basement somewhere and he told me what he had been through at the farm, just awful stuff. He was simply terrified of Larry and was afraid that those people were coming after him. Leon put me in touch with Margo, Carole and Millie, and they all agreed to be interviewed for the series of articles I wrote. I did try and talk to Larry. I went out to the farm a couple times and knocked on the door, but they ignored me. I saw a few people working around the place but they wouldn't speak to me."

Throughout the summer, Leon and others helped their friends escape from the farm and get resettled in the community. On August 30, 1978, the *Ashtabula Star Beacon* reported that Joe and Sandy Markko's complaint against them was withdrawn, clearing them of any neglect of their children. After their children had been examined for signs of abuse, they had been returned home within twenty-four hours with no reported injuries.[47]

During the hearing, the county Children's Services board attorney James M. Timonere said, "Upon investigation, it has been determined that it would be in the best interest of the children that the complaint be withdrawn."[47]

Ohio's oldest county fair, the Great Geauga County Fair, had long since moved on by the time Carole and Millie were prepared to testify in the Ashtabula County Juvenile Court. It was the fall of 1978 and it had taken a great deal of cajoling to convince Millie to testify; she and her family remained in hiding and terrified of being anywhere near Larry Hill or Diane Sullivan.

But Carole was adamant about testifying, telling me, "I drove all the way from Mansfield, Ohio up there. I truly felt like I was on a mission to save Bethy and stop the cult, stop what was going on at Fortney Road.

"The authorities promised us it would be a felony charge or I wasn't going to mess with it. By this time, Sheriff Maynard and I talked quite frequently. The newspapers were all involved and *The Plain Dealer* reporter gave me free phone access so I could get information to him."

When the day arrived to testify, Carole took a deep breath and pulled on the heavy courthouse door. "I remember walking into that courtroom. There was a long, wide hallway with a bunch of benches. And everyone who was left at Fortney Road was sitting there, people I had lived with for six years."

Carole said hello to her friends, but they looked away. No one spoke to her. But she wasn't offended, didn't feel threatened or hurt by their behavior. She didn't feel anything. Having left Fortney Road—wiped the dust off her feet—the people and the place no longer held any power over her. She continued walking past the small group who made up the Church of the Risen Christ. They were the remnant, the lasting generation, secure in their Ark of Safety.

I was once part of that, she marveled.

She caught the eye of the prosecuting attorney and he waved her over. After she sat down and they chatted for a few moments, he cleared his throat, lowered his voice and casually mentioned to her, "Oh yeah, we were only able to get a misdemeanor charge brought against Diane."

Stunned, Carole barely had the chance to open her mouth to respond before a hand was placed on her shoulder. It was Millie. They stood and embraced and tears suddenly appeared in Carole's eyes as she hugged her friend.

Visiting judge of Lake County Juvenile Court, Ross D. Avellone, presided over the trial of Diane Sullivan at the Ashtabula

Court in September 1978. This was a bench trial—there was no jury; the judge alone would decide whether the defendant was guilty beyond a reasonable doubt.

When asked for recollections about the case, the now-retired judge said to me, "I do recall the circumstances and it went on for a couple days. Ms. Sullivan had some pretty good attorneys and there were several local clergy there because a church group was involved. Because of the nature of the case, it was a bit of an educational experience for me. I had no information about the Church of the Risen Christ or any of the people involved. I went into the case cold which is the best way, of course."

Carole recalled, "The attorneys asked me how high the ceiling was in the house where Bethy was beaten. They were trying to convince everyone that it was impossible for a whip that long to be used in the house if the ceiling was too low."

The attorneys asked Millie the same questions and then both women were dismissed.

"We never got called back," Carole said. "We were thanked, excused, and that was it. We never heard what happened."

Weeks passed, and then the newspapers reported the outcome of the trial.

Chapter 31

Judgment Day

Diane Sullivan was convicted of a misdemeanor child abuse violation, and was sentenced to six months and a $500 fine, but the judge suspended all but six days in jail.

Disgusted, Leon said, "I was amazed at how poorly the county addressed this. Only later when I read details of the case in the newspaper would I truly understand how bad the abuse really was, since single men like myself did not live in the house where Larry himself perpetuated the worst abuse."

Judge Avellone told me, "The defense agreed generally that certain events happened but denied any serious injury occurred. And, considering the full facts and circumstances, the actions did not amount to child abuse under the law. The defense said the discipline was really a form of worship. And Diane never intended to seriously harm the child, and intent plays an important role in these cases. Did she have an 'evil intent'? No, she didn't, and she had no previous record. It is treated somewhat like involuntary manslaughter. She had no remorse because she said it was part of her religious beliefs and the state is not about to get involved there in a purely religious issue."

Bethy Goodenough, in accordance with her mindset at the time, corroborated Diane's defense and denied that the beating had hurt her.

"The girl said that it wasn't painful," the judge recalled, "and she and her parents lived at the farm by choice and subjected themselves to the church bylaws. For all I knew, that was the way they handled things in their religion. In Diane's mind, it was purely a religious issue, not a criminal one. But I did determine that she had gone too far and was guilty of child abuse so some punishment needed to be given.

"At that time, six months in jail and a $500 fine was the maximum that could be given. Maximum sentences are usually reserved for repeat offenders or very serious injuries, so I took into consideration a number of factors. For example, the girl denied it hurt and said it was part of her church's beliefs, she and her parents chose to live there, and did we really want the state dictating what a religious group does? However, I wanted to be sure Diane and her group knew that Man's Law was higher than any abusive belief system so I knew she'd have to do some jail time.

"I know a bit about the psychological and emotional impact of jail time. The first three days are the hardest. That first day and night, and then the second and third—they have a real impact to change people. After those first three days, you adapt and it's not as bad. So I wanted her to experience at least three days, and then I decided to double that amount so she'd have those first three bad days plus three more. A suspension of some jail time conditioned on good behavior usually deters a repetition of the same action. When all things were considered, I had to balance the factors and reach a fair sentence."

Ultimately, Diane was convicted of a misdemeanor child abuse violation, with the charge reading:

> On February 16, 1977 Miss Sullivan did cruelly abuse and administer corporal punishment in a cruel manner and for a prolonged period. Also that she did beat the child with a whip, punishment considered excessive under the circumstances and creating a substantial risk of physical harm to the child.[43]

In his published comments, Judge Avellone said he believed Miss Sullivan "had cause to discipline the child, but lost control."[5]

"Several clergy that were there were surprised she got any sentence at all," the judge told me. "They believed she and the church were exercising their religious freedoms and since she did not intend to inflict child abuse, she did not commit a crime."

Following her sentencing, Diane's attorneys had one request.

"Diane's attorneys asked if she could not serve at the local Ashtabula county jail," the judge said. "At the time, it allegedly had a very rural and primitive plumbing and toiletry facility. She was allowed to serve at the more modern Lake County facility."

While Diane was facing her sentence, Larry remained in hiding in Pennsylvania where he was sought by the authorities for his alleged role in the horsewhipping of Bethy.

A local reporter told me, "When Diane was convicted of child abuse and Larry skipped the state, I asked Diane about it for one story. She said Larry had to leave because people wanted to kill him! Ya think? After he beat or ordered beatings of children and women, men, too. Even his own children. Tim was once beaten so bad his ears bled. Mark told me so. I told you, it's awful."

Joe said, "At the trial, every one of us involved perjured themselves in an effort to save Larry. On the stand I was asked if I had ever seen anyone whipped. With my own lashes always fresh in my mind and the knowledge that other adults were beaten as well, I lied and said, 'No.' No one asked me to lie under oath but I did. I promised truthfulness before God, placing my hand on His holy book and I lied."

Larry had often branded Joe as being disloyal and a traitor ever since he had run off in 1972. Joe said, "Now I became disloyal to God that I might be loyal to my fugitive pastor."

He and his wife Sandy and their children stayed as members of Larry's flock until the trial was over. As the verdict was read, Joe sent a letter of resignation to Larry, who remained in Pennsylvania. Since Joe had no idea where Larry was hiding, he had Ben hand deliver the letter to Larry.

Ben told me, "When the few people who remained at Fortney Road heard about the letter, they belittled Joe and what they were told he had written. To them, he was already a traitor to Larry and the Lord, so the letter meant nothing to them, didn't sway them or their commitment to Larry's vision."

In the early winter of 1979, Joe returned to the farm one final time to read his letter of resignation in person to the few remaining members of the church. It was a beautiful, crisp Sunday morning and there were perhaps a dozen people present for church.

As he made his way to the front of the room, Joe tried to catch their eye, tried to connect with them or reconnect. After all, they had been his friends, his family, for several years. They were going to be part of the lasting generation; they were going to survive the Great War together in the Ark of Safety.

But no one looked at him. The women kept their eyes down-cast and the men looked everywhere but at Joe. The few children in attendance were bored and restless. Everyone wondered why this traitor had been allowed back onto their property and what could he possibly have to say to them?

With their prophet in exile and their prophetess falsely convicted of child abuse, the final remnant of Larry Hill's ministry— perhaps just fourteen souls[13]—sat in silence as one more Judas betrayed them and walked away. This was all happening—the Great Falling Away— just as Larry had prophesized so they marveled at the accuracy and wisdom of their pastor.

No one looked at Joe; no one asked a question when he had finished reading the letter, no one challenged what he had said. It had all fallen on deafened ears and after waiting for a response— any response—and hearing nothing but the impatient squeaking and rustling of restless people in uncomfortable chairs, Joe folded up the letter and walked out of the room.

He had met Larry Hill in Chicago more than sixteen years earlier, had been one of his first converts, had formed Preacher and the Witness with him and then the All Saved Freak Band, and they had ministered together in the Church of the Risen Christ community for more than eleven years. Now Larry was hiding out in Pennsylvania, avoiding a police warrant, while Joe, just thirty-one, and Sandy Markko and their five children were leaving behind everyone they knew and heading to a town north of Kent where they would stay with friends until they could get back on their feet.

Sandy found an Assembly of God church five miles away in North Bloomfield and after attending a mid-week Bible study, she returned home excited at the teaching, the people and most of all, the sense of peace and love she had experienced at the meeting.

Encouraged by her report, Joe said, "Our whole family was in church the very next Sunday."

Like Leon, Carole, Daryl, Margo, Jack and the dozens of others who had left Fortney Road, Joe discovered "just how truly out of whack I'd become. My view of myself, my concepts of

Christianity and my understanding of ministry and marriage all needed a significant amount of healing."

A few weeks later, there was a knock at Joe's door. It was Diane Sullivan. The weather was chilly and rainy, and once inside, she refused to be seated.

While the rain dripped off her coat and dampened the carpet, she stood by the front door and told Joe and Sandy she had a message for Joe from Larry.

Sandy remembered Diane read a few scriptures followed by a mini-sermon.

Joe recalled that Diane read two Old Testament verses, the first from 2 Samuel 19:13:

> And say ye to Amasa, "Art thou not of my bone, and of my flesh? God do so to me, and more also, if thou be not captain of the host before me continually in the room of Joab."

The second reading was from 2 Samuel 20:12:

> And Amasa wallowed in blood in the midst of the highway. And when the man saw that all the people stood still, he removed Amasa out of the highway into the field, and cast a cloth upon him, when he saw that every one that came by him stood still.

Diane snapped the Bible shut and standing her tallest and looking her sternest, said, "Joe Markko, God sent me here to tell you, 'Oh, Amasa, why shouldest thou die?'"

That was it.

She kept her gaze locked on Joe and Sandy for a moment, then turned on her heel and left. Joe couldn't make much sense from the puzzling scriptures and what they may or may not mean, but he remembered being caught up short with one word.

"Larry's final word to me through Diane was 'die'?"

Chapter 32

Welcome Home, Glenn

I f Larry Hill's ministry had been an actual building, by the spring of 1979 it would have been condemned. Those who had left Fortney Road claimed it was a dangerous and unfit place for human habitation. For the few that remained, doubts and uncertainty lingered and the longer Larry and Diane stayed away, the easier it was to entertain thoughts of escape.

Carole's friend Janice—who, along with her husband and children, had been a member for several years—decided to leave.

"One morning at breakfast I confronted the few people who were left and told them that the things they had heard about Larry were true and that they should go and check them out," she told me. "It was like I couldn't hold back anymore and I needed to shake myself and everyone else. We needed to wake up! We had been asleep for so long."

The strange thing was that within thirty minutes Diane and a couple of others pulled in the driveway unannounced and unexpected from Pennsylvania.

"It was totally weird that they appeared that day!" Janice said. "But I was on a roll, empowered by who knows what, and I went right over and spoke with Diane immediately and told her all I knew and all I had said and all Diane could do was shout at me, 'How could you tell them that?!'

"For once I stood my ground and there was nothing she could do because I was not afraid of her anymore. Just like that, all that fear and apprehension when I was around her was gone. And she knew that. She didn't try to make me stay or physically do anything to me. I felt the chains drop off and I was free, at least physically."

Janice told me, "At the end, with so many others gone, it was easy to leave. Peter and I packed up our belongings and left. I don't think anyone even tried to stop us."

The public confrontation between Janice and Diane was what sparked Ben to go to Pennsylvania and confront Larry directly.

Ben said, "Ruth and I courted and were married in May 1979 while at the farm, a feat that would have been nearly impossible had not Larry, Diane, and Laura lived in Pennsylvania while we were in Ohio. Their absence allowed our relationship to develop as normally as possible under such bizarre circumstances."

The joy of the newlyweds was cut short when Ruth finally summoned the courage to tell her new husband things that she had kept hidden when she was single. Now that she had a husband, Ruth wanted to unburden these painful secrets and entrust them to Ben.

"In July of 1979, I told Ben about Larry's constant sins of sexual immorality," Ruth said.

"I had a hard time believing this," Ben admitted. "If I believed what Ruth was saying, it meant that the last seven years of my life— our lives—were in vain. But after we talked and prayed about it, I knew that I had to confront Larry with these allegations. I knew no matter what he said that somehow I would learn the truth."

Ben dropped Ruth off at work and then he drove to Pennsylvania.

At the time, Ruth feared that Ben did not believe her and that he was possibly siding with Larry.

Tidioute, Pennsylvania, is a quiet river community of less than a thousand people. Ben drove slowly down the narrow streets, following the directions he had been forced to memorize until he came to the property where Larry was hiding. Nothing could be written down since Larry was convinced the FBI and the CIA were looking for him. Although he knew God would protect him, Larry wasn't taking any chances.

Ben parked the car, honked the horn twice, counted to fifteen slowly and then flashed the headlight beams in the pattern he had been instructed. He waited until he heard the sharp hand claps that signaled all was safe and he could proceed by foot to the hidden location.

Five minutes later, Ben waited for someone to approach him. He knew he was being watched and those hidden from his view in the farmhouse wanted to confirm that he was alone. His mouth dry and heart beating with apprehension, Ben tried to think through again what he would say and how he would say it.

After several minutes, Larry approached. His crutches squeaked loudly in the silent, rural, and isolated area. Ben wondered if Larry still carried a loaded gun, wondered if guns were trained on him right at that moment. But it was too late to back out now.

"Larry and I sat down and talked," Ben told me, no longer remembering how he began the conversation.

For some reason, speaking the truth or stating facts gave those who encountered Larry Hill a calmness and courage they were not expecting to experience. Several have said it was very much like in *The Wizard of Oz* when Toto pulled back the curtain and the wizard is revealed to be an ordinary man. As Ben sat confronting his pastor with the truth, Larry seemed to diminish in size. He was only a man; an awful, sick, dangerous and horrifically abusive man, but still, only a man.

Ben said, "To my surprise he admitted to everything I asked him about. Of course, there was no admission to all the other things that I now know him to be guilty of."

When the confrontation was over, Larry shouted dire prophecies and warnings but they sounded to Ben like fairy tales. "He tried to talk me into staying at Fortney Road, but the prophet and the power of his spell over me had been broken."

The malevolent words Larry had shouted at Ben had no lingering effect, so Ben simply walked away into the trees, feeling the eyes of Larry and others on him, yet he had no reason to turn back or look back. He reached the car and started the engine. Driving back to Fortney Road, he had a lot to think about. He and Ruth had already decided to leave the community if the allegations were true, so in late July 1979, Ben and Ruth—members since 1972— left the farm, just two months after they had been married there.

Ben said to me, "As incredible as it may seem, it was another five years before we could look each other in the eyes because the pain and shame were so great after all those years of abuse."

Within a week, many others left Fortney Road.

A handful—only a remnant—remained: Larry and Diane, Pam and Kim Massmann, Laura Markko, Donald, Ed Durkos, Bob Tidd and Glenn Schwartz.

Unlike his arrival at Fortney Road, Glenn Schwartz's departure was very low key. Carole had married Mike Hough by then and one day during the early spring of 1979, she answered the phone. Glenn's parents were on the line.

"They were so excited! They told us that Glenn had left the farm! He had simply walked off the property one day and kept on moving until he ended up at some bar. He saw a motorcycle parked out front that interested him and it turns out it was his brother Gene's bike." Gene immediately took Glenn home to their parents, which is when they called Carole and Mike and asked them to come over to see Glenn.

"I dressed in my long Church of the Risen Christ farm dress and head covering so I would look familiar to Glenn and not panic him," Carole said. "His parents were concerned that he would go back to the farm just like he had after Ted Patrick had failed to deprogram him. It was the same fear my parents had, that I'd go back. Because I knew the mindset Glenn was struggling with since I had just left, I wanted to look like what he perceived a Christian woman should resemble."

Once Carole had dressed the part, she and Mike hurried over to Glenn's house.

"He was not a famous person to us. He was our brother in the Lord and we loved him and felt his pain. His parents just wanted some reinforcements, some people to surround Glenn and care for him and love him. In my family we have a tradition of making a banner for whatever holiday we're celebrating or for whatever person is visiting. So I made one for Glenn that said *Welcome*

Image 48: From 1979, Glenn Schwartz, Morgan King and Mike Hough, Carole's husband. Photo courtesy of Carole King Hough.

Home, Glenn and took a picture [Image 48] at my house right after Glenn got out of the farm."

Carole and Mike started calling Glenn and inviting him to spend the night at their house, and Carole would set up her keyboards and they'd play together in the basement long into the night. "He was free!" Carole said. "And we were just trying to make him feel comfortable about himself, about his life, about being with us. About not being afraid anymore."

Although Glenn may not have been afraid, his parents were. They screened every phone call and kept a sharp eye on their son.

Butch Armstrong remembers calling Glenn and spending several minutes trying to get past Glenn's father. "They were worried about Larry Hill coming around again, trying to contact Glenn." And they had every right to be apprehensive, for Larry was furious about losing his most prized possession. He was always on the lookout, trying to find out where Glenn was playing.

"I remember that I wrote a story about Glenn for the *Cleveland Scene*," Butch told me. "It was really well received and I was in a record store talking with a friend about it the same day it came out. Only one other customer was in the store so me and the owner were just talking about Glenn and how great it was to see him out playing again after so many years with the All Saved Freak Band and being more or less hidden away at Fortney Road."

As they spoke, the other customer inched closer to them, accompanied by a sharp squeaking sound. "Excuse me?" he asked, his gruff voice startling both men. "I heard you talking about Glenn Schwartz. I'm looking for him. Where is he staying these days?"

A chill went down Butch's neck after he turned to face the man. "It was Larry Hill! Right there in front of me. I realized then that my article had revealed Glenn's whereabouts since I had written that he was playing at Hoopples."

"We both stuttered out that we didn't know where Glenn was," and the owner of the store hid that issue of *Cleveland Scene* behind the counter.

Of course, Larry showed up at Hoopples that week. Glenn's Dark Man was a shadow that seemed to appear at random, always leaving Glenn shaken and apprehensive.

Glenn's son Bob told me, "It's really tough for me to talk about my dad's time at Fortney Road. I just remember that Larry Hill was always creepy and scary looking, and my Uncle Gene just hated what he had done to my dad at the farm. I remember once when I was a kid I was with my uncle in a big old 1967 New Yorker car. Gene saw Larry Hill in his car and we started to follow him. My dad and uncle are both skilled race car drivers and my uncle got closer and closer to Larry and Larry was so nervous, he was driving faster and faster but couldn't shake us. Finally, Larry ended up on a dead end street. He got out of his car and screamed at my uncle, 'What do you want from me? Leave me alone!' I think my uncle just enjoyed messing with Larry."

Glenn didn't stay too long with his parents, Bob said.

"It was fine for a while—they were glad to have him home, but after a few weeks, his constant preaching really bothered his mom and they fought about it a lot. He also had his car parked in the driveway—I think it was a Ford Tourneo—and he had scriptures plastered all over the car. It sort of embarrassed his mom since all the neighbors saw it. So between that car and his preaching, Glenn really didn't want to stay there since he was causing such a fuss, and the family agreed he should move out."

Glenn lived in his car for a while, playing gigs around the area and sleeping in the Ford. But his preaching from the stage clearly rubbed some of the audience the wrong way. He had the car parked out back of a Kmart and one night while he was away playing, someone torched it. He lost everything. Some friends let him live in a broken van that was parked out behind a body shop, so he stayed there for a while.

In 1979, Joe Walsh reached out to his old friend. "He invited Glenn along for a couple legs of the Eagles' tour as they promoted their *Long Run* album," Butch Armstrong told me.

This picture [image 49] was taken at that time. A friend of Bill Jeric's took the photo and Bill said, "The picture was right after *The Long Run* album came out. Glenn and I went to Cincinnati to watch the Eagles' gig and then flew with them in a Lear jet to Indiana for another gig. We had chairs at the end of the stage. The picture was taken in a Cincinnati motel room."[11]

Image 49: Three early James Gang guitarists in 1979: Bill Jeric, Joe Walsh and Glenn Schwartz.

Butch told me, "Joe also surprised Glenn with a 1965 Gibson Riviera guitar, which Glenn immediately decorated with a black Sharpie pen, writing Bible verses all over the front and back."

A couple years later, Butch got a phone call from Glenn. "He said, 'Butch, I gotta sell my Riviera!' I was shocked! He loved that guitar, loved Joe Walsh and he was so grateful for the gift. I asked him why he was selling it but he wouldn't say."

"I'm going to sell it now, for $75," Glenn said.

"Seventy-five dollars?! Glenn, don't do that. It's a gift from Joe."

"I'm selling it and if you want it for $75, come over now," and Glenn hung up the phone.

Butch hurried over, curious as to why Glenn was so adamant about selling the guitar so quickly and so cheaply. When he arrived, Glenn was in the front yard, waiting for him, pacing back and forth.

"You have the $75?"

"Yes, but Glenn, please—"

Glenn cut him off. "If I don't sell it to you, I'll sell it to someone else."

Butch handed over the money and Glenn passed him the guitar, then asked for a ride to a local print shop. Once they arrived, Glenn jumped out of the car and hurried into the store.

"Once we were inside, Glenn handed over the cash I had given him and before the guy behind the counter could count it, Glenn grabbed the box from him and pried the lid off," Butch said. "I looked over his shoulder and couldn't believe what he had purchased."

Inside the box was a stack of 8 ½ by 11-inch flyers, hundreds of them. Each one had the same scripture printed on it in bold, black letters:

For what shall it profit a man,
if he shall gain the whole world,
and lose his own soul?
Mark 8:36

"I was stunned," Butch said to me. "I told him, 'Glenn, I would have loaned you the money, you didn't need to sell the guitar.'

"But he just shook his head, embraced the box of flyers to his chest like it was found treasure. He looked me in the eyes and said, 'I'm going to put one of these on every telephone pole in Cleveland!'"

Bob Tidd finally left Fortney Road on August 5, 1979, a few months after Glenn's departure. "So many of my friends had left that I figured they couldn't all be wrong, they couldn't all be deceived. That was when I confronted Diane and told her that I knew that she was sexually intimate with Larry. And of course, I had heard so many other things.

"When I left I called Larry from the cheese factory where I worked part time. Larry yelled into the phone, 'You have the spirit of Judas on you! God told me a year ago that you would leave and now it's that time!'"

Bob told me, "It took me about six months to finally go to a church service after I got out. When I heard some good, basic

Christian teaching, I began to understand about God's love, and it broke through. It just made sense to me."

Because so many members of the community and band had left Fortney Road by 1979, the All Saved Freak Band no longer existed. Their famous guitarist had departed along with many of the vocalists, songwriters and other musicians.

But Larry had some never-released songs that had been recorded between 1970 and 1974. And since the public at large hadn't had any music from the All Saved Freak Band since 1976's *Brainwashed,* he thought he'd test the waters and release a new album to see what type of interest—if any—it generated.

Chapter 33

Sower

The final All Saved Freak Band album, *Sower*, was released in 1980. Previously, the All Saved Freak Band albums had been released under the band's own label, Rock the World Enterprises, but now Larry claimed to have had a message from God, and as a result changed the name of his record label. It was now ominously called "War Again."

According to Larry:

> In 1975 the Holy Spirit said, "Take Starr, your State Champion Mare, to be bred to Hirzan. The result of that breeding shall be a Palomino stallion foal. You shall name him War Again for he and his name shall be a prophetic sign of the war coming to America."[20]

One thing that remained constant was Larry repeating his fable about Jimi Hendrix and Glenn Schwartz. On the back of the *Sower* album, he wrote, "Jimi Hendrix wanted the best. That's why he asked Glenn Schwartz to play for him at what turned out to be his last birthday party."[20] Larry goes on to write about Glenn's time in PG&E and the James Gang and his previous, high-prolife life in the music business. For those who didn't know better, it reads as if Glenn Schwartz is still an active part of the band.[20]

The album concludes with producer Rob Galbraith's earthy and earnest rendition of "Old Rugged Cross," recorded back in 1972. Though Rob wasn't even aware of the album's release, he, Larry Hill, and Joe Markko share production credits, even though Joe and his family had severed ties with the community in 1979.

241

Looking over the tracks on the album, Joe said, "'Children of the Day' was written in 1969, and the balance of the songs for *Sower* were written between 1970–74."

Band members credited on the album are Larry Hill (vocals, keyboards), Joe Markko (vocals), Kim Massmann (vocals, acoustic guitar, strings), Pam Massmann (vocals, strings), Ed Durkos (rhythm guitar), Tim Hill (percussion), Tom Eritano (drums, percussion), Carole King (keyboards), Norris McClure (bass), and Glenn Schwartz (lead guitar).

Although *Sower* could have been nothing more than an album of leftovers or outtakes, Larry put all of his prophetic promotional zeal behind it, stating in the liner notes:

> *Sower* is a divine announcement! America has crossed the line and must pass through the refining fires of chastisement! That is not a prediction, it is a prophecy! It is likely that a devastating war on America will shatter the security of the masses so strongly that the Antichrist will be able to rise up to world prominence and find world-wide acceptance of his "policy" even as Hitler did in Germany after the first World War.[20]

The liner notes conclude with Larry announcing the creation of a Jesus Music Fellowship:

> This fellowship will form a platform of ministry for Christians on every level. This fellowship will be open to Jesus Musicians, Disc Jockeys, Producers, Engineers, Composers and members of the listening audience. The fellowship was created in response to a growing burden brought about by the influx of mail to the All Saved Freak Band, [which] is preparing to minister to the obvious hunger for spiritual things in the Jesus Community worldwide. [20]

Since the All Saved Freak Band had disbanded years earlier and had released no music in four years, it was doubtful there had been any significant "influx" of mail. No Jesus Music Fellowship was formed.

After reacquainting himself with the liner notes after more than thirty years, Joe said to me, "What Larry wrote is pretty amazing. I love the other comment on the back cover, 'It is the belief of the present members of the All Saved Freak Band . . .'

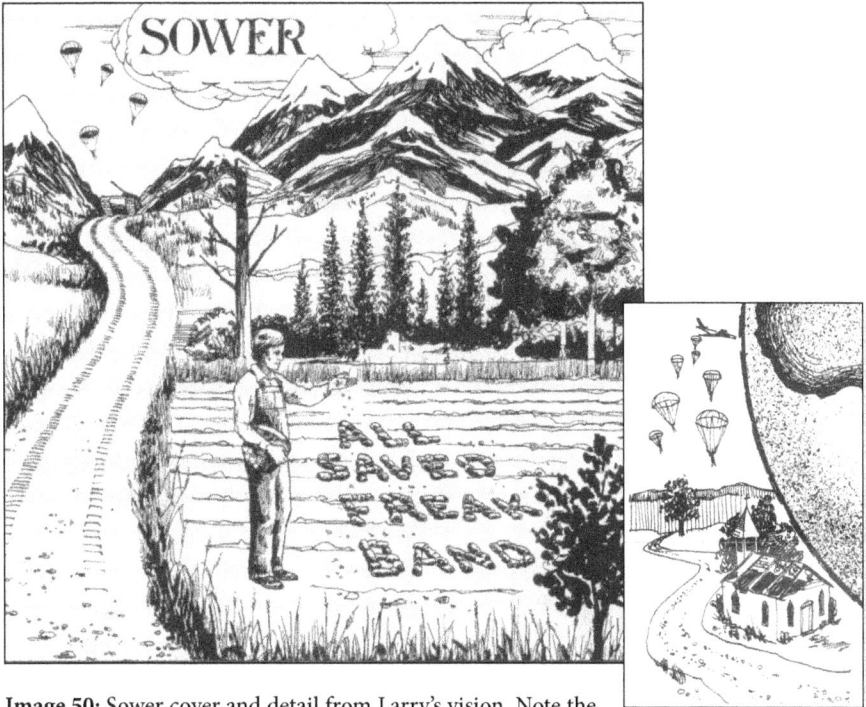

Image 50: Sower cover and detail from Larry's vision. Note the similarities between the 1980 Sower album cover and the insert, which illustrated the third of Larry's four 1965 visions.

meaning Larry, Ed and Kim and Pam Massmann. Everyone else was gone."

The black-and-white, pen-and-ink album cover for *Sower* was charming if you didn't examine it too carefully. A farmer is sowing seeds and piles of rocks spell out the band's name. Behind the farmer is a road that leads off into the horizon. And over that vista, a tank is approaching. Because there are already tracks in front of the tank, it's implied that the area has already been invaded and more vehicles are coming. Army parachutes fall from the sky. The innocent and unsuspecting farmer who is sowing seed doesn't even know he's been invaded. Some also claim to see a hammer and sickle—the symbolism for communism—in the tree on the right below the mountains.

Included in the album was an offer for "a program to encourage growth in soul winning." For $33.50, you'd receive all four All

Saved Freak Band albums, a commentary on the *Sower* album, the Skeleton tract that Larry had been using since 1968, a copy of his *Scripture Lessons for Modern Man* workbook, music and Bible seminars, access to a Larry Hill-led "Bring the Power Down!" prayer meeting held every third Friday from 9 p.m. to midnight ("Be sure to send us your prayer requests!"), and a special Soul Winning Seminar in your area if you provided the place and financial support.

Sower was released in 1980 and eventually joined *My Poor Generation* and *Brainwashed* as part of the *Top 50 Collectible Jesus Music Albums of All Time*. The All Saved Freak Band is the only group to have three albums on the list.[46]

Brainwashed had its centerpiece with "Don't Look Back" and *Sower* had one with "Prince of the International Kaleidoscope."

"Kim Massmann and Larry wrote that," Joe said. The song captured everything that made the All Saved Freak Band stand out in the musical landscape of the time. No one else was singing about Black Madonnas, the Rockefellers, the Pope, or the John Birch Society—or at least not in one almost stream-of-consciousness song.

"To be very honest, though Kim sings the words, they were things we'd been hearing about at almost every church service for years," Joe told me. "Larry was always extremely conspiracy-oriented and was constantly warning us about groups and individuals he considered false and dangerous. They sang from their orientation, trying to warn the world with what they'd been taught."

Because of the bizarre lyrical content and Larry's decision to include information about his visions, reaction to the album was mixed, with critics praising the music but bewildered by the theology.

Jon Trott of the JPUSA community and a lyricist for Resurrection Band told me, "The last All Saved Freak Band album I saw, the lyrics and liner notes struck me as quite odd, and unlike earlier albums I heard, overtly heterodox."

Mark Allan Powell wrote in the *Encyclopedia of Contemporary Christian Music*:

By the time *Sower* was released, the community had denigrated into infamy and the band was no more. Nevertheless, the album presents what critics consider to be their best work, with Joe Markko dominating the vocals and other members exercised by an apocalyptic fervor that seems to ratchet everything up a few notches.[48]

Ken Scott wrote in *Vintage Vinyl Jesus Music (1965–1980)*:

A superbly strong finish for the Freaks. The centerpiece of the album would have to be the apocalyptic "Prince Of The International Kaleidoscope," a powerful haunting minor-key acoustic-rock piece that includes cryptic references to Jesuits, the Pope, the John Birch Society and "black Madonna of the night" (the track also features what is perhaps the most convicting vocal performance on record by the Massmann sisters). Extensive end-times commentary on the back cover and sleeve, including among other things a rather bizarre prophecy they received to breed two specific horses, the resulting foal (named War Again) being a prophetic sign of the war coming to America.[35]

Bob Felberg wrote in *the Acid Archives*:

Man, these guys were just so good! Wailing away one minute, folk mood, jazz lightness the next. Seems impossible on paper, but with the All Saved Freak Band, it works. All tracks are stand-outs. Bizarre liner notes describing prophesies to mate horses.[49]

A 1980 issue of *Harmony* magazine reported that a fifth All Saved Freak Band album titled *Vow* was being recorded, but nothing with that title was ever released.

At the same time, rumors had circulated that Larry pulled together the four remaining musicians—himself, Pam and Kim Massmann and Ed Durkos—and formed a new group called The Magi (Image 51).

However, before The Magi could write any songs or record any music with Ed, Larry abruptly dissolved the foursome by kicking Ed out of the band and the church.

Ed told me that Larry had approached him one morning and told him to get dressed in some good clothes and said they were going for a ride. Ed had learned long ago not to ask any questions so he sat in the back seat while Larry and Diane were in the front.

Image 51: Pam Massmann, Kim Massmann, Ed Durkos and Larry Hill in the post-All Saved Freak Band group, The Magi.

Soon Diane pulled the car over in front of a house and Ed was surprised.

They were parked at Ed's father's house.

Puzzled by what was going on, Ed waited for instructions. Without turning around, Diane told him to get out of the car.

"What?" Ed asked, uncertain if he had heard correctly.

"Get out of the car!" Larry yelled.

Ed fumbled with the door latch and jumped out. He barely had time to get out of the way before Diane drove off.

Ed had been with the community and the All Saved Freak Band since 1973 and as more and more people left, his workload only increased. By 1980, his body was so worn out that he couldn't keep the paying job he had in town. With no money coming in from Ed, Larry felt he was useless and only a drain on the ministry.

Like an animal that was too sick and was put down, Ed Durkos was put out of his misery by being the only member ever to be personally escorted off Fortney Road by Diane Sullivan and Larry Hill.

He watched as the car drove down the street. Neither Larry nor Diane looked back.

Still dazed but elated by what had just happened, Ed hurried into his dad's house and within moments, father and son were locked in a tight embrace.

After dumping Ed off, Larry and Diane discussed the future. They knew Larry needed to be out of state for at least seven years, enough time for the statute of limitations to run out on his alleged involvement with the 1977 beating of Bethy Goodenough. It was risky for him to spend any time at all in Ohio.

They decided to move the remaining members—he, Diane, Pam and Kim, Laura and Donald—permanently to Pennsylvania. On November 20, 1981, Larry filed in Pennsylvania to establish a church under the familiar name of the Church of the Risen Christ. Ohio was listed as the domestic state and more than three decades later, the status of the filing is listed as active.

In Ohio, without a pastor or a congregation, the original Church of the Risen Christ ceased to exist. A real estate agent was contacted to rent out the Fortney Road property.

Larry wasn't sure if he would ever return.

In April 1984, a group called The Magi released a single from a proposed fall 1984 album that was to be called *Girlflower*. No *Girlflower* album was ever released and this is believed to be the only recording by The Magi.

The A-side of the single was "The Lord's Prayer (The International Affirmative)" written by Kim Massmann and Larry Hill, and the B-side was "Children Who Are Crying Inside" written and performed by Kim Massmann. The single was released under the Hopestar Productions label with a P.O. Box address in Tidioute, Pennsylvania.

Joe told me, "I have to fight my anger when I read what Larry wrote in the liner notes: 'All forms of life are tested and purged and, through the mercy of Providence, some survive to fulfill their mission, the rest die.' Larry was careful to take advantage of every opportunity he could to 'harmlessly' share his side of the story, to color all of us who left as 'damned.' Too bad people didn't know the address on the bottom of the recording jacket was the 'hideout' from prosecution for child abuse charges in Ohio.

"'The rest die.' That's a pretty stiff penalty for the crime of changing churches. All these years later he maintains his same story. It's tough to forgive someone who refuses, at every turn, to acknowledge their wrong, instead painting the rest of us as ongoing purveyors of evil."

Joe added, "And those are both songs they used to do while all of us were still there. Seems like nothing new has come out of Fortney Road for quite some time."

Chapter 34

The Nicest Person
I Had Ever Met

I n 1989, Larry Hill's mother, Thelma, died.

Tim Hill told me, "Larry called me in Arizona to tell me Grandma Hill had passed away. I went back for the funeral and it was the first time I had seen him since I ran away in 1978."

According to Tim, Larry treated the situation as if it was a family reunion and wanted to catch up on the past decade. Larry approached his son and haltingly said, "Maybe I wasn't the best father."

Tim thought his father was going to finally admit all that he had done, all that had already been made public, all that had already been reported and discussed in the local community for years. Instead, Larry finished his sentence with, ". . . I was so busy always preaching the gospel and helping drug addicts and other people."

"So he just has no idea who he really is or what he's done to so many people," Tim said.

Soon after that encounter Diane Sullivan left a message on Tim's sister Rebecca's answering machine. "Your dad wants to get hold of you and mend relationships. It's disrespectful for you to treat your father like this!"

Rebecca never returned the call.

January 1990 brought the type of attention Larry feared most.

He and the remaining members of his ministry—Diane Sullivan, Pam and Kim Massmann, Laura Markko and Donald—

were keeping a low profile in the small hamlet of Tidioute, Pennsylvania.

But in January 1990, dozens of influential residents in the small rural community—members of the clergy, real estate agents, auctioneers, teachers and school board members, public officials including mayors and heads of local governments and local council-persons, prosecuting attorneys and child warfare agents—received oversized envelopes in the mail, all postmarked Ashtabula, Ohio.

A cover letter printed on the front of the stapled pages was addressed to *Dear Western Pennsylvania Resident*: "I want to warn you about 'Reverend' Larry Hill, a one-legged man who now lives in Tidioute, PA. Formerly, Hill led a cult in Ohio."

Stapled to the letter were several photocopied 1978 newspaper stories about the Church of the Risen Christ. The residents of Tidioute read the grisly headlines and the details of the almost unbelievable story that followed:

Ex-wife of leader bares tortures
Cult cruelty probed
Ex-cult members describe 'white judge' beatings
Taught to use whip, ex-cultists say
Ex-members say brainwashing was a part of Hill's cult

The articles were filled with accounts of torture, physical and sexual abuse, brainwashing and beatings.

Cults? This brutal cult and its leader, Larry Hill, was now living in Tidioute?

Because a law enforcement officer stated in the cover letter that he had produced and distributed the material, the community took it all very seriously. Phone calls to the local police department shed no light on who had distributed the flyers. In fact, the local authorities had no knowledge of the documents and denied printing them. It turns out that the identity of the "law enforcement officer" was actually one of the former members of the cult.

"I did it," Leon admitted to me. "Once I knew where Larry had relocated, and that he was actively trying to start a church and recruit people again, I printed up the flyers. I anonymously posed as the law enforcement officer so that the information would be taken seriously."

Leon's letter seemed to work—by 1991, Larry and what was left of his flock left Pennsylvania and returned to Ohio. Fortunately for Larry, the statute of limitations had run out, allowing Larry to return to Fortney Road without risk of arrest.

However, the property—once so cared for that the women scrubbed the floorboard cracks with toothbrushes—had fallen into ruin.

Donald told me, "We were shocked when we saw the property the first time. It had become a bit of a dump. The people who had rented it—who were not associated with Larry or the church—had left it in a mess but we all tried to fix it up as best as we could."

Larry's demands for early morning exercises and following the twenty godly disciplines and late night prayer meetings all fell to the wayside after the mass exodus of the late 1970s. Donald remembers his final years at Fortney Road strictly as a time for maintaining the farm and the animals and keeping income sources steady. Ironically, it was one of Larry's own horses that helped free Donald from Fortney Road.

In the summer of 1991, Larry wanted to sell a man a horse but first Donald had to break or tame the animal so he could be easily saddled and ridden.

"It was a stubborn and strong horse and I was thrown hard from it once and suffered serious whiplash," Donald told me. "The doctor said that I was not to do any physical labor for a couple of months."

Donald made arrangements to stay with his mother while he recuperated from the injury. "She lived a few hours away so I started to spend the week with my mom and because I couldn't do any heavy physical labor, I got a desk job at the local sawmill. As I got better, I'd go to Larry's for the weekend to do what I could for the livestock. I was sort of in limbo at this time, going back and forth between my mom's house and Larry and the farm. Five days with her, the weekend with Larry."

One day an Amish fellow Donald worked with said he had a sister and he wanted Donald to meet her. She had formerly been Amish but she had left the sect, a process called "yanking over." Her name was Brenda and she had left the Amish sect to become a born-again Christian. While the Amish believe that one can only "hope" to be saved and enter heaven upon death, a born-again

Christian believes that by putting one's faith in Jesus Christ, he or she is certain to enter heaven, no questions asked.

Because Donald had spent almost twenty years with Larry near the Amish communities in Ohio and Pennsylvania, he felt that if he ever married, his ideal mate would be an "ex-Amish" woman, so Brenda sounded ideal.

Without telling Larry what he was doing, at the end of October 1991, Donald and Brenda had their first date. They immediately clicked.

Over dinner at the Spaghetti Factory, Brenda (not her real name) told me she innocently asked Donald, "Where do you go to church?"

"In Windsor. It's a small church, only about eight people," Donald answered.

"Who's the pastor?" Brenda asked. It was a small town and she knew most of the churches and leaders.

"Larry Hill is—" Donald started to say.

"Larry Hill!" Brenda cried, almost choking on her food. "You're in a cult?!"

Donald was startled by her reaction. He tried to stammer out an explanation. Visibly shaken, Brenda quickly excused herself before Donald could say anything. Brenda went to use the public phone and called her best friend Marie, who confirmed what all the Amish families knew: stay away from Larry Hill and keep your children from him.

Over the phone, Marie quieted Brenda down, telling her that her brother knew and trusted Donald or he never would have suggested they meet in the first place. Brenda returned to the table and Donald was relieved to see she appeared to be more relaxed. She changed the subject and they finished the evening with no more discussions of religion, churches, or cults.

When it came time for a second date, Brenda said yes, but Donald had no idea of the angst she had been through since their first meeting. "I knew that I shouldn't go out with him again because he was involved in Larry's cult," she said to me. "But I also felt compelled to see him again, almost like a calling or something. Perhaps God would use me to help Donald get free, so I agreed to another date."

A second date led to a third and it was then that Brenda brought up Larry's church again. "I asked Donald, 'Would you want me to attend your church?' and that one question seemed to turn on some very bright lights in his heart and mind.

Donald told me, "Her question caught me off guard, which of course was key. And even though I was loyal to Larry all those years, it was an eye-opening question. Would I want Brenda to be part of what I had experienced? What Diane, Pam, Laura, and Kim were experiencing? Would I want Brenda to be part of that? No. No, of course not! And I told her so. I would not want her to attend Church of the Risen Christ! And I would not want her to live at Fortney Road."

That night, Donald didn't sleep well.

"It was like God brought to my remembrance twenty years' worth of images from my time with Larry Hill. Horrible, awful things that I had done, had been done to me, or I had seen done to others or had heard about. And then all of my excuses played over and over in my head, all the futile reasons as to why I had done some of the things I had done."

Saturday morning, after an anxious and restless night, Donald drove to Fortney Road from his mother's house.

"I remember that there was a big picture window in the front of the farmhouse and when I pulled into the driveway, no one was there. There was no one around, but then I saw Pam Massmann coming around from the back of the house. I went over to her and sort of blurted out, 'I've prayed about it and what we're involved with here is a cult!'

"Pam looked shocked at what I said and she was literally speechless. But I wasn't there for a reaction or discussion. I quickly grabbed the few things I had and left. And I never had to see or speak to Larry Hill again."

A couple days later, Larry and Diane paid a visit to Donald's boss and his wife, telling them stories about Donald in an attempt to defame him. "Of course, my boss and his wife had known me for years and didn't believe a word Larry or Diane told them," Donald said.

In November 1991, Donald left Larry Hill and the Church of the Risen Christ. He had been a member since September 1972.

Soon after, Donald married Brenda, the woman who had helped yank him over from darkness to light.

While Larry and the few that remained with him tried to re-establish themselves on Fortney Road, Leon remained relentless in monitoring Larry's whereabouts and activities.

"I happened to make the acquaintance of a female private investigator. I told her about my experiences with Larry's church, something at that time that I rarely did with anyone. She and I began planning an operation to investigate Larry's current activities."

The detective's daughter happened to have recently given up her horse, so the investigator, playing the role of a mother looking for another horse for her daughter, knocked on the farmhouse door and asked to see Larry, expressing her interest in buying a Morgan horse.

Larry cheerfully obliged and led her to a corral to show her a few horses that he would be willing to sell. She began talking with Larry about her life and how she recently lost her father to cancer. Without missing a beat, Larry told her how he understood, because he had lost his right leg to cancer.

"By his own account, Larry told us repeatedly that he lost his leg in a car accident," Leon said.

The detective was successful in gaining Larry's confidence and she was invited to church services at the farm. "After she attended several weeks of services, we concluded that there were only six people living at the farm," Leon told me, "and only a few living outside the farm that attended the services, which did not include any children. With this information in hand, I was satisfied that no other children were being victimized."

For those who believe they could not be fooled by someone like Larry Hill—myself included—the detective's final analysis of her investigation was chilling.

Leon said, "She told me, 'If I had not known you, Leon, and understood your story, I would have thought I had met the nicest person I had ever met in my life.'"

Now only Larry, Diane, Kim, Pam and Laura Markko remained at the farm. In 1999, they had a visitor from their past. Carole King Hough and her husband Mike were in Ohio for a wedding. They decided to drive down Fortney Road.

Chapter 35

Loose Ends

"The place was very shabby looking," Carole remembered, "like it was deserted. In my mind I remember all the flowers I planted in the front yard and how hard the guys worked on the fence. The whole place was not the same."

Larry's lost his free labor, she thought. And then she saw him. Reverend Larry Hill, now sixty-five, came out onto the front porch.

With the car still moving and before she lost her courage, Carole jumped out and quickly approached him. "How are you doing?" Carole asked.

"Fine . . ." Larry spoke hesitantly. He had shielded his eyes against the afternoon sun to get a better look at her. She could tell he was trying to figure out who she was—he hadn't seen her since she left in 1977—and then all at once he recognized her.

Larry started to ask about her family—her brothers John and Morgan, and her parents, one after the other as if it was a normal conversation, two chance encounters by old friends with more than twenty years of catching up to do.

"After he asked all his questions, I noticed that he started to repeat himself," Carole said. "He just kept asking me over and over what was I doing there, what was I doing there."

She kept telling him they had been at a wedding.

"But it was his old paranoia kicking in. What he really wanted to know was what I was up to. Who was I working for? Who assigned me to spy on him?"

Carole looked past Larry and saw a woman walking toward the barn.

It was Kim Massmann.

"She looked to be in a bad way, walking stiffly and even from a distance, I could see there was something that wasn't healthy about her. Something wasn't right."

Carole called out a greeting and Kim looked up. "Carole?" Kim asked. Carole nodded and waited for Kim to come be a part of the conversation. Instead, Kim put her head back down and continued toward the barn.

Larry invited them to come in—the perfect host—but they declined and returned to their car. They sat there talking for a few minutes and watched as Larry got into his car and backed out of the driveway.

"I was surprised to see Larry driving alone because he never went anywhere by himself, always afraid someone was going to kidnap him or kill him."

Mike started the car and they pulled onto the road behind Larry. "I realized then that he probably thought we were following him," Carole said. "And sure enough, he kept putting his foot on the brake, checking us out in his rearview mirror. I know we were totally freaking him out."

They sped up and passed Larry without looking at him.

"Mike was in awe that I would stop and talk to Larry like that," Carole said. "Actually, so was I! But like I've always said, I'm Miss Spontaneous! It was destiny calling me, I guess. I don't know why I wanted to do it, to bring closure perhaps. Of course, there will never be closure."

But there was something better than closure.

Freedom.

"Yes," Carole said. "Suddenly, I knew I was free. Larry no longer had any power over me. It was finished. God set me free. I'm not the same person I used to be. Yes, I did forgive Larry and anyone associated with Fortney Road. Forgiveness is where it's at! I totally got rid of all the fear left over from Larry."

In the May 19, 1999, issue of the Ohio *Valley News*, there was an article about a mare giving birth to twin foals. The story stated:

Twin foals were born Monday morning to a Belgian mare at CRC farm. Dee Dee Sullivan, owner of the Fortney Road farm in Windsor Township, said the breeding was part of an experiment she and her husband set out to accomplish. The two were trying to raise a better breed of show jumper, and bred the Belgian mare with a Registered Morgan stallion. Sullivan said the twins are doing really well. She said she has to check on them every two hours to make sure they are eating, but so far they have been eating and doing great.

The foals were named Fred Astaire and Ginger Rogers.[50]

Tim Hill said, "In 2000, my Mom worked at the country clerk's in Ashtabula County and she got a call from a woman requesting a marriage certificate. My mom recognized the woman's voice immediately—it was Diane Sullivan. Diane said, 'I have to have a certified copy of the divorce decree from my fiancé's former wife.' My mom told her, 'I'll leave all of the notarized paperwork on the desk downstairs.'"

According to Tim, his mom printed out the copies, put her stamp on it and signed her first, middle and maiden name in big, easy-to-read letters. And she attached a note: "You can have him!"

On March 18, 2000, Diane Sullivan married Larry Hill after living with him for decades.

A local reporter told me, "Yes I know he married Diane after years of fornication with her in the cot beside his son's Mark's bed at the farm. Then he only married her when he had prostate troubles. But Laura Markko lives with them. Go figure that arrangement."

Of Diane's three siblings, only one attended the ceremony, accompanying her parents. The three of them arrived just before the ceremony began and left immediately after. None of Diane's family members took any pictures to commemorate the day. The sister who attended said, "We didn't care. We didn't care to remember the moment so we didn't even bother to bring a camera."

Larry Hill has never been allowed into any of their homes.

In May 2000, Richard Acevedo had obtained the rights from Joe to release CDs of the All Saved Freak Band's music on his Hidden

Vision label. He contacted Kim Massmann at Fortney Road to see if she had any photos of the band, and she responded:

> As far as old band pictures—this will take me some time to locate, then make some more copies so bear with me, I won't forget. I just wanted to tell you that I felt very encouraged after all these years hearing that our music was a blessing to you! It has always been worth doing and three of us have continued in our Christian walk. This coming September I will have been saved 29 years.
>
> We are all still inspired from Jesus to write numerous songs. We have enough material to do a lot more albums. Our next album is either going to be called *Closing of the Gentile Age* or *The 4 Horsemen*. It is dealing with prophecy, etc.
> Love in Christ,
> Kim

Five weeks letter, Richard received a letter from Larry Hill:

> Dear Brother,
> I write this letter as we travel on our weekly mission to teach God's word in a New York state prison. The round trip from Ohio is approximately nine hours. Please excuse the unclear writing— as Barry McGuire once said, "When you're reading in a bus, you read the same word seven times."
> Concerning your effort there, I have the question of what your purposes and goals are.
> Thank you,
> Larry Hill

When I asked Richard what happened after he received Larry's letter, he said, "They never sent out any photos. When Larry found out I had released the ASFB on CD, he closed me down." No new music by Larry, Kim and Pam was ever released.

Pam Massmann eventually moved off the property but still attends church services. Pam's sister Kim remains at Fortney Road with Larry and Diane, as does Joe's sister, Laura.

In April 2013, Pam and Kim's brother, Mark reached out to me when he heard about this book:

My name is Mark Massmann, a brother of Pam and Kim Massmann who were part of the All Saved Freak Band. I still to this day have no idea of the sinister events that happened on that farm, and happened to my sisters, who are still under Larry's iron grip some 30 years later! I'd like to finally know the truth about it. Who knows? I still may be able to reach my sisters, whom I love dearly and who need to leave the farm and make albums on their own!!

I really wish to know about some of the abuse they and others were exposed to, which has kept them imprisoned by Larry to this day. Please help me understand why they refuse to leave!! Do you know much about Larry Hill? What is your opinion of him and should he have been jailed for child abuse (or other) charges?

After sending Mark some chapters about his sisters, he wrote back:

I am in shock of what my sisters have gone through with Larry's group. I need some time to think about this before talking with you. Can I let you know when I'm ready to talk?
Thanks, Mark

Before we were able to speak, Mark Massmann, 49, died in a motorcycle accident on October 5, 2013.

Larry Hill continues to deny any allegations of abuse.

When questioned about Diane Sullivan's 1978 conviction, Larry said, "She never hurt anyone and children fought to be with her. It was not a cult. We were helping kids come off drugs."[51]

In October 2006, Larry's second-oldest son Mark wrote to Joe about his Aunt Claudine and his father:

I spoke with my dear Aunt Claudine tonight. She's 83 with 83-year-old health problems but what a broad! I have the utmost and profound respect for her. Fourteen years Dad's senior, they've never gotten along. The reasons are obvious. She's respectable, loving, disciplined, classy and, ah—did I say loving!! LOL. Opposite of her devilish brother.

I am convinced that the angels of darkness speak to Dad, giving him the appearance of an angel of light. Wouldn't surprise me a bit if he worships the occult.

In September 2011, the Ashtabula County Treasurer filed a civil foreclosure action against the Church of the Risen Christ in the amount of $9,518.37. The church likely missed a real estate tax payment and a lien was placed on the property by the county to collect it, but the reduced amount due—$1,191.96—was paid in December 2011, and the lien dismissed.

The summons had been sent to Larry Hill, Diane Sullivan-Hill and Laura Markko, who all resided at 8179 Fortney Road.

Epilogue

A Light from
the Shadows

Thanks to you all for starting it, the end of it. I
heard all kinds of stories.
When you are ready I sure would like to know what
you have to tell.
What are the kids and you up to now days? If ever
you get to Atlanta, come on down.
Come in the summer. We can swim.

> —*Statement by a former member of Larry Hill's Church of the
> Risen Christ*

I n May 2006, the for-
mer members of the
Church of the Risen
Christ and the All Saved Freak
Band and their spouses and
friends gathered together for a
reunion in Lynchburg, Virginia.
Many of them had not seen
one another or been in contact
since they had left Fortney Road
twenty-five to thirty years earlier.

Image 52: Some former members
of the Church of the Risen Christ
and All Saved Freak Band and their
spouses and friends at a reunion in
2006. Photo courtesy of Joe Markko.

Joe said, "The first reunion required a profound amount of
courage to tell some of the stories. It also required courage to
listen. There were many sobering moments but also much reflection, much joy."

When I asked for an update after the former members' last reunion, I received the following:

Joe Markko has recorded two albums and written eight books since leaving Fortney Road in 1978. He and Sandy divorced and Joe has remarried. He also served as pastor with the Assemblies of God for a decade. He is now retired, a grandfather of ten and lives with his wife near Cleveland.

Bethy Goodenough said of the 2006 reunion, "Thanks to all of you who made my visit to Virginia a blessed experience. I spent most of the time taking everything in and trying to fill in the voids. Honestly, I didn't know I had as many voids as I did! I want to help people who read this book understand that even though we have been through these things, with God's help, we have become stronger people. I'm sure there are people from those days who can give a more accurate story of what happened, but for now what's in this book is the version that an abused, broken-spirited eleven-year-old girl remembers."

Morgan King was one of the first to escape from the farm in 1975 and he went on to help more than a dozen people leave. Married for more than thirty years, he and his wife have two adult children and live in Tennessee. Morgan works in television and real estate. His wife, Linda, is an RN specializing in pediatrics.

Carole King Hough married Mike Hough soon after she left the farm in November 1977. Today Carole continues to write music and sing for her own enjoyment. She and her husband live in Georgia. She lost track of **Millie Romanchik** and her friend **Anne** over the years.

Every one of Larry Hill's children have profoundly painful issues they continue to deal with and have shared unbelievable stories of abuse. Tim Hill is the only family member who agreed to be interviewed and quoted for this book.

Tim Hill is married with children and lives on the West Coast. "For the most part since leaving Dad's, I have put my childhood in a box, locked it and thrown away the key. A lot of the stuff has come back out of the box this year after reading the All Saved Freak Band website and this book. I don't know if the book will matter to the public but it made me cry and made me angry like I haven't been in a long time.

"When I left Fortney Road, I was determined not to ruin the rest of my life but instead press on with three desires: to have a good life, have a great family, and to make a difference rather than be a detriment. I've been extremely lucky. It's worked out as good as any other life except that I always have this little additional monkey that I am carrying around.

"Because I have children, I have had to tell them that their grandfather is a bad man. I've had to warn the schools they have attended to never allow Larry near my children, and if Larry ever shows up, they are not to get close to him. The amount of pain and destruction that Larry has caused in his immediate family is more than any former member can probably comprehend."

When it comes to religion, Tim said, "I can spend only about fifteen minutes in a Protestant church before I want to throw up. My wife is Catholic so that's where I go, to a Catholic church. I don't get a lot out of it but I believe in Jesus, know He died for me, the basics.

"For a while, I can get away with telling most people that my dad lives back east, but when I was dating my now-wife, at one point I finally said, 'Okay, there are some things you need to know.'"

In February 2007 at the age of 46 **Mark Hill** died suddenly after a long illness. Since the family didn't want Larry to know, no obituary was posted in the *Ashtabula Star Beacon*.

Many of the people Mark knew while at Fortney Road reached out to him during what proved to be his last Christmas. When friends spoke to him during the first week of January, he could not get over the fact that so many remembered him with such fondness. He received cards, letters and simple gifts, and was said to be overjoyed by the love shown him, perhaps the last spot of joy he experienced.

Joe said, "I find some consolation that, in what proved to be the final year of his broken life, Mark was reintroduced to those of us who had left Fortney Road, the only group of people on the planet who could understand his pain. He did not die alone or abandoned. He knew there was a group of people who loved him."

Those who had lived with Mark at Fortney Road sent their condolences:

> So sorry to hear about Mark. He was one of the good memories from my time at the farm. Always friendly, kind and understanding in a way that was so much beyond his years.

> How in the heck can I not be angry about this? It has taken me years to get through the mess with the church and I still think about the woman, children and men that Larry ruined in so many ways. I remember after I left the church talking to Mark and listening to how he felt about everything, he had so many issues about his Dad back then. How sad.

> I will miss him so much! I am glad that I did get a chance to talk to him since our experience on the farm and I had the chance to tell him that I loved him . . .

> I'm so thankful we were able to reach out to him and let him know he was not forgotten.

Mark's remaining siblings and their families returned to Ohio for the burial of their brother. Tim said, "While I was up there I had to drive to Fortney Road. I had to. It was like, 'Did any of this stuff really happen?' And then I saw the place."

Daryl Pitts met and married Connie two years after leaving Fortney Road in 1978. Daryl had been the Counseling and Recovery Pastor of Thomas Road Baptist Church since 2000, and a professor at Liberty University since 2001. "I hope those who read our story are first of all warned and secondly can understand the difference between the real and the counterfeit." Daryl and Connie have been heavily involved in adoption homes and agencies in several states, and have two adopted sons.

Daryl passed away on Thursday, August 5, 2010.

Norris McClure played bass on three of the four All Saved Freak Band albums, picking up when Morgan left Fortney Road. He and

Daryl left the farm in May of 1978. Norris and his family live in Ohio and are faithful participants in their local church fellowship.

Joan Dolch Marks never lived at Fortney Road and when she left the Kent New Generation Church in 1973 she told me she felt as if she "fell away from the Lord . . . I am telling you, you just have no idea how disturbed I was for years about the church and all. It was never a closed chapter for me." Today Joan is married and has been a secretary in the medical field for more than fourteen years. She has three grown children, a stepdaughter and seven grandchildren.

Bob Tidd eventually found a home with a fellowship of believers in Indiana after leaving Fortney Road in August 1979. For more than twenty years he has been serving as a missionary, working among the poor in Guatemala, Argentina, and the Dominican Republic. All on-line funds raised from the sale of All Saved Freak Band music (AllSavedFreakBand.com) go to support Bob's ministry.

Ben and Ruth (not their real names) knew one another before they joined the community in 1972. They eventually married at the farm in 1979 but left a few months later. Ben told me, "When we have spoken to people about the atrocities that happened on Fortney Road, they could not understand why or how we would stay. Now, having the whole story told, I believe it will reveal the true desire of everyone's heart. We were there to give God our all."

"I think that our 2006 reunion had a profound effect on many of us," Ruth said to me. "All of us are at different levels in our healing process. I found that I wasn't as whole as I had thought, so I've got some work to do."

Today, Ben and Ruth live in Tennessee and their entire family is involved in their thriving home construction business while maintaining a small farm where their children raise horses.

Leon (not his real name) left Fortney Road in June 1977 and was one of several members instrumental in alerting the FBI and local authorities as to what was occurring on the farm. Today Leon is married and the owner of a successful graphics and print shop, and an official with Cult Information Services of Northeast Ohio.

After they left Fortney Road in 1977, **Jack and Margo** (not their real names) eventually divorced.

Jack remarried and lives in California. He is actively involved in his home church and works as a financial planner. Margo is single and lives on the West Coast where she is an editor in Christian print media.

Donald (not his real name) was the last male to leave the farm and was one of two men Larry made responsible for executing his disciplines. He and his wife **Brenda** (not her real name) live in Ohio with their two children and they are actively involved in a local church.

Peter and Janice (not their real names) met at Fortney Road and married. While many marriages didn't survive, they have built a strong family with six children. Peter has been a union carpenter for twenty-five years while Janice home-schooled their children until it was time for their higher education.

Mike and Carol Berkey lived at Fortney Road from 1972 to 1978. They divorced a short time after they left. Mike served as the All Saved Freak Band's soundman and came on stage to perform with his acoustic guitar while the band backed him up.

In 2003, Mike released a CD appropriately titled *Let Go*. It consists of 11 tracks he wrote between 1973 and 1980 and recorded "in a room about the size of a clothes closet using one mic and a cheap cassette recorder. If anyone is encouraged by these tracks, then I am a happy camper. Thanks to all those who have encouraged me."

Ed Durkos left Fortney Road in 1980 and lives in central Ohio, working for an electronics firm. He had not been in touch with any of the former members until the spring of 2007 and said he has not picked up a guitar for twenty-five years.

"It's taking me a little while to absorb what is going on with all the brothers and sisters I used to know so well. I guess after we parted, I never thought I would ever see or hear from any of you again. Then, suddenly, as if in a dream, everyone is here again. Maybe that's the feeling we all had, after we left, a feeling that everything was all over."

Glenn Schwartz left Fortney Road in 1979 and now usually lives with his brother, Gene, and together they play occasionally as the Schwartz Brothers around the Cleveland area, and Glenn also plays with other pick-up bands. His son Bob often plays drums with his dad and uncle. "We get along okay," Bob told me. "I have no bad feelings toward him. He's more laid back now, too, and while he still preaches, he's not as judgmental or harsh as he used to be when he first left the farm."

Glenn and his ex-wife Marlene are also friendly. Bob said, "She goes to his shows sometimes and when he sees her from the stage, he still introduces her as his wife, and will tell the crowd, 'My wife is here tonight!'"

Bob told me, "When Joe Walsh is in town, he usually comes by to see Dad and my uncle Gene at the house. When I've seen Joe in concert, I'm able to get backstage when the stage manager lets Joe know that Glenn Schwartz's son is here. Joe's always been really friendly toward my family and my dad."

In 2005, Joe Walsh reunited with the James Gang and they were scheduled to play at Peabody's Downunder. When Joe showed up in Cleveland for a private rehearsal, Butch Armstrong told me he got the call that Joe needed some equipment.

"I'd met Joe before and brought along what he needed, and then I handed him the 1965 Gibson Riviera he'd given Glenn back in 1979."

Joe Walsh's eyes looked closely at the guitar. "Is this—?"

Butch laughed, "Yep, that's the one you gave to Glenn."

Joe looked it over and noticed all the Bible verses and Christian stickers plastered all over the guitar.

He grinned and said, "Yep, that's our Glenn!"

In June 2007, Joe Markko told me, "So I'm standing on the sidewalk, looking in the side door of Hoopples they kept open for ventilation, waiting for Glenn to finish his last song. The cramped, ten-foot section given for the band to set up is just inside the door so Glenn is only about that distance from me. He ends his set and steps outside with me, his guitar still plugged in. After greetings he starts to play All Saved Freak Band songs! He just starts playing "Sower," then "Beautiful Morning" and he asks me, 'What were those words again?' So I start to sing with him. After a few minutes, I'm not certain how long, I looked up and there are people standing inside the door, listening to us under the streetlight. It was beautifully surreal. And I saw him laugh last night, too. I had given him the sections of your manuscript that were about him and he had nice things to say. It's proven a positive experience for him and for that I thank you."

On October 23, 2008, David Byrne, founding member of Talking Heads, posted on his Web site:

> "I was tipped via an email sent by a man named Tim Rossiter to my office. Tim wrote: 'I've got to tell you about a special Cleveland treasure, Glenn Schwartz. Glenn started the James Gang in the 60s, then moved to California and was in the Pacific Gas & Electric Co. He flipped out soon afterward and was in religious communities. Now Glenn plays in a blues trio and he is jaw-droppingly amazing to see.'
>
> "Well, Tim didn't exaggerate. Sure enough, between amazing and inventive Hendrix-like solos, he would admonish the audience and prophesize 'blood on the moon and War in America.' He may have lost his mind but his fingers are firing on all cylinders."

Ohio-based guitarist Frankie Starr was 12-years-old when he first saw Glenn Schwartz play in 1982. "He actually took a liking to me and would come over to my house and showed me some things on the guitar," Frankie told me. "He wouldn't necessarily teach, he was more watch and learn and pick up what you can."

Frankie recently spoke to Glenn. "He was so happy to see me, we talked all night until daylight. We reminisced about everywhere he's played and all of his experiences. He taught me so much when I was young and made such an impression on me that I think of him often when I play."

Glenn doesn't talk much about his time at Fortney Road. Frankie said, "He calls it 'the Farm,' refers to Larry as 'the Dark Man,' and I know from what he shared with me that it was not a message of God's love that he got there."

Joe Markko said, "Glenn was always such a good man with such a gentle, tender heart. I think if Glenn had never encountered Larry Hill, he would have made music that could have really influenced his entire generation."[10]

Kim Massmann and **Laura Markko** still reside at Fortney Road.

Pam Massmann lives nearby and regularly attends Reverend Hill's services.

Larry Hill still lives at Fortney Road with his wife, **Diane Sullivan-Hill.**

Afterword

Oz the Great
and Powerful

For years we've all sort of been embarrassed and shamed by our experiences, like we were wearing scarlet letters. But I realized today, being with everyone and seeing how well we are all doing . . . in reality we are all wearing red badges of courage.

—*Statement by a former member of Larry Hill's Church of the Risen Christ at the August 2007 reunion*

A t Joe Markko's invitation, in August 2007, I attended the second reunion of those who had lived at Fortney Road. It was held at Meadow Ridge, a beautiful outdoor event and catering facility in Windsor, Ohio, about fifteen minutes from the farm.

Joe told me, "We'll have the entire 135 acres to ourselves. Ought to be memorable. Wait 'til you hear the stories."

About a dozen had gathered in May of the previous year, which was the first time many of them had seen one another since leaving Fortney Road. For this second gathering, more than forty adults, teenagers, and children came from Georgia, Tennessee, Virginia, California, Indiana, and towns throughout Ohio.

To have so many more make the trip said much about the healing process that had possibly occurred as a result of the previous reunion—plus the curiosity factor. Some attendees told me that they had come to "test the waters," to see one another again, to talk about what had happened, and to see if some of their memories and nightmares would be laid to rest. Over and over I was told, "It's hard to believe it happened. It doesn't seem real. Even when I see everyone here, it still seems like a horrible dream."

They hoped that by meeting face to face—for the first or second time in so many years— they could try to make some kind of sense out of what had happened to them at Fortney Road.

One woman said to me, "It's weird because once I left, I had no more contact with anyone, and so I never knew anything about what had happened to anyone. My husband and I just fled for our lives."

Another former member said, "Seeing everyone now, it feels like we're this small group of survivors who share something that no one else understands. It must be what prisoners of war feel like."

At the time of the reunion, I had already spoken on the phone with Joe and several other survivors, but hadn't met any of them in person. Once word got around that I was intending to write an article—and then a book—about Larry Hill, the Church of the Risen Christ, and the All Saved Freak Band, a few of them read early rough drafts of sections and offered corrections and clarifications. As the project grew in scope, many decided to come forward publicly for the first time while others wanted to share their stories but remain anonymous.

I stayed at the same hotel where Margo and Bethy Goodenough were and Saturday morning, August 11, I met them for the first time. Margo drove the three of us to Meadow Ridge and we talked easily in the car, they very matter-of-factly discussing the book I was writing.

Margo surprised me by wanting to visit Fortney Road right then and there.

"It's on the way," she said casually and I wondered how Bethy felt about making the trip, but she seemed fine with the idea. Neither had been back to the farm since they had left in the late 1970s.

We passed the sign for the township of Windsor, and Bethy and Margo made subdued comments about the growth of the area but also remarked that much had not changed over the years. I wondered how they felt, if they were apprehensive or fearful but both women seemed somewhat distracted from whatever they were about to encounter. Maybe because for so many decades they had both tried to shut out the experience of Fortney Road, it was impossible for it to impact them emotionally. That box of memories was tied down and locked securely.

We made a right turn onto Fortney Road and slowly passed a number of homes. Then Margo and Bethy realized they had gone too far.

We had passed right by the house and barn.

Margo had to turn around on the one-lane dirt road and backtrack. Then she slowed down in front of a house.

"Is that it?" one of them asked. "Yeah" was the uncertain answer. Then more assuredly, "Yes, that's it." A woman wearing a baseball cap and sweatpants and T-shirt was mowing the lawn. Two women were chatting on the front steps with a heavyset man. They all glanced at us when we drove by but didn't appear to have much interest.

"Who were those people?" I asked, but Margo didn't know. Bethy thought one of the women was Kim Massmann but couldn't be certain.

Because neither had reacted, I had to ask. "How did it feel driving by the house?" "It's gotten old," Bethy said. "Sort of run down." Margo agreed. That was their only response. Within twenty minutes we had arrived at the reunion site.

At the venue, we found an assortment of picnic foods and drinks set up in a shaded area along with a cake inscribed with words from Philippians 3:13: *"This one thing I do, forgetting what lies behind me and straining toward what is ahead."*

Throughout the day, as each car arrived, heads would turn to see who was about to join us. Joe Markko; Carole King Hough and her husband, Mike; her brother Morgan and his wife and children; Leon and his new bride; Margo's ex-husband, Jack, and his wife; Ben and Ruth and their children; Daryl and Connie Pitts; Donald and his wife, Brenda; Ed Durkos, and many more. Bob Tidd, Glenn Schwartz, and Tim Hill were not able to make the reunion but sent written greetings that were passed around.

By that time I'd compiled an annotated, 578-page manuscript that Leon had copied and given the others to read.

Weeks later, the remarks and corrections started to arrive.

Some people wondered why I had to be so explicit, saying, for example, *We would like our friends and family to read [your book], but not the way it is. The sexual content does not have to be relived to know that it went on.*

I later learned that, after the reunion, there had been much discussion among the former members about what and how much to tell. Some, like the person quoted above, wanted to soft-peddle the truth, while others felt exactly the opposite. One, for example, wrote in an email:

> What is wrong with all these people??? I will not help any of them protect the child molester. COWARDS!!!!! Everybody feels bad for Bethy, Mark and the children but nobody wants to inconvenience their own lives to work justice for them at last . . . Larry Hill's greatest ally has been our silence.

It's important—and was of interest to me—to note that those who objected to the explicit contents of the book did not share any of their own personal experiences of sexual abuse nor did they choose to go public with their names.

And in the midst of the opposition to tell the whole story of what occurred at Fortney Road, several former members also felt their impact on the demise of the cult was given short shift. In other words, a few members felt they alone were the reason for the final breaking apart of the community.

Each of their stories is included and it's up to the reader to determine who—if anyone—dealt the fatal blow to the Church of the Risen Christ, if it even matters.

I couldn't leave Ohio without at least attempting to speak with Larry Hill face to face. Ironically, it was one of Diane Sullivan's sisters who offered to take me to Fortney Road. I later found out that throughout the reunion, several former members of the cult had taken time out to drive by the house on Fortney Road.

Once we got in the car, Diane's sister asked if I minded if she smoked. "I need this," she said grimly, lighting up.

Ten minutes later, we parked the car in front of the house. I recognized Laura Markko, who was sitting on the front steps. She was wearing a yellow blouse, a long green dress, and tennis shoes. I introduced myself.

"I have a five-thirty appointment with Reverend Hill," I lied. Larry and I had never communicated or scheduled a meeting. He had never returned my phone calls or responded to the letters I had sent him.

Laura seemed hesitant and puzzled, but she got up and went inside.

A moment later, from inside the house, I heard him. "I don't want to talk to him!"

Laura reappeared and took her seat again on the front steps. "He has no appointment with you. He doesn't want to talk to you."

I noticed that she kept her eyes fixed on the ground. Then there was a movement behind the screen door, and I saw it was Larry Hill.

His short-cut hair and groomed beard were snow white and he wore round, gold spectacles. He seemed a bit gaunt, his cheekbones his most arresting facial feature. "Go away! I looked into you and you're a liar!"

I found I was very calm. It was as if I could not wrap my mind and emotions around the idea that this fragile old man was the one who had done so much harm to so many people. Many of his former followers had told me that once they decided to leave, Larry Hill could no longer terrify or intimidate them. Like the mighty Oz, he was really just a man after all.

Image 53: Laura Markko at Fortney Road in August 2007.

"Hi, Larry. I wanted to get some information about these visions you had in 1965."

"I said to go away! Do I need to call the police?"

I noticed that even with all of Larry's yelling and threats, he never put a hand on the screen door or made a move to come outside. Clearly he was trapped in the house and had nowhere to go.

"Get off my property!" Larry yelled from behind the screen door. "I said to go away! Do I need to call the police? Get off my property!"

But not once did he make a move to come outside.

Knowing I had gone as far as I could with them, I said, "Okay. Goodbye, Laura. 'Bye, Larry."

As we pulled away, I grabbed my camera and snapped a photo of Laura on the front steps.

Larry saw me take the picture, and, with one final salvo, his hoarse, raspy voice followed us down Fortney Road.

"I hope you sell a lot of books!"

Acknowledgments

T his book is based on interviews and correspondence with former members of the Church of the Risen Christ, the Kent New Generation Church, members of the All Saved Freak Band, and others who know the principals involved; on the published writings of Reverend Larry Hill and community and band members as found in the *Freedom Bell* newspapers and other community documents and teachings; on audio tapes of Reverend Larry Hill, Pam Massmann, Kim Massmann, Laura Markko, Glenn Schwartz, and Diane Sullivan which were made with their knowledge at the Kent New Generation Church on July 15, 1973, at Fortney Road services on June 9, 1974 and August 18, 1974, and at an undated 1974 service; and on published interviews, articles and books.

In 2007, when the first draft of this manuscript was shared with those who lived at Fortney Road, everyone generously provided feedback and corrections, taking much time and effort as they relived a painful part of their lives. But it's important to remember that these events occurred more than forty years ago under almost unbearable conditions. Memories did not always line up with one another or with the facts my research revealed. For example, there were two completely different versions of how Larry's wife escaped. Others don't recall the FBI's involvement at all. There was another family whose children were beaten and abused as much as Bethy but they refused to provide any information and were not willing to speak to me. Some had no recollection of Diane Sullivan's trial even though they said they were still living at Fortney Road when it occurred. Others objected to the description of the pain the White Judge caused, saying it wasn't as bad as depicted.

Ultimately, I made all the corrections that were sent to me and lined up the conflicting stories against the detailed timeline I had managed to create with the documents that were available to me. Using that as my plumb line, I let the narrative align with those facts. To the very best of my ability, this book is the factual story of what happened at Fortney Road.

I am grateful to many, many people for trusting me to tell a painful part of their life stories:

Thank you to Joe Markko for all his help and generosity with his time, insight, and memories. In February 2007, he asked me to read, critique, and make suggestions to his manuscript *When Someday Comes: Memoirs of a Survivor*. Other than making some recommendations for chapter titles and breaks in the content, there wasn't much to change. How can you suggest edits to some-one's life? Since the book covered his entire life—of which time at Fortney Road was only a portion—I found myself asking him questions about his experience on the farm, in the All Saved Freak Band, and interactions with those he lived with. He kindly and patiently answered all my questions, and then sent along photos, letters, recordings and the *Freedom Bells* that Mike Berkey had saved. And then Joe invited others to share their story with me. Without his help, this book would never have been written. And if I hadn't read *When Someday Comes*, I never would have known about Fortney Road. Joe graciously granted me permission to quote from his manuscript since it provided some of the skeleton upon which I built this narrative. I began this project as an article, never knowing it would grow into a book. When I started, Joe wrote, "I really hope your article turns out well and can find a national publication to unveil itself. Everyone I've talked to says, 'It's about time.'"

I encourage readers of this book to seek out Joe's memoir—what happens after he leaves the farm makes for a compelling tale and his story of survival is unlike any you've ever read.

Leon provided photos, documentation and a sharp memory. And his dogged pursuit of Larry over the years is why I gave him the name Leon, which means "lion."

Thank you to members of the All Saved Freak Band and former members of the Church of the Risen Christ, and the Kent New Generation Church and those who told their stories but did not want their names used. I know it was difficult to talk about what happened and I appreciate your willingness to correct me until I got it right.

Much appreciation also to Bethy Goodenough, Tim Hill, Carole King Hough, Daryl Pitts, Morgan King, Bob Tidd, Cookie Markko, and Joan Dolch Marks for their willingness to go public with all they experienced and relive some very painful memories.

Unless otherwise referenced, the following provided documentation or quotes (sometimes anonymously) or were author interviews conducted between February and September 2007, June and July 2008, June 2012, and July 2014. Genders of pseudonyms have not been changed: Deanna Adams, Butch Armstrong Richard Acevedo, Judge Ross D. Avellone, retired, Ben and Ruth (pseudonyms), Darryl Berk, Arthur Blessitt, Brent Block, Alan Canfora, Frank Cook, Donald and Brenda (pseudonyms), Dick Feagler, Jim Fox, Rob Galbraith, Georgia (pseudonym), Bethy Goodenough, John Griffith, Tim Hill, Mike and Carole King Hough, Jack and Margo (pseudonyms), Mark Jones, Glenn Kaiser, Rick Kalister, Morgan King, Leon (pseudonym), Cookie Markko, Joe Markko, Joan Dolch Marks, Mark Massmann, Danny McFadden, John Miller, Tim Miller, Eric Pement, Peter and Janice (pseudonyms), Scott Ross, Bob Schwartz, Gene Schwartz, Glenn Schwartz, Marlene Schwartz, Ramona Shay, Jeremy Spencer, Frankie Starr, Shelley Terry, Bob Tidd, Jon Trott, David Wilkerson, and Dale Yancy

In John Griffith's October 1978 series of articles published in the *News-Herald of Willoughby*, the names "Jane" and "Tom" are pseudonyms. Those same individuals are quoted extensively in this manuscript and out of respect for their privacy, their names have not been used yet they are referred to as "Margo" and "Leon" in this document.

In my efforts to document and confirm the events and timelines in this book, many phone calls were made and many emails were sent. For those who took the time to respond, I'm very grateful:

The reporters, who said they have never forgotten what happened more than forty years ago and were eager to help and greatly encouraged me to tell the whole story: David W. Jones for getting me in touch with John Griffith of the *News-Herald of Willoughby*, and John for agreeing to an interview while you were fishing; Shelley Terry of the *Ashtabula Star Beacon*; Dave Simms of the *Palm Beach Post*; Thomas Francis of *Cleveland Scene*; Michael Sangiacomo, Richard C. Widman, Karl R. Burkhardt, Thomas Fladung, Chris Quinn, Jo Ellen Corrigan and David Kordalski of the *Cleveland Plain Dealer*, and Dick Feagler, who also agreed to an interview; and Jean Mlincek of the *Kent Record-Courier*.

The researchers, who turned out to be loyal fans of Glenn Schwartz: Ted Diadiun and David Jardy of the *Cleveland Plain Dealer*; Vern Morrison of Cleveland State University Library for copies of the *Cleveland Press*; and Howard Fields of rockpaper.net for researching *Rolling Stone* magazine.

The musicians, including Brent Block, Ken Utterback, Frank Cook and Frank Petricca of Pacific, Gas and Electric, and the late Paul "Mr. Rock 'n' Roll" Sobieraj who watched over their site; Jim Fox and Ron Silverman of the James Gang; Rick Kalister; Michael Bacon who responded to my email and put me in touch with Rob Galbraith; Jeremy Spencer; Darryl Berk; Butch Armstrong; Mark Jones; Frankie Starr; Danny McFadden; Sam Andrew of Big Brother & the Holding Company; Melody Green for your Friday night potlucks in Woodland Hills which introduced me to Glenn Kaiser and Resurrection Band; Joe Walsh, who was kind enough to read all that pertained to his friendship with Glenn Schwartz, and Smokey Wendell for passing the pages on to Joe.

The contributors: David Wilkerson's spokesperson, Barbara Mackery; Stephanie Landry who provided the photo of Glenn; George Caldwell for the photo of Tom Miller; Glenn Kaiser and Jon Trott of *Cornerstone* magazine and JPUSA for your quick response and sharp memories; David Di Sabatino for our shared interest in the All Saved Freak Band and that "whole other era"; Dave Hollandsworth and his Jesus Music site (http://one-way.org/jesusmusic/); Scott Ross for responding; Dr. Mark Allen Powell, Professor of New Testament studies, Trinity Lutheran Seminary in Columbus for your *Encyclopedia of Contemporary Christian Music* resource and providing the *Harmony* magazines; Ken Scott for permission to cite your reviews as published in *Vintage Vinyl Jesus Music*; Richard Acevedo of Hidden Vision Music for the inserts and graphics from the *Brainwashed* and *Sower* albums; Bob Felberg for your encouragement and support of the All Saved Freak Band; Patrick Lundborg for allowing me to quote from *The Acid Archives* and your high regard for the All Saved Freak Band; Dale Yancy for remembering so much from so long ago; Arthur Blessitt for clarifying where and when Glenn first met you and providing the much needed documentation.

The website: FortneyRoad.com was designed to be an interactive experience to help viewers find out what really happened at Fortney Road. It was a tremendous challenge to get it out of my head and heart and onto the Internet. Thank you John Niernberger (consciousimages.com), Nathan Bleigh (@nnnnathann) and Jim Button (http://cargocollective.com/jimbutton) for creating a truly unforgettable experience; it's better than I ever could have hoped for. And Justin Gardener (@jpgardner), for all the great suggestions to help get the word out. Thanks for understanding my vision and vetting all those tweets!

Thanks to all who have followed along on Twitter @FortneyRoad and @CultHistory.

The analog men: Jose Gonzalez and Don Gordon for the postcards and business cards and utilizing your amazing analog skills in a digital age.

The lawyers: Ira Schaefer, Eric J. Lobenfeld and Allison Schoenthal who read, explained and counseled me to expunge when necessary.

Special appreciation to Judge Ross D. Avellone, retired.

Miriam Parker, your class helped confirm that I was on the right track and your exhortation for your authors to tweet is infectious (and I hope they are all minding you).

Thank you to my family and friends who took the time to read all or a portion of this manuscript in its earliest form and provided invaluable support and criticism: My mom and dad (wish you were here); my aunt, Dona Killeen; sisters Jan Laidlaw and Jill Stevens; and my niece, Kim Buczkowski; Dale Levey (I guess I have Lou to thank for you!), Ron and Carolyn Wunner (still the safest place on earth); Kim MacDonald (a wise and loving friend for so many years); Bruce Morrison (editor extraordinaire, great friend and VI to all); Steve Doty for patiently listening about this project for years; and Joe Watkinson for the use of his phone so I could speak to Diane Sullivan by foiling her caller ID. And Sydney, of course. And Wendy, always.

Special mention goes to Jeff Dunn for connecting me with Adam Palmer. Adam, thank you for editing out some of my favorite sections (some of which I put back in!) and for challenging me to look a little deeper.

Thank you, Neil Salkind, for walking the road with me for a time.

Paul Bulos, who put on two hats—agent and author—and wore them both so well. Thanks so very, very much for your help with the contract.

Dick Marek for a suggestion that significantly changed the entire structure of the book and made for a much more compelling story, and Bill Thompson for confirming I was on the right track.

Alice Peck put her hand to the plow and polished and revised and made a very dark story shine bright. Thank you for your skills, sensitivity and willingness to spend time on Fortney Road.

Dave Cullen, whose book *Columbine* inspired me to rewrite *Fortney Road* one more time, and it's so much better because of your example of accurate, factual reporting and characterization. Thank you.

Toward the end of the road, Susan Ginsburg and Stacy Testa introduced me to Judy Kern, who helped me to smooth out the rough patches and polish up the proposal and manuscript. Thomas Tessier generously provided me with key observations and some tips on narrative structure that made the story much more compelling.

Fortney Road's journey to publication was an educational one. The mainstream publishers wanted to excise much of the religious content while the Christian publishers wanted to remove the brutality that was documented in the story. Turning down offers for publication is extremely risky but I knew I needed to hold out until I could tell the whole story of what really happened at Fortney Road.

So I am very grateful for the staff at Freethought House who immediately saw the importance of this project and wanted the events told exactly as they transpired: Publisher Bill Lehto had excellent suggestions to help me to focus on the core of what transpired; Elizabeth Stiras copyedited it (and taught me about the use of italics); Robaire Ream designed the compelling cover that proved once again that a picture is worth a thousand words; Eric Jayne got the word out far and wide; and James Zimmerman proofed and corrected me and helped me to clarify what I already thought was clear and taught me much about useless quotation marks!

And David Young. I'll never forget when I introduced myself to you and you said (weeks later!) what you did for a living and I immediately responded with, "Have I got a book for you!" Your encouragement, insight, good humor, dinner, drinks and willingness to answer my endless questions about publishing has been invaluable and I'm so grateful for your friendship. Pushing the sled with you? Not so much. The Burden is lucky to have you.

Those who know me know that this story has been an obsession of mine for many years. Thank you for patiently listening to me.

None of the people listed above are in any way culpable for errors of fact or interpretation in this biography.

Although this book is dedicated to Mark Hill, it is, of course, also for Brett Hill, Randy Markko and Tom Miller, and for every child and adult who suffered or was mistreated at Fortney Road.

Thank God for the Internet and email. You brought so many people together at just the right moment and I very clearly saw Your hand in this. You constantly amaze me.

Notes on Sources

Portions of this document—including stories about Larry Hill and Diane Sullivan and quotes attributed to Joe Markko—have been freely adapted and modified with permission from Joseph G. Markko and his manuscript, *When Someday Comes: Memoirs Of A Survivor* available at Amazon.com.

Unless otherwise indicated, all Internet postings and quotes are verified to be from former members of the Church of the Risen Christ (aka Christ Farm), the Kent New Generation Church or the All Saved Freak Band. Where requested, first name pseudonyms have been used. Genders have not been changed. Some postings have been edited for clarity.

Claims and postings—anonymous and otherwise—made by individuals on the Exchristian.net forum and any other site are unable to be verified yet are believed to be true and accurate as posted. Some postings have been edited for clarity.

Verbatims other than Internet postings were obtained from published newspaper transcripts and are believed to be accurate as originally stated. Some statements have been edited for clarity.

All non-referenced quotes and statements were obtained via email response to my queries or acquired from Internet postings from a variety of sites. Although any Internet posting (such as a blog or email) can technically be considered copyrighted unless explicitly stated otherwise, the act of posting can be taken to imply consent and the waiver of copyright, and it has been construed so for the writing of this document. Some communications have been edited for clarity.

Although individuals may have been identified by name in published interviews thirty or forty years ago, for the purposes of this document, identities made public in the primary source may have been altered to mask the identity out of respect for his or her privacy.

All excerpts from *"Everything You Always Wanted To Know About The All Saved Freak Band (But Never Had The Chance To Ask)"* by Jeff C. Stevenson ©2006 Joe Markko/All Saved Freak Band, allsavedfreakband.com, and Well Done Productions are not individually sourced yet are used with permission.

Freedom Bell was the newspaper published by the Church of the Risen Christ between approximately 1968 and 1977 and given away free at concerts and during evangelism crusades. Because no volume or issue number is provided, the year of the issue cited is estimated unless a year could be accurately determined. Articles were frequently reprinted so the first or earliest appearance was used as a source. No copyright is known to exist so reproduction of the art, graphics, photographs and written contents are used under the fair use copyright principle. Editions have been referenced according to the front page headline.

Larry Hill, Laura Markko, Pam Massmann, Kim Massmann, and Dianne Sullivan were not interviewed for this document, although I did seek to verify the contents with them on numerous occassions. I did speak briefly with Diane Sullivan on the phone, and Larry Hill and I conversed at Fortney Road, but neither encounter could be considered an interview. All quotes and statements attributed to them are public record.

The CSE Citation-Sequence System of reference documentation was used in this book.

References Cited

1. Cotter H. Through rose-colored granny glasses. The New York Times. 2007 May 25.

2. Sharlet J. Through a glass, darkly: how the Christian right is reimagining US history. Harper's Magazine. 2006 Dec.

3. Khong R. Holy rollers rock: they're on a mission from God. The Yale Herald. 2004 Oct 15.

4. Davis E. I'd like to dedicate this next song to Jesus. The freaky origins of Christian rock. Slate magazine. 2007 July 31.

5. Griffith J. Taught to use whip, ex-cultists say. News-Herald of Willoughby. 1978 Oct 3.

6. Freedom Bell. All quotes or statements are from these issues and may have been edited for clarity or grammar.
   - Freedom Bell circa 1968, "A reverberant sounding Jesus said ye shall know the truth and the truth shall make you free"
   - Freedom Bell circa 1970, "Harold Fuller seeks re-election: member of anti-drug committee"
   - Freedom Bell circa 1970, "The All Saved Freak Band"
   - Freedom Bell circa 1973, "Son of God–high priest–prophet–savior–soon coming king"
   - Freedom Bell circa 1976, "July 4, 1976 will we celebrate the ride of this horseman . . . or of these horsemen?"
   - Freedom Bell circa 1976, "Jesus Christ is raised from the dead"

7. Griffith J. Ex-wife of leader bares tortures. News-Herald of Willoughby. 1978 October 3.

8. Lyrics to the Doors' "Not To Touch The Earth". 1968. Doors Music, Inc.

9. Adams D. Rock 'N' Roll and the Cleveland Connection. 2002. Kent State University Press.

10. Francis T. Lord of the strings. Cleveland Scene. 2004 Dec 8.

11. JamesGangsters Yahoo Group. Retrieved 2007 April 10 from http://launch.groups.yahoo.com/group/JamesGangsters/.

12. Simms D. Yeah, yeah turns to no, no; Christ inside me now. Palm Beach Post. 1969 Dec 1.

13. Griffith J. Cult cruelty probed. News-Herald of Willoughby. 1978 Oct 3.

14. Lyrics to "There Is Still Hope In Jesus" by Joe Markko and Larry Hill/All Saved Freak Band. 1973.

15. Hill L. Scripture Lessons for Modern Man.

16. Griffith J. Ex-cult members describe white judge beatings. News-Herald of Willoughby. 1978 Oct 3.

17. Tolkien J.R.R. All that is gold does not glitter. 2001. Houghton Mifflin Company.

18. Spencer J. Out of the blue. 2002–2005. Activated Ministries.

19. Liner notes from Brainwashed. 1976.

20. Liner notes from Sower. 1976.

21. http://www.rocksoff.org/jimi.htm. Retrieved 2007 July 30.

22. Widman R, Burkhardt K. Kidnap can't end rhythm of singer's life with Jesus. The Plain Dealer. 1975 Feb 27.

23. Liner notes from My Poor Generation. 1973, 1976.

24. Griffith J. Ex-members say brainwashing was part of Hill's cult. News-Herald of Willoughby. 1978 Oct 3.

25. Audiotape transcript from a 1974 Sunday evening community meeting at Fortney Road; date unknown.

26. Audiotape transcript from an 1974 Aug 18 Sunday morning service at Fortney Road.

27. Feagler D. Guitarist is shielded by his new family. Cleveland Press. 1975 Feb 27.

28. Terry S. The journey to heal. Ashtabula Star Beacon. 2005 Aug 7.

29. Audiotape transcript from Kent New Generation Church service. 1973 July 15.

30. Fusetronsound review retrieved 2007 from http://www.fusetron-sound.com/label.php?whomart=ALLSAVEDFREAKBAND.

31. http://ccms500bestalbums.wordpress.com/2010/11/30/228-my-poor-generation-the-all-saved-freak-band/ Retrieved 2014 July 31.

32. Audiotape transcript from 1974 June 9 community meeting at Fortney Road.

33. Liner notes from For Christians, Elves, and Lovers. 1976.

34. Lyrics to "Tom Miller" by Morgan King/All Saved Freak Band. 1973.

35. Scott K. Vintage Vinyl Jesus Music (1965–1980; 3rd Edition). 2003.

36. Felberg B. review retrieved 2007 July 11 from www.one-way.org/jesusmusic/index.html.

37. Feagler D. Kidnap plan fails to bring back son to family. The Plain Dealer. 1975 Feb 26.

38. Widman R. Son's kidnap prompted by judge, mother says. The Plain Dealer. 1975 Mar 13.

39. Conway F, Siegelman J. Snapping: America's epidemic of sudden personality change. 2nd Edition. 1995. Stillpoint Press.

40. Lyrics to "Ode To Glenn Schwartz" by Joe Markko/All Saved Freak Band. 1976.

41. Lyrics to "Don't Look Back" by Joe Markko and Larry Hill/All Saved Freak Band. 1976.

42. Lyrics to "Stephen" by Mike Berkey/All Saved Freak Band. 1976.

43. Lundborg P, Milenski A, Moore R. The Acid Archives. 2006. Lysergia.

44. Proctor R. Harmony magazine. 1976 May.

45. Proctor R. Harmony magazine. Date unknown.

46. Di Sabatino D. List of the Top 50 Collectable Jesus Music Albums Of All Time retrieved 2007 July 11 from www.one-way.org/jesusmusic/index.html.

47. Donley L. Hearings continue in abuse case. Ashtabula Star Beacon. 1978 Aug 30.

48. Powell MA. Encyclopedia of contemporary christian music. 2002. Hendrickson Publishers.

49. Felberg B. review retrieved 2007 July 11 from www.one-way.org/jesusmusic/index.html.

50. Fair DE. Mare gives birth to twin foals. The Valley News. 1999 May 19. Vol. 109, No. 20.

51. Terry S. Cult-like sects not new to area. Ashtabula Star Beacon. 2005 Aug 5–7.

About the Author

J eff C. Stevenson works as a freelance copywriter for various New York advertising agencies. He is also a writer, photographer, and film publicist and producer. His work has appeared in *PRISM* magazine, where his article "Bury Me Standing" was awarded the editor's choice, and he has contributed entertainment items to the New York Post's Page Six. He spent seven years researching and writing Fortney Road. Jeff lives in New York City.

www.ingramcontent.com/pod-product-compliance
Lightning Source LLC
Chambersburg PA
CBHW050510270326
41927CB00009B/1981